**NATIONAL
GEOGRAPHIC**

Backyard
GUIDE TO THE
Birds of North America

Backyard
GUIDE TO THE
Birds
of North America

JONATHAN ALDERFER AND PAUL HESS

NATIONAL GEOGRAPHIC

WASHINGTON, D.C.

Contents

Adult male Baltimore Oriole (Texas, April)

previous pages: Male and female Eastern Bluebirds (Connecticut, January)

Color Index

In this index, male birds are labeled by their predominant color. The bird head may have a different color than its label states. That's because the body—the part most noticeable in the field—is the color labeled.

MOSTLY BLACK

 Black Vulture, *56*

 Turkey Vulture, *57*

 Black Phoebe, *110*

 Fish Crow, *128*

 American Crow, *129*

 Common Raven, *130*

 European Starling, *210*

 Brewer's Blackbird, *212*

 Red-winged Blackbird, *213*

 Great-tailed Grackle, *214*

 Common Grackle, *216*

 Brown-headed Cowbird, *218*

 Bronzed Cowbird, *219*

 Orchard Oriole, *223*

MOSTLY BLACK AND WHITE

 Acorn Woodpecker, *93*

 Red-bellied Woodpecker, *94*

 Yellow-bellied Sapsucker, *95*

 Red-naped Sapsucker, *96*

 Ladder-backed Woodpecker, *98*

 Nuttall's Woodpecker, *99*

 Downy Woodpecker, *100*

 Hairy Woodpecker, *101*

 Pileated Woodpecker, *105*

 Eastern Kingbird, *112*

 Black-billed Magpie, *131*

 Violet-green Swallow, *135*

 Spotted Towhee, *182*

 Eastern Towhee, *183*

 Rose-breasted Grosbeak, *208*

 Black-headed Grosbeak, *209*

MOSTLY WHITE

 Ring-billed Gull, *70*

 California Gull, *71*

 Herring Gull, *72*

MOSTLY BROWN

 Canada Goose, *50*

 Northern Bobwhite, *53*

MOSTLY BROWN AND WHITE

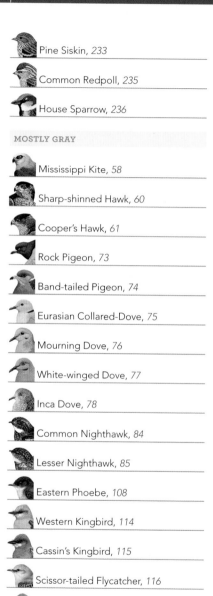
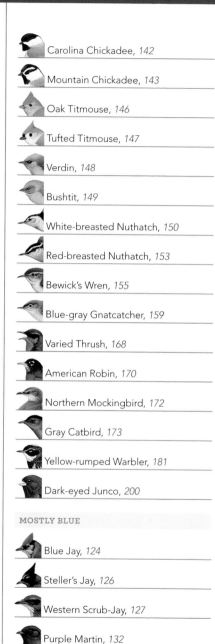

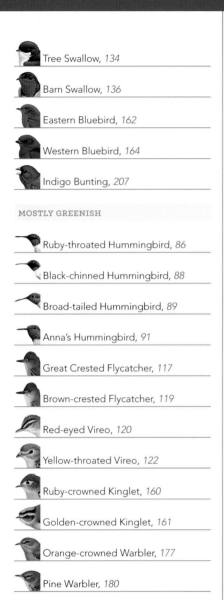

How to Use This Book

Of all the creatures in nature, birds are the most visible and accessible. Right in your backyard these wonderfully complex and beautiful animals are going about their daily lives. With minimal effort and expense, your life can intersect with theirs, and both you and the birds around you will benefit. This book is a concise guide to enjoying and identifying the common birds in your backyard wherever you live in North America, north of Mexico.

BACKYARD BASICS

The first section of this book presents basic information on bird-feeding, birdhouses, landscaping for birds, and birding skills. Installing a bird feeder in your backyard is a sure way to get great looks at some of your backyard birds, and a pair of binoculars will multiply your enjoyment. Enticing a pair of birds to raise its family in a birdhouse you have provided and maintained is a special joy, and bird-friendly landscaping will coax even more species to take up residence in your yard. All the information you need to get started is located here.

GUIDE TO 150 SPECIES

Millions of people have discovered that the pleasures of bird-watching increase when they know what they're looking at. We have designed the identification section to help you along that path. The features found in every species account are detailed on the sample page opposite. The following additional features will help you locate any of the 150 species using different search criteria.

■ Color Index Following the Contents. Images of bird heads arranged by each species' dominant color, followed by a page number.
■ Visual Index Inside book covers (front and back). Images of all 150 species shown in taxonomic order, followed by a page number.

■ Quick-Find Index Front cover flap. Alphabetical listing of common bird names.
■ Map Key Front cover flap. Key to the colors used on the range maps. A full-size map key appears on page 12.
■ Parts of a Bird Back cover flap. Illustration labeled with the names of the various feather groups.
■ Glossary Page 238. Definitions of specialized birding terms.

The sequence of birds in the identification section may seem arbitrary to the beginner, but it is based on taxonomy—the science of evolutionary relationships—and proceeds from the oldest (most primitive) species to the most recent in origin. Almost all birding field guides follow this convention, so it's helpful to become familiar with it. You can always turn to the Visual Index on the inside covers for a quick reminder of the sequence. The sequence is subdivided into bird families—scientific groupings of related bird species—and each family is introduced with a short description.

ONLINE RESOURCES

For all 150 species found in this book, the National Geographic website features complete recordings of birdsongs as well as an interactive identification guide, which helps users identify birds based on their color, month, state, or size. Visit nationalgeographic.com/birding for more information.

SPECIES
The common name for each bird is given, followed by its official genus and species designations in Latin. Sizes (lengths) are also indicated.

ILLUSTRATION
Paintings of each species, often shown with common variations within species, are drawn to highlight noteworthy characteristics.

♂ male

♀ female

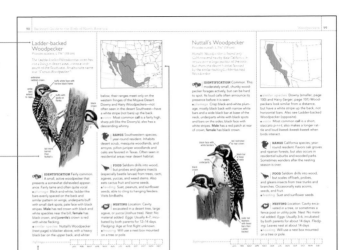

SIGHTINGS
A row of boxes at the bottom of each species description allows you to keep track of your own sightings by month throughout the year.

RANGE MAP
The extents of each species' range and migratory routes aid identification in your part of the country. See the key on the following page.

FAMILY
Common groupings of bird species are described in greater detail at the start of their section.

SIDEBAR
Interesting or helpful information about birds and birding is highlighted in side essays throughout the field guide section.

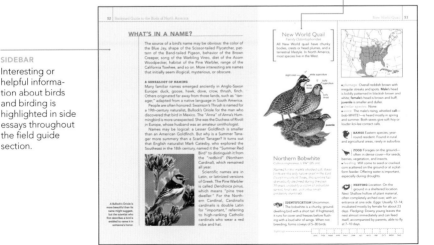

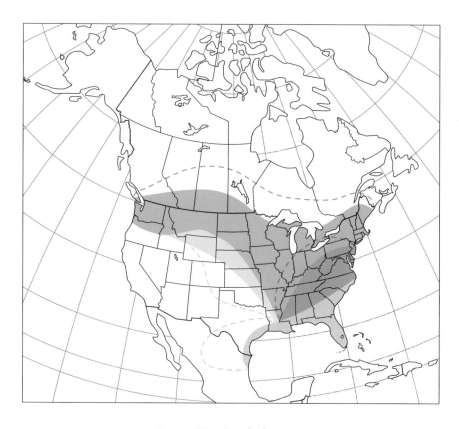

Range Map Symbols

 Breeding range, generally in spring and summer

 Year-round range

 Winter range (if no winter or year-round range is shown, winters outside North America)

 Migration range

 Extent of irregular breeding range, or of post-breeding dispersal in summer and fall

 Extent of irregular year-round range

 Extent of irregular or irruptive range in some winters

 Extent of irregular migration

[BACKYARD BASICS]

PAUL HESS

[Bird-watching]

Perhaps your backyard is a small lot in a big city or a suburban lawn with flower beds and trees; perhaps it's in a woodland, along a seashore or lake, high on a mountain, low in a desert, or amid farmland. No matter where your yard is, you are sharing it with birds—all just outside your window, waiting for you to spot and enjoy.

IN YOUR BACKYARD

There are about 10,000 different species of birds in the world, including more than 900 in North America north of Mexico, probably as many as 300–500 in your state or province, and 100 or more in a large park. How many different kinds of birds come to your backyard depends on where you live. But one thing is certain: If you pay attention to them and make your yard attractive by landscaping and adding feeders, nest boxes, or a birdbath, you will see more than you ever thought possible.

Besides the basic treasures of their beauty and behavior, your backyard birds can offer you a perennial treasure hunt: What new birds will I see today? Will there be a species that has not visited the yard since last winter, or—much more exciting—might there be a species I have never seen anywhere at all?

WHY WATCH BIRDS?

People enjoy backyard birds for different reasons. Some seek relaxation in watching them; others focus intently on their visual and vocal beauty. Many learn to identify species. In a spirit of conservation, some help the birds thrive by providing food and shelter. Often, people become inspired to delve into natural history, reading books that deal with ornithology, the science of bird study.

Truly, any path you take in enjoying birds is the correct one. Whichever one you choose, a wonderful world of birding awaits you—starting right in your own backyard.

Watching these downy Eastern Screech-Owls peer curiously at the world outside their nest tree would be a highlight of any backyard observer's day.

[Where & When]

B irds live everywhere, even in the highest Arctic latitudes and in the hottest deserts—but which birds you'll find in your yard depends largely on where you live. Of the species described in this book, expect to see only those that occur where and when the range maps indicate. Each species has its special place and time.

GEOGRAPHY

Some birds, such as American Robins and House Finches, live in many regions, almost anywhere on the continent. Others can be found only in particular areas. Each bird's geographic distribution—its "range"—is linked precisely to its tolerance for heat and cold, dryness or humidity, and other environmental conditions. For instance, an American Tree Sparrow is adapted to breed at the edge of Arctic tundra, while a Lesser Nighthawk lives only in arid deserts of the Southwest. They could not trade places and survive.

As a result, the list of birds you will easily see in your backyard depends largely on your local environment— how your surroundings, with their particular combination of food and vegetation, match that which each species prefers.

Spring: a hearty robin-style breakfast

Summer: a goldfinch and sunflower day

SEASONS

Birds bring us special ways to observe and celebrate the changing of the seasons. After a long winter with few birds on the bare branches and none in the dried-up grasses, plants blossom and the chorus of birdsong begins, even in the lingering chill of early spring mornings. Birds that vanished for the winter after traveling far southward return, adding their own sometimes dazzling colors to the greening forests and brightly budding trees. Even the backyard's birds that remained all through the winter are newly active and a joy to watch as they pair off for the summer breeding season.

CHANGING PLACES

If you pay close attention throughout the year, you will see that most bird species follow strict seasonal patterns. Bullock's Orioles and Baltimore Orioles, for example, allow us to see their stunning beauty only during the summer months. By early fall they have departed on a long journey southward to spend their winter in the tropics. When fall arrives in the southern U.S., they will be replaced by less bright but still dapper species such as White-crowned Sparrows and White-throated Sparrows that remain all winter.

Be careful: Watching this lively annual panorama of birds' comings and goings can become addictive!

Fall: a chickadee snacking

Winter: a Cedar Waxwing's berry treat

YEAR-ROUND BIRDS

Steller's Jay

Great Horned Owl

Carolina Wren

Northern Cardinal

Some of our most beloved birds stay with us throughout the year. Black-capped Chickadees remain in the North, Mountain Chickadees in the West, and Carolina Chickadees in the Southeast. Downy Woodpeckers and Hairy Woodpeckers are present year-round throughout almost the entire continent. All of those species are well adapted to survive cold winters without your help, but if you offer them food, they will welcome it and will enliven your yard even on winter's coldest, snowiest, or rainiest days.

YEAR-ROUND BY REGION

Folks fortunate enough to live in the Northern Cardinal's year-round range find their darkest December days brightened by the classic bird of the Christmas card. For backyard bird-watchers in the West, tame Western Scrub-Jays and gregarious Black-billed Magpies are similarly familiar and fun to watch all year.

Some of the year-round species in your area are not always the same individuals that spent the summer in your yard. Blue Jays may bring their boisterous bluster into your yard during every month of the year, but scientists have learned that many of those present over the winter are birds from farther north that have moved south to join their local counterparts. Birds that depend on water such as the Belted Kingfisher and the Herring Gull withdraw just far enough south to reach lakes and rivers that remain unfrozen. There, they join the kingfishers and gulls that are your year-round residents.

Yet, most birds that populate our backyards year-round are in fact permanent residents, and many of us can rightly consider them our lively little neighbors and companions.

Yearly Variations A few species have no typical seasonal pattern at all. The Purple Finch and Evening Grosbeak, for example, live in northern latitudes and migrate south only when the conifer seed crop is poor. You may see them locally only once every few years.

MIGRATORY BIRDS

Birds such as American Tree Sparrows across the northern U.S. and Palm Warblers in the southeastern states are true migrants that nest in Canada and come south only for the winter. Birds that live with us just in the summer, such as Western Tanagers and Scarlet Tanagers, are also migrants that journey south—in some cases, far south—for the winter months. The most abundant group of migrants are the species that travel far south in fall and far north in spring between their breeding and wintering areas: Purple Martins, during their long-range autumn passage to South America, for instance, or Broad-winged Hawks, streaming overhead along a mountain ridge during their fall migration.

LISTEN FOR MIGRATION

To get the most out of backyard birding, don't limit your observations to the daytime hours. If you have sharp ears, you might hear the sounds of migration.

Stand in your backyard on a clear night in the spring or fall before the dawn's first light. In the darkness, you may hear cheeps and chirps of hundreds of small birds passing over during their all-night migration. You will likely have no idea what species these are, but that doesn't matter. Your ears will be witnessing one of nature's great spectacles.

Broad-tailed Hummingbird

Eastern Kingbird

Western Tanager

[Feeding Birds]

I f there is one great symbol of backyard bird-watching, it is the bird feeder—and with good reason. Nothing enhances the enjoyment of backyard birds better than watching them easily and closely through your window. Birds quickly discover which yards have feeders, and they will return to them again and again.

TYPES OF FEEDERS

A single feeder will bring a nice variety of birds, but an array of different kinds will attract many more species. Install as many different types of feeders as you can, but space them at least 15 feet apart.

■Tube Typically tubes of clear plastic 16 to 24 inches long, with perches and small holes in the sides, these feeders do not attract squirrels because the holes are so small. Tubes that are relatively wide in diameter with larger holes hold mixed seeds to accommodate many different species.

■ Finch feeder This type of tube has very small holes designed to dispense only tiny black "thistle" or nyjer seeds, best for American Goldfinches, Pine Siskins, and Common Redpolls.

American Goldfinch

■Hopper Often made of cedar wood, these attractive feeders look like roofed pavilions with large feed compartments—hoppers—made of clear plastic, a tray that extends out, and rails for the birds to stand on. They come in many sizes, materials, and shapes and are best for sunflower seeds. A disadvantage is that when hanging from a tree, these are not safe from squirrels, raccoons, deer, or even bears. In a short time, any of those mammals can empty a feeder. In general, it is best to fill a feeder in the morning rather than leave it full for an invasion of nocturnal prowlers.

■ **Table** One of the simplest feeders is a platform of heavy plywood mounted on short legs. It will attract Mourning Doves, Song Sparrows, and Dark-eyed Juncos, which typically feed on the ground. A low rim keeps the seeds from spilling over onto the ground. Using a table is better than merely tossing seeds out into the yard, because uneaten seeds spoil and can host mold and bacteria, which can sicken your birds.

■ **Globe** Made entirely of clear plastic, small inexpensive globe feeders are surrounded by a thin perch and are designed for the smallest birds such as chickadees. The perches are so thin and placed so close to the globe that large birds such as jays can't reach and gulp down the seed. Globe feeders can accommodate either sunflower or mixed seeds.

■ **Window feeder** Apartment dwellers and others who have no actual yard can still enjoy feeding birds. Their best choices are plastic feeders with suction cups for attaching to window panes or small covered trays for window sills. Unfortunately, these feeders are often so small that they require frequent filling. They may also attract large birds such as jays, which may be too heavy for the feeder to hold.

Rufous Hummingbird

■ **Hummingbird feeder** Among the most delightful feeders of all are those especially designed for hummingbirds: small, red plastic containers that hold sugar water, offered to the birds through tiny tubes or holes at the bottom. Hummingbird feeders can be placed anywhere, even on porches a few

Uninvited Guests Bird feeders can attract unwanted guests: squirrels, chipmunks, and even less appealing birds like crows and starlings that scare off other birds. Makers of bird feeders have tried diligently to create squirrel-resistant feeders, but sometimes the creatures outsmart everyone. Tube and globe feeders with the smallest holes are one way to confront the problem, since larger birds and animals usually can't get into them.

Tubes hold large seeds.

Finch feeders have tiny holes.

Hoppers may tempt mammals.

Tables attract mockingbirds.

Globes keep seeds dry.

Window mounts bring birds close.

Hummingbirds crave nectar.

Suet cakes nourish woodpeckers.

Fruit beckons orioles.

feet from a window or door. A frequent question is whether maintaining a feeder too late in the fall will encourage the hummers to stay around until dangerously cold weather sets in. Although there are very rare exceptions, usually when a bird is already unhealthy, hummers instinctively know when to migrate and will depart on their normal schedule—and you will have helped them add energy for their long migration.

■**Suet and peanut butter cakes and logs** Square cakes of beef suet, often mixed with seeds, are favorites of woodpeckers. These are generally hung in metal screen-type containers that are the same size as the cakes. A variation is the suet or peanut butter log, which can be purchased or easily made by drilling large holes in a length of tree branch and packing the holes with a mixture of suet, peanut butter, and seeds. Large pinecones packed with the same mixture work well, too. Carolina Wrens have more trouble maintaining energy in very cold weather than many other birds, and these logs and cones will be especially welcome to them.

■**Fruit hangers and bowls** Special hangers are sold for holding fruits such as orange or apple halves. Homemade versions made of wire from coat hangers will work just as well; bend one end of the wire to hang from a branch and the other end to hold the fruit. You can even attach a shallow fruit bowl filled with grapes, blueberries, or cherries. These may attract woodpeckers, thrushes, mockingbirds, catbirds, Cedar Waxwings, and many other species that often prefer fruits over seeds.

Bird Feeder Hygiene Clean all feeders at least once a month. Moldy mite- and bacteria-infested feeders are dangerous to backyard birds. Scrub and rinse plastic feeders in hot water with a dash of chlorine bleach. Use a weak disinfectant in hot water on wooden hoppers, scrubbing to remove dirt and seed remnants. Flush out hummingbird feeders with hot water (but no soap) once a week, especially around the holes. Replace suet/peanut butter logs regularly, and rake up hulls and uneaten seeds under feeders often.

BEST BIRD FOODS

Seeds, staples of backyard bird feeding, come in a some-times confusing variety. Yet a few basic types will satisfy a diverse clientele. Other foods may attract different birds.

■ Sunflower seeds These come in two kinds. The smaller black-oil sunflower seeds will bring the greatest variety of species, from chickadees and titmice to jays. The larger striped type is better for strong-billed birds such as Purple Finches and Evening Grosbeaks. Even woodpeckers will visit a hopper or tray feeder for sunflower seeds.

■ Mixed seeds A birdseed mix should be an important part of any backyard menu, but quality varies greatly. The best mix-tures are combinations of black-oil sunflower, white proso mil-let, bits of nuts and corn, and perhaps safflower as well. Avoid the least expensive mixtures, which are filled with the small globes of red milo, which very few birds except doves eat.

■ Nuts and corn Almost all seed-eating birds will enjoy unsalted nuts broken into bits with a rolling pin, and larger birds including jays will like cracked corn (although rake it up if it gets wet). Scatter the nuts and corn on the ground and hope that the birds will get their fair share before the squirrels arrive for breakfast.

■ Suet and peanut butter These are high-energy winter foods loved by many species. See page 23 for tips on how to provide them. Suet is favored especially by woodpeckers. Peanut butter is a source of crucial energy for birds in winter, and it can be lifesaving for Carolina Wrens at the northern end of their range in a harsh season.

■ Fruits Oranges cut in half or apples and other fruits cut in pieces are favorites of orioles, especially when they return in the spring to breed. Berries are a favored winter food for thrushes, Cedar Waxwings, and Yellow-rumped Warblers, but these are best provided by landscaping with shrubs that will be loaded with berries during fall and winter.

Black-oil sunflower seeds

White proso millet

Nyjer for finches

High-quality mix

Nuts and large seeds

Peanuts for jays

Suet-and-nut cake

Fruits of all kinds

Mealworms, packed with protein

■ **Specialties** Experiment with other types of foods: mealworms, which parents feed to nestlings; crushed oyster shell, a source of calcium; or stone grit, which various birds require to crush foods in their gizzard. Avoid using old bread.

■ **Hummingbird food** Nothing beats the classic, simple recipe of one part white granulated sugar to four parts water. Boil the water, then add the sugar and stir. Don't use food coloring or artificial sweetener.

Birdhouses

As your enthusiasm for watching birds grows, take the next step and invite birds to nest in your yard. All through the spring and the summer, watch the passing parade. First, adults haul nest material into a birdhouse. Then they fly back and forth, carrying food to the nestlings. Finally the chicks fledge and fly away.

TYPES OF HOUSES

First decide which birds you would like to attract. Birdhouses are suitable only for species that naturally nest in holes or cavities, but many of our most beloved birds will use birdhouses: chickadees, titmice, nuthatches, wrens, swallows, and bluebirds. To see what you might attract, check the range maps and nest types of the common species described here.

There are three main types of birdhouses: a nest box, for a pair of birds and their young; an apartment house, for a Purple Martin colony; and a simple sheltered shelf, for species that prefer to nest on a flat, open surface.

■Nest box This is the typical wooden birdhouse, available ready-made or in kits for building. Plans are also available in books, at your local Audubon chapter or bird club, and on the Internet. Nest boxes can take many shapes and sizes, depending on the species they are meant to attract.

The length, width, and height are important. The diameter of the entrance hole is critical, and often needs to be smaller than might seem appropriate: for example, only 1 inch for a House Wren or a Black-capped Chickadee and 1½ inches for an Eastern Bluebird—if it's any larger, House Sparrows or European Starlings may usurp the box.

Use untreated, unpainted wood such as cedar or pine. It should have a sloped, overhanging roof, ventilation holes at the top of each side under the eaves, and small drainage holes in each corner of the floor. The roof should be hinged for cleaning. Don't add a perch—nesting birds don't need it, but predators such as jays might use it to poke into the hole.

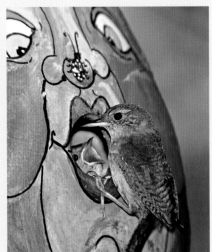

Eastern Bluebirds use a classic nest box.

House Wrens don't mind gaudy colors.

One of the most gratifying conservation success stories is the comeback of the Eastern Bluebird, which was vanishing from the countryside in recent decades as the availability of natural nest holes in old trees declined. But the bluebird population is now increasing because bird lovers are building special houses for them. Some people have even started "bluebird trails," installing dozens of boxes on fence rows along roads in parks and rural areas where volunteers monitor them. Western Bluebirds and Mountain Bluebirds have declined in parts of their ranges, too, and nest boxes can help them as well. The key online resource for information on bluebird conservation is the nonprofit organization Sialis (the species name for the Eastern Bluebird).

■ **Purple Martin house** These familiar bird "apartment buildings" can attract colonial martins that chatter, swoop, and dart about, gulping down thousands of flying insects daily. Martins in the East nest only in human-made houses, while those west of the Rockies use natural cavities.

Unfortunately, a martin house can easily disappoint. The amount of open space around the house is critical, and absolute precision is required in the dimensions of each

A mansion awaits Purple Martins.

Martins use hanging gourds, too.

nest compartment and its entrance hole. The house must be designed to be raised on its pole in the spring and lowered to the ground in fall—and it is critical to raise the house during the particular week when the martins typically return to your locality from their spring migration. Furthermore, special efforts must be made to prevent European Starlings and House Sparrows from moving in and taking over a Purple Martin house. These and other details make being a martin landlord a difficult, yet rewarding, occupation.

Martins will also nest in a structure of gourds hanging from cross arms on a tall pole. These are less expensive on average than the full-scale houses, but they have the

House Cleaning Birdhouse cleanliness is crucial to birds' health and safety. Clean out the box or shelf in early spring. March is a good month, before the birds begin to breed. As with feeders, clean them inside and out with a weak chlorine bleach solution. Resist the temptation to line the inside of the nest box with a chemical coating to seal the wood or kill insects; evaporating solvents—usually toxic—may linger inside the closed box for a long time, and birds are very sensitive to them.

same strict requirements as houses for size, seasonal timing, and placement within your yard.

Providing housing for Purple Martins is a true hobby, incomparably enjoyable if you are so inclined. Just keep in mind that expert advice is needed to improve your chances of success. The essential resource for well-researched information is the Purple Martin Conservation Association, which offers extensive information online.

■Shelf or ledge Some species will nest on an open platform under a sheltering roof. You can attract Eastern Phoebes, Black Phoebes, Say's Phoebes, and Barn Swallows with nothing more than a flat piece of plywood, 6 inches square, placed under an eave. Since these species tolerate nearby humans, as long as the nest is not disturbed, you can watch the parents feed newly hatched nestlings.

Phoebes often renovate and reuse shelf nests for multiple years. When one of these birds settles into the nest shelf you provide, you may see the same one year in, year out. Barn Swallows and Eastern Phoebes may alternate possession of a nest from year to year, each remodeling it after the other's use.

Eastern Phoebes prefer an open shelf under a roof.

LOCATING THE BIRDHOUSE

Locate a nest box or shelf in the safest place possible. Throughout their lives, birds are faced with the dangers of predators, and a poorly placed birdhouse simply offers them up as prey. Feral cats and house cats that spend time outside present challenges for which birds have never evolved defenses. Here are some birdhouse practices that can offer important protection.

■**On a pole** The best place for a nest box is atop a tall metal pole, and some birds such as House Wrens will readily accept pole-mounted boxes. A wide, slippery, metal baffle surrounding the pole halfway up can help prevent egg-eating squirrels and raccoons from climbing to the top. Keep the box well away from hanging tree branches and tall shrubbery from which a squirrel could easily jump over to it. Ants and other crawling insects can be kept from invading a birdhouse by wrapping the pole below it with sticky flypaper-type material.

■**In a tree** The fact is that few bird species will nest in a box high out in the open. It is not their natural behavior.

POLE HEIGHT MATTERS	
POLES THIS TALL	ATTRACT THESE BIRDS
6–7 feet	Wrens, Chickadees, and Bluebirds
8–10 feet	Downy Woodpeckers and Ash-throated Flycatchers
9–12 feet	Northern Flickers, Hairy Woodpeckers, White-breasted Nuthatches, and Great Crested Flycatchers
12–20 feet	Red-headed Woodpeckers
15 feet or taller	Larger birds such as American Kestrels and Eastern Screech-Owls

Pole mount for bluebirds or Tree Swallows

Tree mount for Great Crested Flycatchers

They would prefer a nest box mounted on trunk or thick branch of a tree. Space nest boxes widely around the yard. Do not put more than one on a tree, and don't place them near feeders.

The nest entrance should face in a direction helpful to the birds inside. If your wind and rain come most often from the northwest, face the house opening to the east and south. If you live in a region where nights are cool, face the hole east, so the early morning sun can shine into the birdhouse. Birds usually place their nests in a place sheltered from the midday sunshine, and you should do the same.

■On a porch Birds use enclosures not only for nesting but also for shelter in the winter. A birdhouse gives them a place to roost and survive the coldest days and nights. People in the Northeast can create roosting structures for chickadees and wrens by lining a basket with soft material, covering it in waterproof material with a one-inch hole on one side, and placing it on a south-facing porch. Cover a pinecone with peanut butter, suet, and seeds, and leave it by the hole on the snowiest days.

[Bird-Friendly Yards]

With feeders and nest boxes, we provide food, nesting opportunities, and shelter for birds. Your backyard is not just a home but a neighborhood—in the language of science, a habitat. All birds require specifics in their habitats, and if you know how to fulfill those needs, you can make your backyard more bird friendly.

CREATING A HABITAT

Begin by considering the sorts of plants that attract the birds you want to watch. A yard with tall trees can attract tanagers or orioles. A yard with shrubs can attract Gray Catbirds and Song Sparrows. If your yard is nothing more than a wide open, manicured lawn, it may attract American Robins, European Starlings, and Common Grackles to poke around in the grass for worms and grubs, but that's about all. A smooth, closely mowed lawn is not a prime habitat for any bird.

ATTRACTING BIRDS
Some species are remarkably adaptable—for example, House Finches live in cities, suburbs, and deserts—but most are very particular, and this gets to the essence of landscaping for birds. If you provide the largest possible diversity in habitat—a combination of different, carefully planned types of vegetation—you will attract the greatest variety of birds.

Assorted heights are one factor: trees, shrubs, and low understory plants. A range of food is another: plants that provide different kinds of berries, fruits, and seeds as well as supporting caterpillars and insects. Seasonal diversity matters, too: Nectar-bearing flowers attract hummingbirds in summer, and berry-laden trees and shrubs attract Cedar Waxwings in winter. Landscapes designed for diversity not only offer food and shelter but also provide varied locations, attracting different birds that stay to carve out or build a nest.

Yards with a variety of shrubs and trees—here a birch and a maple—will appeal to many different birds, including Blue Jays.

BIRDBATHS

Water is essential for birds in every season, whether it is provided in an elaborate pond or a simple birdbath. Of all the habitat requirements, this is one shared by all birds and essential to their existence. Birds both drink and bathe in water, and they will visit your yard more often and in larger numbers if you provide it.

If you can, provide a birdbath on a pedestal—even a container as simple as a shallow pan placed on a low table. Some units are quite elaborate, with heaters and circulators. In arid regions water is especially crucial, but all birds require drinkable water every day, even in cooler and damper regions.

A Scarlet Tanager fluffs after bathing.

Western Bluebirds like dripping water.

The Allure of Water Attract small songbirds at migration time by offering water in different forms when thirsty flocks pass through your neighborhood. You can create a temporary moving-water feature in five minutes by propping your lawn hose nozzle on a foot-long stick and letting it drip or spray onto the grass in an open area of the lawn. Take care to keep birdbaths filled in hot weather. The water will disappear rapidly as birds splash avidly, and filling baths twice a day is not too often.

REGIONAL PLANTS

The vegetation of large forests and small woodlands, high and low elevations, cool and warm climates, scrubby meadows, old pastures and farms, prairies, marshlands, ponds, shorelines, and deserts—all must be considered in your landscaping scheme, depending on the habitat you are creating in and around your yard. Particularly in northern latitudes, the emphasis should be on plants that serve the needs of birds throughout the year, not just at the height of the warm-weather growing season.

■ **Trees and shrubs** Add trees first when you begin a planting program, putting in a mix of evergreens and deciduous species. Then, go down to the shrub layer. Again, add both evergreens and deciduous bushes to fill in and shape the open spaces.

■ **Annuals and perennials** Next, add perennial and annual flowers. Consider growing vines over fences, up the sides of a house or garage, or on trellises out in the open, as space and your tastes allow. If you have any non-native flowering plants, consider removing them and replacing them with native varieties.

■ **Native plants** Plants that are native to an area will establish easily, require the least care, and support bird species that have co-evolved over thousands of years to feed on these plants' seeds, fruits, and nectar. If space permits, include an area where you can let ordinary local weeds colonize and mature. Birds have fed on these plants habitually, and the weeds may serve up nutrients that birds need.

Also keep in mind that yesterday's weeds often become tomorrow's favored perennials. The word "weeds," after all, is merely a disparaging term for unwanted plants, some of which may have attractive flowers. Not long ago gardeners were aggressively ripping out goldenrod, joe-pye weed, and mullein as weeds—now all are featured in upscale nursery catalogs. You may be leading a trend when you cherish a few stalks of pokeweed behind the garage.

LANDSCAPING FOR BIRDS IN THE NORTHEAST

The northeastern states host many nesting birds in the warmer months, temporary migrants in spring and fall, and a smaller number of species year-round. Recurrent and persistent winter frost, variable summer heat, and year-round precipitation make this a variable habitat for the birds.

TREES	SHRUBS	GRASSES	ANNUALS AND PERENNIALS
yellow birch *Betula alleghaniensis*	Bartram serviceberry *Amelanchier bartramiana*	little bluestem *Schizachyrium scoparium*	New England aster *Aster novaeangliae*
red pine *Pinus resinosa*	red chokecherry *Aronia arbutifolia*	Indian grass *Sorghastrum nutans*	beebalm *Monarda didyma*
black cherry *Prunus serotina*	winterberry *Ilex verticillata*		foxglove penstemon *Penstemon digitalis*
eastern hemlock *Tsuga canadensis*	bayberry *Myrica pensylvanica*		black-eyed Susan *Rudbeckia species*
eastern red cedar *Juniperus virginiana*	staghorn sumac *Rhus typhina*		goldenrod *Solidago canadensis*

A pond or lake will attract ducks, geese, herons, and other waterbirds.

LANDSCAPING FOR BIRDS IN THE SOUTHEAST

The southeastern states experience hot and humid summers, mild winters with periodic yet less persistent frost, and year-round precipitation in the form of rain. Permanent bird residents are joined for the winter by those that have migrated south to overwinter in this warmer clime.

TREES	SHRUBS	GRASSES	ANNUALS AND PERENNIALS
serviceberry *Amelanchier laevis*	American holly *Ilex opaca*	northern sea oats *Chasmanthium latifolium*	false indigo *Baptisia* species
river birch *Betula nigra*	winterberry *Ilex verticulata*	switchgrass *Panicum virgatum*	coreopsis, tickseed *Coreopsis* species
live oak *Quercus virginiana*	smooth sumac *Rhus glabra*		coneflower *Echinacea* species
saw palmetto *Serenoa repens*			joe-pye weed *Eupatorium fistulosum*
			hairy sunflower *Helianthus hirsutus*
			goldenrod *Solidago* species

A diverse array of trees, shrubs, and flowers is perfect for many birds.

LANDSCAPING FOR BIRDS IN THE NORTHWEST

The interior mountains and valleys and the northern plains are snowy and cold in winter, and dry and hot in the summer. Along the coast, the Pacific Northwest is wet and often chilly. In forested landscapes, pines, cedars, and spruces supply shelter, nest sites, and food across the whole of this sector.

TREES	SHRUBS	GRASSES	ANNUALS AND PERENNIALS
mountain dogwood *Cornus nuttallii*	serviceberry *Amelanchier alnifolia*	little bluestem *Andropogon scoparius*	sagebrush *Artemisia ludoviciana*
desert olive *Forestiera neomexicana*	Oregon grape holly *Mahonia aquifolium*	blue grama *Bouteloua grama*	purple aster *Aster bigelovii*
juniper *Juniperus* species	wax myrtle *Myrica cerifera*		Indian paintbrush *Castilleja* species
piñon pine *Pinus edulis*	fragrant sumac *Rhus aromatica*		plains coreopsis *Coreopsis tinctoria*
Gambel oak *Quercus gambelii*	elderberry *Sambucus canadensis*		

Junipers and other shrubs with berries serve birds well in moist climates.

LANDSCAPING FOR BIRDS IN THE SOUTHWEST

The southwestern region is rich in natural wonders and wildlife. Generally mild, this sector experiences cold temperatures at higher altitudes and suffers brutally hot summers. The precipitation is seasonal, with summer rainfall rare. Resident and migratory birds seek water above all.

TREES	SHRUBS	GRASSES	ANNUALS AND PERENNIALS
mountain dogwood *Cornus nuttallii*	century plant *Agave chrysantha*	sideoats *Bouteloua curtipendula*	sage *Artemisia species*
California juniper *Juniperus californicus*	ocotillo *Fouquieria splendens*	blue grama *Bouteloua gracilis*	purple aster *Aster bigelovii*
piñon pine *Pinus edulis*	cholla, prickly pear *Opuntia species*	buffalo grass *Buchloe dactyloides*	plains coreopsis *Coreopsis tinctoria*
western white pine *Pinus monticola*	common chokecherry *Prunus virginiana*	switchgrass *Panicum virgatum*	California poppy *Eschscholzia californica*
California live oak *Quercus agrifolia*			sunflower *Helianthus species*
western hemlock *Tsuga heterophylla*			black-eyed Susan *Rudbeckia species*

Cacti and other plants of arid lands are essential in desert environments.

Birding Skills

Your feeders are installed, your birdhouses are in place, and you've invited the birds with attractive landscaping. Now there are three more keys to full enjoyment: Sighting the birds in your backyard; learning to identify the most common visitors; and then learning their songs, so that you know a visitor even without seeing it.

HOW TO SEE THE BIRDS

Watching birds from inside a window can be endlessly entertaining, but you'll miss many other opportunities to find birds if you stop there. You'll be seeing only one small part of a larger—sometimes much larger—bird community that is in and near the yard. These birds are in the air, high and often camouflaged in the trees, lurking in the shrubs, and feeding in the flower bed around the corner of your house.

To maximize awareness and recognition of what's there, go outside and look carefully—high and low, and at different times of the day. Begin by studying birds' daily patterns of activity. As you become aware of how they behave at various times, your enjoyment will be enhanced immeasurably.

TIME IT RIGHT

Songbirds have a typical pattern of behavior within the 24-hour span of a day. They are most lively in the early morning, even before dawn in the spring and summer, not long after they awaken. Like us, birds wake up hungry after a long night of sleep and fasting. They spend the morning feeding, and then—in both midsummer heat and midwinter cold— many of them disappear from view, moving back into the bushes and trees to rest all afternoon. Finally, in the early evening until sunset, they come out and spend a short time foraging for the day's last meal before withdrawing out of sight again for the night. The lesson here is that if you are a late sleeper and look for birds only in the afternoon, you will see only a fraction of your yard's birds.

Seeing birds can be as easy as watching hummers at a bleeding heart.

THROUGH THE SEASONS

During migration season, look intently into the trees—right at eye level, you might see a well-camouflaged greenish-and-yellowish Orange-crowned Warbler that is passing quietly through the yard. Look straight up, where a Broad-winged Hawk may be circling silently, during a migration that covers thousands of miles. Peek carefully down into shrubbery, and you could see a Gray Catbird or a Spotted Towhee creeping from low bush to low bush.

Especially in the breeding season, be sure to look high into deciduous trees. You may spot a Bullock's Oriole or Baltimore Oriole hanging its pouch-like nest from a branch. If your yard borders a marsh, gaze out in the early morning for a burst of activity as male Red-winged Blackbirds vie for territory in the cattails. If you can see a lake or pond in the West, watch for Violet-green Swallows in search of insects, skimming over the water. Spring and summer—breeding season—represents the peak of watchable bird activities. Look around in winter, too. Besides the birds at your feeders, some may lurk in the shrubbery.

KEYS TO IDENTIFYING BIRDS

Eight basic characteristics of a bird can lead to its identification: size, shape, colors, color patterns, behavior, song, habitat, and geographic range. Of course, you don't need to consider all of these for every bird; one or two will clinch the identification in many cases.

Let's use the American Robin as an example, because it is found just about everywhere in North America and is a bird that you likely recognize already. You might even find a robin in your yard, to serve as a living example as you read these words.

A robin is considered a medium-size bird—smaller than a pigeon and larger than a sparrow. In shape, it is what we might call "medium" as well—rather bulky, especially in the breast, with bill, legs, and tail neither very long nor very short. But that information isn't much help, is it? "Medium" applies to many birds, so we must look further—primarily at colors and color patterns.

For colors and patterns, look carefully at the next robin you see. It has the famous red breast, and is entirely dark gray on the upperparts, with a white throat faintly streaked in black, a bright yellow bill, and a broken white ring around the eye.

Now let's look at a robin's behavior: This is a bird often seen walking through the grass, intently seeking, and often finding, and pulling up a worm.

American Robin

Finally, let's listen. Robins are almost everywhere, month after month, so you may know their song—something like *cheedily, cheedilo, cheedleup, cheedlit,* sung over and over again for minutes on end.

Use these eight features when you want to identify any bird. You usually don't need to concentrate on all eight, because not all will be necessary. Here are three examples of different paths to identification, based on the illustrations in this book:

DISTINGUISHING BETWEEN SIMILAR SPECIES

	DOWNY WOODPECKER	HAIRY WOODPECKER
+ Size is the key for distinguishing these two. + They look almost the same, except that the Hairy is substantially larger, with a distinctively longer, heavier bill. + Song helps, too. If they give a long call, the Downy's will be a descending whinny, but the Hairy's whinny will be harsher and all on one pitch.		
	GAMBEL'S QUAIL	CALIFORNIA QUAIL
+ Size, shape, and behavior are not appreciably different, so the keys to distinguishing these two are color and color patterns. + Note the distinctive plumage pattern on the underparts of each bird. + The California Quail has a chestnut-colored patch on its belly center. + The Gambel's Quail is plain, with a large black patch on the male.		
	CAROLINA CHICKADEE	BLACK-CAPPED CHICKADEE
+ These two birds are nearly identical in look and behavior. + Their songs differ slightly, but it takes experience to recognize them, if they are heard at all. + Look at the range map. In Minnesota, it's a Black-capped; in Mississippi, a Carolina.		

Rose-breasted Grosbeak

HEARING BIRDS SING

Go outside just before sunrise in the spring, and you may hear a disorganized symphony of birdsong that is called the dawn chorus. Males of dozens of species are singing all at once, trying their best to establish nesting territory and attract mates. In some places, there is so much noise that it's hard to sort out even a few of the dozens of different songs. That is why a better approach is to learn one song at a time.

IDENTIFYING BIRDS BY THEIR SONGS

Almost all birds sing most often in the spring—and some sing *only* in the spring. Others, such as the Carolina Wren, can be heard throughout the year: *tea-kettle tea-kettle tea-kettle*.

Some birds sing all day long, such as the Red-eyed Vireo and the Common Yellowthroat. Other birds sing all night long—not only owls but also, for example, the Northern Mockingbird. And still others, such as the Hermit Thrush, sing primarily before midmorning and then again in early evening.

If you hear a bird, try to figure out where the song is coming from. If you can find the bird, you can put song and species together. Above all, when you begin to learn songs, have patience. Watch one bird singing at a time. The more slowly you learn your yard birds' songs, the longer will be your joy in day-by-day, year-by-year discoveries.

Birdsong Online All 150 species of birds identified in this book can be explored on the National Geographic Society's Backyard Birding website, http://animals.nationalgeographic.com/animals/birding. There you can search for each bird species, read details about every one of the eight keys to identification, see detailed illustrations and photographs, and hear recordings of representative birdsongs.

CHOOSING BINOCULARS

For the best backyard bird-watching, use binoculars. If a bird is more than 15 or 20 feet away, you may not see sufficient details of plumage, color, and pattern to identify it. And you will appreciate its full beauty with a closer look.

Invest in a set of binoculars in the $150 to $200 range. To prove to yourself that the investment is worth it, go to an optics dealer and look through a cheap model and then a more expensive one. What a difference!

While you're at it, try out various models. Think about comfort first. The binoculars should be comfortable to hold, should have an easy-to-turn focus wheel, should adjust properly for the distance between your eyes, and should

Encourage your children to share your enjoyment of birds and all nature.

provide a single, unshaded circle when you look through the two eyepieces. Eyeglass wearers, make sure the image is not vignetted by the black tube that surrounds the lens.

Binoculars are described as 8 x 32, 7 x 40, 10 x 40, and so forth. The first number simply represents the power of magnification—the higher the number, the closer the bird will appear. The second number is the width of the light-gathering lens in millimeters—the higher the number, the brighter the image will be. But don't get too caught up in the numbers. An 8 x 32 or 7 x 40 model will be satisfactory for almost every backyard bird-watcher.

[Citizen Science]

As your experience in backyard bird-watching grows, your enthusiasm will grow as well, and you will want to share it with others. Get your children involved at an early age. Share the pleasures with your spouse or a neighbor. Then get to know the larger birding community—others just as interested in birds as you are.

THE BIRDING COMMUNITY

You may never have met them. You may not even know they exist. But in the area where you live, there may be dozens—even hundreds—who call themselves "birders": the term for people who go beyond their yards to make watching birds, traveling to see new birds, and studying birds a major passion in their lives.

Who are these birders? How can you get in touch? If there is an Audubon Society chapter or other nature center in your area, contact it for information on bird-oriented activities. Search the Internet for bird clubs in your state or local area. Look for scheduled bird walks led by experienced birders.

Two of North America's most important birding organizations are the American Birding Association (ABA; www.aba .org) and the Cornell Lab of Ornithology (www.birds.cornell .edu). The ABA publishes a magazine, *Birding*, for birders of all levels of experience. The Cornell Lab sponsors a host of "citizen science" projects, such as the Great Backyard Bird Count and eBird, highlighted on the next two pages.

Ornithological organizations are often scientifically oriented, but all offer programs and welcome new members.

Keeping a Journal Some birders like to keep a journal of where and when they first saw a bird, with notes on its habitat, behavior, and other information. Add up all the species you have seen, and you have a "life list." In the pages of this book, we offer a system that can help you keep a record of the months when you spot your favorite species in your backyard.

A Blue Jay offers a gift to his mate.

■ The Christmas Bird Count The most famous and longest lived birding activity for participants amateur and professional alike is the annual Christmas Bird Count, sponsored by the National Audubon Society. Going for 110 years, the Audubon CBC now boasts tens of thousands of volunteers throughout the Americas who go out on a scheduled day in late December or early January and count all the birds they can find.

This is "citizen science" at its best, an opportunity to get outdoors and at the same time contribute important data that scientists can use to determine which species are increasing and which are declining.

Learn how to join the fun, experience nature's winter beauty, and help to find out how our bird populations are faring. Visit the Christmas Bird Count website at http://web4.audubon.org/bird/cbc.

■ Project Feeder Watch Here is a scientific project that you can enjoy simply by looking out the window periodically from November through early April and counting the birds that visit your feeders. Submit your counts online to the Cornell Lab of Ornithology, which sponsors the project along with Bird Studies Canada. Feeder Watch data help scientists track broadscale movements of winter bird populations and long-term trends in bird distribution and abundance. Anyone with an interest in birds is welcome to participate.

Which species are reported most often at feeders in different regions? They are the Black-capped Chickadee in the North Atlantic, Northern Cardinal in the Southeast, Dark-eyed Junco in the Central Midwest, and House Finch in the Southwest. Without backyard watchers like you reporting their observations, no one could know those answers.

Learn how to participate by visiting the project's website: www.birds.cornell.edu/pfw.

■ **The Great Backyard Bird Count** This project, sponsored by the Cornell Lab, Bird Studies Canada, and the National Audubon Society, is an annual four-day event in February that captures an annual snapshot of birds across the continent. Anyone can participate, from beginners to experts. Count birds in your yard or anywhere you'd like to visit, for as long as you like each day of the count, even if you only spend 15 minutes doing so.

Then send your checklist to the organizers, through their website: www.birdsource.org/gbbc. There you can also find more details on how to participate, and you can learn which species are seen in states, cities, and towns across the United States and Canada.

Here's a tidbit from the 2010 GBBC: Across the continent, the Northern Cardinal was reported on the most checklists, and American Robins were reported in the largest numbers.

■ **eBird** Sponsored by the Cornell Lab and National Audubon Society, eBird is a living encyclopedia of what species are being found where. It is an online checklist program that allows birders to enter their own bird lists online at www.ebird.org. Individual bird lists are tallied, and in January 2010, participants reported more than 1.5 million bird observations across North America.

Besides contributing to scientific knowledge, the submitted records are a treasure of information for the average birder. Let's say you plan to visit a certain town, park, or wildlife refuge next week. Enter the location on eBird, and you will find out which species have been seen there in recent days or recent weeks. Other website features include interesting articles about birds and birding.

WEBSITES
+ American Birding Association *www.americanbirding.org*
+ American Ornithologists' Union *www.aou.org/checklist/north/*
+ Birding on the Net *www.birdingonthe.net*
+ Breeding Bird Survey *www.pwrc.usgs.gov/BBS*
+ Cornell Laboratory of Ornithology *www.birds.cornell.edu*
+ eBird *www.ebird.org*
+ Frontiers of Identification *www.birdingonthe.net/mailinglists/ FRID.html*
+ National Geographic Society *animals.nationalgeographic.com/animals/ birding*
+ SORA (Searchable Ornithological Research Archive) *elibrary.unm.edu/sora/index.php*

GUIDE

TO 150 SPECIES

JONATHAN ALDERFER

Ducks, Geese, & Swans
Family Anatidae

A worldwide family of web-footed, gregarious birds, ranging from small ducks to large swans. Largely aquatic, but some species also graze on land.

long, black neck

white chin strap

honking calls lower pitched than Cackling Goose

Canada Goose
Branta canadensis, L 30–43" (76–109 cm)

Nonmigratory populations have exploded in the last 50 years and are regarded as pests in many locations.

IDENTIFICATION Common and increasing. "Canadian Geese" or (as hunters often refer to them) "honkers" are well known and easy to identify.
■ **plumage** Long black neck (like a black stocking); black head with white "chin strap"; brown body, paler below. Downy **goslings** are a patchy blend of yellow and brown.
■ **similar species** Cackling Goose (not illustrated) is a tiny look-alike that occasionally winters with "normal-size" Canada Geese.

■ **voice** Call is a deep, musical but nasal *honk-a-lonk* or two-syllable *ka-ronk*.

RANGE Widespread species; year-round resident throughout much of its range. Nonmigratory (feral) geese abound in many suburban locations, such as parks, golf courses, and reservoirs, as well as more natural locations. Flocks of wild migrating birds fly in V-formation. Spring **migration** of wild geese: February–April; fall migration: September–November.

FOOD Grazes on grass, but diet is usually supplemented with a variety of pond plant life. Migrating birds seek out waste grain in agricultural fields.
■ **feeding** Canada Geese are very attracted to corn and other grains.

U-shaped rump band

NESTING *Location:* On the ground near water. *Nest:* Bulky construction of plant material. *Eggs:* Usually 5–6; incubated by female for 25–30 days, while male stands guard. *Fledging:* Downy gosling leaves the nest soon after hatching and can feed itself; able to fly at about 9 weeks. Parents and young remain together as a family group until the following spring.

Sightings

JAN	FEB	MAR	APR	MAY	JUN	JUL	AUG	SEP	OCT	NOV	DEC

blue speculum—

Mallard

Anas platyrhynchos, L 23″ (58 cm)

♂
♀

The Mallard is the most abundant duck in world and the ancestor of almost all domestic ducks. The world population is estimated at over 30 million birds, with about 18 million in North America.

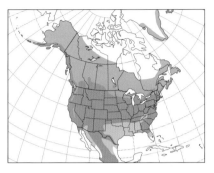

♀
dark saddle on orange bill

mostly white tail

IDENTIFICATION Common. The Mallard and related ducks, known as dabbling or puddle ducks, are strong, agile fliers able to spring directly into flight.

■ **plumage** **Male** has metallic green head, chestnut breast, and yellow bill; **female** is a nondescript, mottled brown, with orange bill with a black saddle mark. **Ducklings** are flightless, fluffy balls of yellow and brown.

■ **similar species** City and suburban parks host a bewildering mix of Mallard-like domestic ducks with plumages from all white to ancestral looking, and everything in between.

■ **voice** Male's **call** is soft, raspy *rab*; female gives the loud, familiar *Quack!*, often in a descending series *Quack, Quack, quackquackquack.*

RANGE Widespread species. Mallards are found around almost any freshwater habitat, and many birds are year-round residents. Spring **migration** is very early, with breeding birds usually arriving during the spring thaw; fall migration: September–November.

FOOD During the breeding season, feeds almost entirely on animal pond life (insect larvae, snails). At other seasons, they are opportunistic feeders that seek out seeds from wild plants and farm crops. Most food is obtained by "tipping up"—using the familiar "butt-in-the-air-and-head-underwater" position that allows food to be gleaned from the pond bottom.

■ **feeding** In many city and suburban parks, the local birds will see you coming and demand a handout, even if it's only some bread crumbs. Cracked corn makes a healthier meal.

NESTING *Location:* On the ground, usually near water. *Nest:* Hollow of plant material, lined with feathers and down. *Eggs:* Usually 10–12; incubated by female for about 28 days. *Fledging:* Duckling can swim and feed itself soon after hatching. The female accompanies young until they can fly at 7–8 weeks.

yellow bill
♂
curled central tail feathers

Sightings—

JAN	FEB	MAR	APR	MAY	JUN	JUL	AUG	SEP	OCT	NOV	DEC

WHAT'S IN A NAME?

The source of a bird's name may be obvious: the color of the Blue Jay, shape of the Scissor-tailed Flycatcher, pattern of the Band-tailed Pigeon, behavior of the Brown Creeper, song of the Warbling Vireo, diet of the Acorn Woodpecker, habitat of the Pine Warbler, range of the California Towhee, and so on. More interesting are names that initially seem illogical, mysterious, or obscure.

A GENEALOGY OF NAMING

Many familiar names emerged anciently in Anglo-Saxon Europe: duck, goose, hawk, dove, crow, thrush, finch. Others originated far away from those lands, such as "tanager," adapted from a native language in South America.

People are often honored: Swainson's Thrush is named for a 19th-century naturalist, Bullock's Oriole for the man who discovered that bird in Mexico. The "Anna" of Anna's Hummingbird is more unexpected. She was the Duchess of Rivoli in Europe, whose husband was an amateur ornithologist.

Names may be logical: a Lesser Goldfinch is smaller than an American Goldfinch. But why is a Summer Tanager more summery than a Scarlet Tanager? It turns out that English naturalist Mark Catesby, who explored the Southeast in the 18th century, named it the "Summer Red Bird" to distinguish it from the "redbird" (Northern Cardinal), which remained all year.

Scientific names are in Latin, or latinized versions of Greek. The Pine Warbler is called *Dendroica pinus*, which means "pine tree dweller." For the Northern Cardinal, *Cardinalis cardinalis* is double Latin for "important," referring to high-ranking Catholic cardinals who wear a red robe and hat.

A Bullock's Oriole is more beautiful than its name might suggest, but the scientist who first describes a bird is entitled to name it in someone's honor.

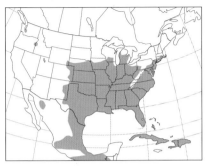

New World Quail
Family Odontophoridae

All New World quail have chunky bodies, crests or head plumes, and a terrestrial lifestyle. In North America, most species live in the West.

slight crest — ♂ — white supercilium
♀ buffy supercilium
white throat
buffy throat

juvenile

Northern Bobwhite
Colinus virginianus, L 9¾" (25 cm)

Named for the male's whistled call, these birds are the only native quail in the East. Except in parts of Texas, this species has dramatically declined during the past 30 years, probably a victim of suburban sprawl, feral cats, and other small predatory mammals.

IDENTIFICATION Uncommon. The bobwhite is a chunky, ground-dwelling bird with a short tail. If frightened, it runs for cover and freezes before flushing with a loud whir of wings. When not breeding, forms coveys of 5–30 birds.

■ **plumage** Overall reddish brown with irregular streaks and spots. **Male's** head is boldly patterned in blackish brown and white; **female's** head is brown and buff; **juvenile** is smaller and duller.
■ **similar species** None.
■ **voice** The male's rising, whistled **call**—*bob-WHITE!*—is heard mostly in spring and summer. Both sexes give soft *hoy* or louder *koi-lee* contact calls.

RANGE Eastern species; year-round resident. Found in rural and agricultural areas, rarely in suburbia.

FOOD Forages on the ground—often in dense cover—for seeds, berries, vegetation, and insects.
■ **feeding** Will come to seed or cracked corn scattered on the ground or at a platform feeder. Offering water is important, especially during droughts.

NESTING *Location:* On the ground in a sheltered location. *Nest:* Shallow hollow of plant material, often completely arched over, with an entrance at one side. *Eggs:* Usually 12–14; incubated mostly by female for about 23 days. *Fledging:* Downy young leaves the nest almost immediately and can feed itself, accompanied by parents; able to fly at 7–10 days.

Sightings

JAN	FEB	MAR	APR	MAY	JUN	JUL	AUG	SEP	OCT	NOV	DEC

California Quail
Callipepla californica, L 10" (25 cm)

This handsome and sociable quail inhabits westernmost North America. During the nonbreeding season, large coveys form. An old name for it is "Valley Quail." State bird of California.

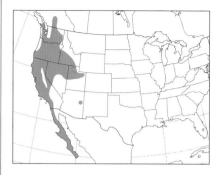

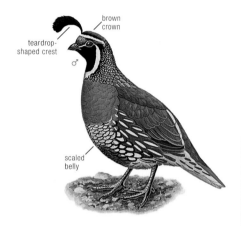

brown crown

teardrop-shaped crest

♂

scaled belly

RANGE Western species; year-round resident. Lives in scrubby lowlands and on brushy slopes to about 5,000 feet. Comes to suburban backyards if there is suitable cover and a supply of water.

FOOD Vegetable matter, especially buds and fresh shoots in spring, and insects. In winter, subsists largely on seeds, small fruits, and berries.
▪ **feeding** Comes to grain scattered on the ground or on a platform feeder.

IDENTIFICATION Common. Ground-dwelling bird that looks beautifully ornate up close. You're most likely to see them at dawn or in the late afternoon; during the heat of the day, they stick to cover.
▪ **plumage** Curved topknot feathers overhang bill; scaly belly. Fancy **male** has dark head with white stripes and chestnut patch on belly. **Female** is browner and more subtly marked, lacks strong face pattern, and has smaller topknot. **Juvenile** is browner and has tiny topknot.
▪ **similar species** Desert-dwelling Gambel's Quail (opposite) overlaps slightly in range. The male Gambel's has a redder crown and a black belly patch.
▪ **voice** The most characteristic **call** is a loud, emphatic *chi-CA-go*—often heard in the background of Hollywood Westerns.

NESTING *Location:* On the ground. *Nest:* Shallow depression lined with grass. *Eggs:* Usually 10–17; incubated by female for 18–23 days. *Fledging:* Downy young leaves the nest almost immediately and can feed itself, accompanied by parents; able to fly at 10–14 days.

small topknot

♀

coastal females are browner

Sightings

JAN	FEB	MAR	APR	MAY	JUN	JUL	AUG	SEP	OCT	NOV	DEC

Gambel's Quail

Callipepla gambelii, L 11" (28 cm)

This close relative of the California Quail is a familiar and beautiful desert bird. Tame and sociable, it has adapted to the increasing human development of its desert home.

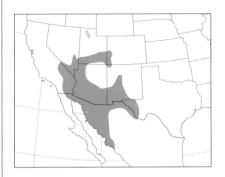

IDENTIFICATION Common. This gregarious bird is often seen in small family groups or large winter coveys. When frightened they scurry for cover, if pressed further, they scatter in all directions on loudly whirring wings. At night, coveys roost in low trees.
■ **plumage** Curved topknot feathers overhang bill. **Male** has white stripes on head, reddish crown, and black belly patch surrounded by white. **Female** is more subtly marked and has an unmarked white belly and smaller topknot. **Juvenile** is gray and tan with a tiny topknot.
■ **similar species** California Quail (opposite), with a small overlap in range, is browner and has a scaly belly.
■ **voice** Most characteristic **call** is a loud, emphatic *chi-CA-go-go*—similar to the California Quail's, but higher pitched and usually with four notes, not three; also a plaintive *qua-el.*

RANGE Desert Southwest and Great Basin species; year-round resident. Inhabits low-lying desert washes, river valleys, and arroyos with scrubby vegetation. Frequents suburban backyards and urban parks with nearby desert vegetation.

FOOD Vegetable matter, especially buds and fresh shoots in spring, and some insects. In winter, feeds mostly on seeds, small fruits (including cactus fruit), and berries.

teardrop-shaped crest

chestnut crown

chestnut sides

black belly

Cannot survive without a permanent water source.
■ **feeding** Is attracted to grain scattered on the ground or on a platform feeder, but is vulnerable to free-roaming cats.

NESTING *Location:* On the ground, sheltered by a shrub, tree, or clump of prickly pear cactus. *Nest:* Shallow depression lined with grass. *Eggs:* Usually 10–12; incubated by female for 21–23 days, with male nearby on sentry duty. *Fledging:* Downy young leave the nest almost immediately and can feed themselves, accompanied by parents; able to fly at 10–14 days.

Sightings

JAN	FEB	MAR	APR	MAY	JUN	JUL	AUG	SEP	OCT	NOV	DEC

New World Vultures
Family Cathartidae

A small family of large soaring birds that primarily eats carrion. All have small, unfeathered heads and hooked bills. Inaccurately, the general public often refers to vultures as buzzards.

soars on flat wings, wing flaps are rapid and shallow

adults

pale grayish legs

short tail

extensive white base to outer primaries

Black Vulture
Coragyps atratus, L 25" (64 cm)

Appropriately dressed in funereal black, this efficient and successful carrion scavenger has a huge hemispheric range extending from southern New England to southern South America.

IDENTIFICATION Common. In flight, short tail barely extends behind the broad wings and feet almost reach tip of tail. Soars high on steady wings held flat. Usually seen in groups, especially when roosting.

■ **plumage** Appears all black when perched, with bare head of wrinkled gray skin; whitish legs. In flight, underwings show large whitish patches on outer wing.

■ **similar species** Turkey Vulture (opposite) has narrower, two-tone wings (not white patches) and a much longer tail, usually flies with up-tilted wings, and almost never flaps rapidly. Adult Turkey Vultures have browner plumage and red facial skin and legs. Immature ones have gray head and legs (like Black Vulture); on perched bird, look for Turkey Vulture's longer wingtips, more slender body, and smaller head.

■ **voice** Essentially silent; nesting birds utter hisses and grunts.

RANGE Mainly Southeastern species; year-round resident. Abundant in the Southeast, but avoids mountainous country and open plains. Range is expanding into southern New England.

FOOD Feeds on animal carcasses, including roadkill; scavenges at garbage dumps. Soars to great heights, locating its food by sight and also by spying on Turkey Vultures that more efficiently locate food by smell. Dominant at feeding sites.

NESTING *Location:* On the ground in a concealing thicket or hollow log; occasionally in an abandoned building. *Nest:* None. *Eggs:* Usually 2; incubated by both parents for 37–41 days. *Fledging:* Leaves nest at 75–80 days; usually accompanied by parents for many months.

Sightings

JAN	FEB	MAR	APR	MAY	JUN	JUL	AUG	SEP	OCT	NOV	DEC

Turkey Vulture

Cathartes aura, L 27" (69 cm)

The most common vulture across most of North America. Unique among vultures, it locates the carrion it feeds on by using its sense of smell, in addition to visual clues.

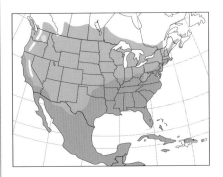

reddish head
adult
grayish
juvenile

IDENTIFICATION Common. A consummate soaring bird that rarely flaps, seeming to catch the slightest updraft by tilting its long wings from side to side. In flight, note its long, narrow wings, long tail, and tiny head; soaring birds fly with wings in a noticeable dihedral V.
■ **plumage** Appears blackish brown when perched. In flight, underwings are two-toned—silvery and black. **Adult** has reddish head of bare skin and pinkish legs. **Juvenile** has grayish head and legs.
■ **similar species** See Black Vulture (opposite), which has a more limited distribution—compare the range maps.
■ **voice** Essentially silent; nesting birds utter hisses and grunts.

RANGE Widespread species. Favors wooded regions (for breeding) with open areas (for foraging). Since birds range far and wide, backyard birders often see them soaring overhead in small flocks or roosting together in a tree. Northern breeding birds migrate south in fall. Spring **migration** peaks in March–early April; fall migration: September–October.

FOOD Feeds on animal carcasses, specializing in small food items that it can eat quickly. Its keen sense of smell allows it to locate carcasses concealed beneath the forest canopy.

soars on slight dihedral, wing flaps are slow and deep

two-toned underwings

long tail

NESTING *Location:* On the ground in an isolated rocky crevice or hollow log; occasionally in an abandoned building. *Nest:* None. *Eggs:* Usually 2; incubated by both parents for 38–41 days. *Fledging:* Leaves nest at 75–80 days. Young birds soon join a nearby communal roost and fend for themselves.

Sightings

JAN	FEB	MAR	APR	MAY	JUN	JUL	AUG	SEP	OCT	NOV	DEC

Hawks, Kites, & Eagles
Family Accipitridae

Worldwide family of diurnal birds of prey with hooked bills and strong talons. Many species are easier to identify in flight, when their different wing and tail patterns can be seen.

juvenile

pale gray head

pale bands on tail

black tail

adult ♂

Mississippi Kite
Ictinia mississippiensis, L 14½" (37 cm)

Kites are a loosely related group of raptors with many different species found around the world; the Mississippi is the most common of the five species that occur in North America.

 IDENTIFICATION Locally common. Buoyant flier with pointed wings. In areas of abundance, these gregarious, crow-size birds often hunt in groups and form loose breeding colonies.
■ **plumage** In flight, upper wing has a whitish secondary patch. **Adult male** is dark gray overall with whitish head and red eyes; **female** has darker head. **Juvenile** has heavily streaked underparts and banded tail.

■ **similar species** Unlike most common hawks (buteos) that have heavier bodies and broad, rounded wings, the Mississippi Kite looks more like a gray falcon.
■ **voice** The two-syllable, high-pitched **call** is whistled: *phee-phew.*

 RANGE Southern Great Plains and Southeastern species; summer resident. Very common around shelterbelt tree plantings, towns, and backyards in Kansas, Oklahoma, and north-central Texas. Its aggressive nest defense sometimes results in diving attacks on people. Migrates to southern South America for the winter. Spring **migration:** early April–mid-May; fall migration: late August–mid-October.

never hovers

adult ♂

whitish secondary patch

FOOD Nimbly captures and consumes large flying insects in flight; also hunts frogs, lizards, snakes, and a variety of small birds and mammals.

NESTING *Location:* In a tree, often at the edge of a woodlot. *Nest:* Loose construction of twigs lined with green leaves. *Eggs:* Usually 2; incubated by both parents for 29–32 days. *Fledging:* Young moves to nearby limbs at 25–30 days; able to fly at 30–35 days.

Sightings

| JAN | FEB | MAR | APR | MAY | JUN | JUL | AUG | SEP | OCT | NOV | DEC |

RAPTOR HUNTING STRATEGIES

Hawks' hunting prowess is legendary, and it is why they are called *raptors*—from the Latin word for "plunderers." The seven raptor species in this book use different strategies to seek, find, and capture their prey.

■**Kites** A Mississippi Kite soars, glides, twists and turns buoyantly, and swoops smoothly, grabbing insects with its bill in midair.

■**Accipiters** The Sharp-shinned Hawk and Cooper's Hawk are often familiar to backyard feeder watchers. These bird-eaters learn quickly which yards have feeders. Usually, the small birds see them coming and dart into the nearest shrubbery. If the birds suddenly disappear and become silent, perhaps a "Sharpie" or a "Coop" is nearby.

■**Buteos** Red-tailed, Red-shouldered, and Broad-winged Hawks usually adopt a perch-and-watch strategy, rather than searching from the air. When a small animal moves through the grass or leaves, even if the animal itself is not visible, the hawk spots the vegetation moving and swoops down instantly to make the kill.

■**Falcons** The American Kestrel, a kind of falcon, has two strategies. One is the perch-and-watch method from a pole or wire. The other is hovering 20 or 30 feet above ground. After spotting a large insect or small rodent, the kestrel zooms down at high speed to grab its prey.

This composite photo illustrates a Cooper's Hawk in pursuit of a Northern Flicker.

Sharp-shinned Hawk
Accipiter striatus, L 10–14" (25–36 cm)

This is one of the accipiters—bird-eating woodland hawks. Winter bird feeders are favorite hunting locations. Although some bird-feeding enthusiasts vilify the feisty "Sharpie," our advice is to marvel at the drama of the hunt. These predators serve a needed function by keeping wild bird populations healthy and wary.

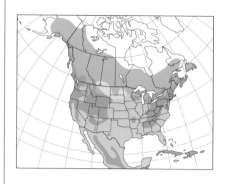

small head — adult ♂
juvenile ♀
thin legs

below. Sharpies are about the size of a grackle; Cooper's are closer to crow size. In direct flight, Sharpies have fast, flicking wing beats; Cooper's have noticeably slower, stiffer wing beats.

■ **voice** A high, chattering *kew-kew-kew* call heard around the nest.

 **RANGE** Widespread. Breeds in northern and western forests, but thinly distributed and declining. More widespread and commonly seen in winter, particularly around bird feeders. Northern breeders migrate south in fall. Spring **migration:** mid-April–early May; fall migration: September for juveniles, October for adults.

IDENTIFICATION Fairly common. Small hawk with short, rounded wings and long tail that allows it to maneuver rapidly around tree trunks and branches.

■ **plumage** **Adult** is bluish gray above and rufous below; dark cap blends into nape. **Female** is larger than male (close to size of male Cooper's Hawk). **Juvenile** is brownish above with coarse brown streaks below.

■ **similar species** Cooper's Hawk (opposite) has longer round-tipped tail, heavier legs, larger head, and longer neck. Juvenile Cooper's has thinner, darker streaks

FOOD Preys mainly on small, woodland songbirds. Attacks from a perch or cruises low, using shrubs or even buildings for cover.

 NESTING *Location:* Most often concealed high in a conifer. *Nest:* Platform of sticks. *Eggs:* Usually 4–5; incubated mostly by female for 30–35 days. *Fledging:* Leaves nest at about 23 days.

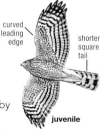

curved leading edge
shorter square tail
juvenile

Sightings

JAN	FEB	MAR	APR	MAY	JUN	JUL	AUG	SEP	OCT	NOV	DEC	

Cooper's Hawk
Accipiter cooperii, L 15–18" (38–46 cm)

Cooper's Hawk and the similar Sharp-shinned are swift and effective bird ambushers that patrol bird feeders and woodlands in search of a meal.

IDENTIFICATION Fairly common. Cooper's and Sharp-shinned Hawks hunt in a similar fashion, but the larger Cooper's favors larger prey—doves, jays, and robins rather than chickadees, titmice, and sparrows.
■ **plumage** Adult is bluish gray above with rusty bars below; blackish cap contrasts with paler nape (more blended in Sharp-shinned). **Juvenile** is brownish above, often with orangish highlights on the head, and thin, dark streaks below.
■ **similar species** See Sharp-shinned Hawk (opposite) and Red-shouldered Hawk (next page).
■ **voice** Chattering, strident **call** *kak-kak-kak,* reminiscent of Sharp-shinned Hawk but lower pitched.

RANGE Widespread species. Inhabits forests and forest edges, even around urban locations. Year-round resident throughout much of North America, but northern populations migrate south in fall. Spring **migration:** mainly in April; fall migration: September–October.

FOOD Preys primarily on birds up to the size of a flicker, and small mammals up to the size of a squirrel. Hunts much like a Sharp-shinned, but often perches more openly, even on telephone poles.

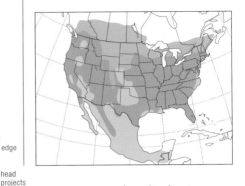

straight leading edge

head projects

long rounded tail

juvenile

NESTING *Location:* In a tree. *Nest:* Bulky platform of sticks. *Eggs:* Usually 3–5; incubated mostly by female for 30–36 days. *Fledging:* Leaves nest at 30–35 days. Young learn to hunt in about 3 weeks.

larger head, longer neck, and tawny nape

juvenile ♀

female larger than male

blackish cap

adult ♂

Sightings

JAN	FEB	MAR	APR	MAY	JUN	JUL	AUG	SEP	OCT	NOV	DEC

Red-shouldered Hawk
Buteo lineatus, L 17" (43 cm)

The colorful Red-shouldered Hawk is a vocal bird with a loud voice. Backyard birders often hear them calling in flight from high overhead.

 IDENTIFICATION Fairly common. Medium-to-large hawk. Soaring bird holds wings cupped forward and has rounded wingtips.

■ plumage In flight, there is a pale crescent ("window") visible at the base of the primaries. West Coast birds are more richly colored and checkered; those in south Florida, paler with whitish head. Adult has rufous upperwing coverts ("red shoulders") and densely barred rufous underparts. Wings and tail are dramatically barred in black and white. Juvenile has brown-streaked underparts and a dark tail with numerous pale bands.

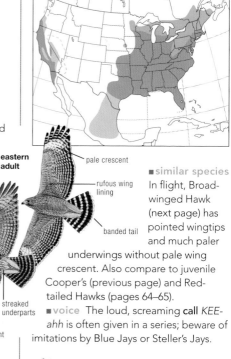

eastern adult

pale crescent

rufous wing lining

banded tail

eastern juvenile

streaked underparts

pale crescent

■ similar species In flight, Broadwinged Hawk (next page) has pointed wingtips and much paler underwings without pale wing crescent. Also compare to juvenile Cooper's (previous page) and Redtailed Hawks (pages 64–65).

■ voice The loud, screaming call *KEE-ahh* is often given in a series; beware of imitations by Blue Jays or Steller's Jays.

RANGE Widespread species. Inhabits well-watered woodlands, suburban areas with nearby woodlots, and oak and eucalyptus groves in the West. Year-round resident in many areas, but northern breeders in the East are migratory. Spring **migration:** February–early April; fall migration: mid-October–late December.

FOOD A perch-hunter of the forest understory, it feeds on frogs, snakes, lizards, and small mammals.

NESTING *Location:* In a high tree crotch. *Nest:* Bulky platform of sticks. *Eggs:* Usually 3–4; incubated mostly by female for about 33 days. *Fledging:* Leaves nest at about 6 weeks.

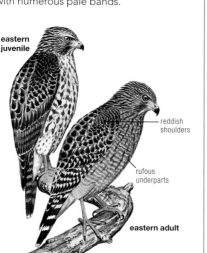

eastern juvenile

reddish shoulders

rufous underparts

eastern adult

| JAN | FEB | MAR | APR | MAY | JUN | JUL | AUG | SEP | OCT | NOV | DEC |

Broad-winged Hawk
Buteo platypterus, L 16" (41 cm)

The smallest North American buteo hawk, and a rather nondescript bird. It is spectacular in migration, entirely vacating North America and traveling in large "kettles"—spiraling clusters of birds that ride upward on warm air currents and then glide gradually downward in their desired direction.

juvenile

adult

dark malar stripe

rufous-brown barred underparts

black wing tips; more pointed than Red-shouldered

IDENTIFICATION Fairly common. This small woodland hawk has a chunky, compact shape, short tail, and broad-based wings with pointed tips. When breeding, it is inconspicuous and would often go unnoticed if not for its loud whistled call.

variable whitish underwing

juvenile

black trailing edge

adult

■ **plumage** Dark malar stripe (moustache). In flight, has pale underwings with a dark border. **Adult** is dark brown above and has rufous-brown barred underparts and a blackish tail with two white bands. **Juvenile** has breast variably streaked with brown and indistinct bands on tail.

■ **similar species** Compare juvenile to juvenile Red-shouldered (opposite), Cooper's (page 61), and Red-tailed Hawks (pages 64–65).

■ **voice** **Call** is a thin, shrill, slightly descending whistle *pee-heeeee* that carries well; imitated by Blue Jays.

RANGE Central and Eastern species; summer resident. Inhabits forested areas and migrates to Central and South America for the winter. Migrating kettles often pass over suburban and urban locations. Spring **migration:** mid-March–mid-May; fall migration: early September–early October.

FOOD A patient, perch-hunter specialist of the forest understory, often near watery edges. It feeds on frogs, snakes, lizards, small birds, small mammals, and insects.

NESTING *Location:* At mid-level in a large tree. *Nest:* Small platform of sticks. *Eggs:* Usually 2–3; incubated mostly by female for 28–31 days. *Fledging:* Leaves nest at 5–6 weeks.

Sightings

JAN	FEB	MAR	APR	MAY	JUN	JUL	AUG	SEP	OCT	NOV	DEC

Red-tailed Hawk

Buteo jamaicensis, L 22" (56 cm)

The Red-tailed Hawk's extensive breeding range makes it the "default" raptor in most of the U.S. and Canada. Juveniles lack the adults' trademark reddish-orange tail feathers.

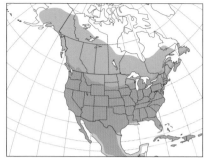

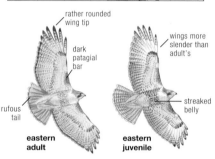

rather rounded wing tip

dark patagial bar

rufous tail

eastern adult

wings more slender than adult's

streaked belly

eastern juvenile

IDENTIFICATION Common. This bulky, broad-winged, broad-tailed hawk is built for effortless, languid soaring over open country. It perches in the open and is often seen sitting atop roadside utility poles or fence posts. Get to know the Red-tail's shape, silhouette, and posture and you'll be able to identify many birds without inspecting their plumage. If you are enthusiastic about raptors, purchase a specialized hawk guide and take a trip to a popular hawk-watching location, where scores of hawks can be seen in a single fall day and there are usually experienced birders on hand to help out.

■ **plumage** Eastern adult is brown above, with large white patches on the scapulars that form a broad V across its back. The pale underparts are crossed by a dark belly band. The Great Plains **"Krider's Red-tailed"** is much paler above and below (no belly band); its tail has a pale reddish wash. Farther west, **rufous morph** or **dark morph** birds are often encountered, or even the uncommon, blackish **"Harlan's Hawk."** All of this can be a bit confusing, but almost all adults have at least some reddish orange color on the tail. In flight, the best field mark is the distinct dark patch on the leading edge of the underwings; this dark patagial bar is visible on all ages and morphs, except for the very darkest birds. **Juveniles** have gray-brown tails with many blackish bands, and most show some white on the chest and dark mottling on the belly.

■ **similar species** In the East, a juvenile Red-tailed might be mistaken for a smaller Red-shouldered juvenile (page 62), but that species lacks the patagial bar and has a rangier body and longer tail.

eastern adult

eastern juvenile

whitish on scapulars

rufous tail

brownish banded tail

Farther west, Red-tailed are more variable, but the dark patagial bar is a good mark on most birds.

■ **voice** Distinctive **call**—a harsh, descending *keee-eerrrrrr*—is often given by flying birds.

RANGE Widespread species. Lives in various habitats, from mountains and woodlands to prairies and deserts, as well as suburban and urban locations with trees and open space. Year-round resident in much of its range. Breeders from Alaska and Canada move south in the fall, so there are more Red-tails in the Lower 48 during the winter months. Spring **migration** begins as early as February, but the northern-most breeding areas may not be occupied until early June; peak fall migration is from mid-October to late November.

western dark-morph adult

FOOD Most hunting is done from an elevated perch that allows a visual search of the surrounding area, but Red-tails also hunt by cruising over open

Broad wings and powerful muscles are required to get a Red-tailed Hawk's 2½-pound body aloft.

areas or soaring at higher altitudes. Prey includes small mammals (ground squirrels are a favorite in the West), reptiles, and larger birds. Most prey is captured and dispatched on the ground, then taken to a feeding perch to be eaten.

NESTING *Location:* Usually high up in a large tree, but cliff ledges, saguaro cacti, power-line towers, and building ledges are also utilized. *Nest:* Bulky platform of sticks. *Eggs:* Usually 2–3; incubated by both parents for 28–35 days. *Fledging:* Young birds move out of the nest at about 6–7 weeks, but are not strong fliers until about 9 weeks. They continue to receive food from their parents for a month or more, while they hone their flying and hunting skills.

"Krider's Red-tailed" adult

pale head

paler rufous tail

This adult Red-tailed has taken its meal to a feeding perch to be plucked and eaten.

Sightings

	JAN	FEB	MAR	APR	MAY	JUN	JUL	AUG	SEP	OCT	NOV	DEC

Falcons
Family Falconidae

Falcons are distinguished from hawks by their long wings, which are narrow, pointed, and bent back at the "wrist." Females are larger than males.

all with two dark facial stripes uniformly

male has bluish gray wings

adult ♂

American Kestrel
Falco sparverius, L 10½" (27 cm)

This petite and colorful raptor lives in open habitats from coast to coast and is North America's most common falcon. Its north–south range extends from Alaska to the southern tip of South America.

IDENTIFICATION Fairly common. The American Kestrel is a buoyant flier with slender pointed wings and a long tail. It is capable of hovering on rapidly beating wings while searching for prey.

■ **plumage** Two black facial stripes. **Adult male** has blue-gray wings, chestnut back with black bars, chestnut tail with a black bar near the tip, and apricot underparts with dark spots. **Juvenile males** are similar, but with paler underparts, more dark bars on the back, and streaked breast. **Adult female**

has reddish brown upperparts and tail with dark bars; reddish streaks on underparts.

adult ♂

frequently hovers

■ **similar species** None.

■ **voice** Distinctive **call** is a shrill, rapid *killy-killy-killy*.

adult ♂

RANGE Widespread species. Lives in rural and suburban areas with open fields; often seen hunting along roadways. Declining in the East. Spring **migration:** April–mid-May; fall migration: August–September.

FOOD Prey consists of large insects, lizards, rodents, and birds. Most prey is attacked on the ground and carried off to a feeding perch.

adult ♀

uniformly rufous brown

NESTING *Location:* In an old woodpecker hole or natural cavity. *Nest:* No material added. *Eggs:* Usually 4–5; incubated mostly by female for 29–30 days. *Fledging:* Leaves nest at 28–31 days.

■ **housing** Will use a nest box fastened to a tree or pole 10–20 feet off the ground.

rufous tail

Sightings

	JAN	FEB	MAR	APR	MAY	JUN	JUL	AUG	SEP	OCT	NOV	DEC

WHY DO BIRDS MIGRATE?

The simplest answer is: because they must. Twice a year, hundreds of millions of birds embark on long, treacherous journeys north or south between different regions where seasonal food and climate enable them to live. The idea that a Rufous Hummingbird could fly between Alaska and Mexico, or that a Ruby-throated Hummingbird could travel between Newfoundland and Costa Rica, seems preposterous. But they in fact make such flights, and enough survive that their species is preserved.

WHERE THE FOOD IS

It is easy to understand that insect-eating flycatchers, vireos, thrushes, and warblers are not likely to survive during a snowy winter in the north, so they must leave. These are basically tropical species whose breeding ranges gradually expanded northward in the past 20,000 years as the ice sheet that covered Canada and much of the northern U.S. retreated. They now can breed at very high latitudes because their insect food is plentiful in spring and summer.

ONGOING CHANGE

The climate continues to warm, as it has for 20,000 years, and the ranges of birds such as the Red-bellied Woodpecker are still expanding farther into the northern U.S. and southern Canada. If their physiology and a regular food supply enable them to survive northern winters, the birds become year-round residents.

Various species, including the Eastern Bluebird, are partial migrants, whose populations in the northernmost range may need to migrate southward to areas with sufficient food, but whose populations living in more southerly regions can remain year-round.

Migrating Tree Swallows form immense flocks along the Atlantic coast, where 750,000 were estimated on one autumn day at Cape Charles, Virginia.

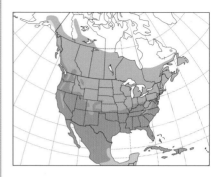

Plovers
Family Charadriidae

This family is part of a much larger assemblage of birds collectively known as shorebirds, which includes stilts, avocets, sandpipers, curlews, godwits, dowitchers, and snipes, among others. Many of these species occur in coastal and freshwater locations but are beyond the scope of this book.

two breast bands

Killdeer
Charadrius vociferus, L 10½" (27 cm)

The Killdeer—a type of plover—is a conspicuous shorebird that doesn't require a watery location for breeding or feeding. It prefers open, often human-altered habitats. In fact, few native birds have benefited more from the fragmentation of the American landscape.

 IDENTIFICATION Common. Easily recognizable by its shape—slender and horizontal—and distinctive plumage. While feeding, it moves with a jerky, run-stop-run cadence. Its noisy call is often the first signal of its presence. Migrating and wintering birds sometimes form loose flocks of 20 or more birds.

■ **plumage** Two prominent black bands on chest and black bar on forehead. Brown upperparts, white underparts, and a reddish orange rump, most noticeable in flight or during a broken-wing display (see opposite). Flightless **downy young** have single breast bands and leave the nest shortly after hatching.

■ **similar species** None. Downy young with a single breast band could be mistaken for a different species of plover, but an adult Killdeer is usually nearby and probably making a fuss.

■ **voice** Loud and piercing *kill-dee* (for which it is named) or *dee-dee-dee* **call** is easy to recognize. The Killdeer is often active at night—look for it on lighted playing fields and parking lots—and can be heard calling in the darkness, especially in spring and summer.

RANGE Widespread species. Although often seen around ponds and puddles, the Killdeer prefers

A downy young Killdeer has a single breast band; the adult has two breast bands.

to breed in heavily grazed meadows, large lawns, golf courses, sod farms, airports, and parking lots, among other unnatural landscapes. Northern breeders are migratory, retreating southward for the winter months. Spring **migration** is early, with birds showing up in the middle latitudes with the first bit of warmth after mid-February; fall migration peaks in August–September. Many birds linger in the north until November or later, if warm weather persists.

The Killdeer's ostentatious "broken-wing" display serves to lead a predator away from its nest.

FOOD Diet consists mostly of invertebrates, especially earthworms, grasshoppers, beetles, and snails picked from the ground or mud.

NESTING *Location:* Open ground (gravelly areas are favored). *Nest:* Shallow scraped indentation, lined with pebbles and nearby debris—especially white objects, including shells, plastic items, even cigarette filters—and well camouflaged. *Eggs:* Usually 4; incubated by both parents for 22–28 days. *Fledging:* Downy young leave the nest almost immediately and can feed themselves, accompanied by parents; able to fly at 30–40 days.

■ displays When protecting its nest or flightless young, the feisty Killdeer has evolved some effective and easily observed tactics. During a **"broken-wing" display,** it drags a partially open wing on the ground, spreads its long tail, and exposes its bright, reddish-orange rump, leading a potential predator away from the area before suddenly flying off. The **"ungulate" display,** another theatrical performance, seems designed to divert a large grazing animal (or person) from trampling its nest: The loudly screaming bird rushes toward the animal; if that doesn't work, it lowers its breast, raises its long tail, and beats the ground with its wings, continuing to give high-pitched calls. Bravo!

long tail and reddish orange rump

The "ungulate" display probably evolved to divert large animals from trampling the Killdeer's nest.

Sightings

	JAN	FEB	MAR	APR	MAY	JUN	JUL	AUG	SEP	OCT	NOV	DEC

Gulls
Family Laridae

Identifying gulls can be complicated. Some species take more than three years to reach adult plumage, and the intervening immature plumages are often quite different.

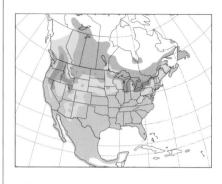

Ring-billed Gull
Larus delawarensis, L 17½" (45 cm)

The Ring-billed Gull is the most widespread and familiar gull over much of North America. Its population probably exceeds four million birds.

IDENTIFICATION Common to abundant. Ring-billed are the typical gull at inland locations in winter. They notoriously hang out around shopping centers, parks, and garbage dumps, as well as the standard watery locations.
■ **plumage** Takes just over two years to reach adult plumage. **Winter adult** is pale gray above, white below; bill is yellow with a prominent black ring, and legs and eyes are yellow. **First-winter** bird has a pale gray back, pinkish legs, mottled brown head and underparts, pink bill with a black tip, and variable, brown tail band.
■ **similar species** Discernible from California and Herring Gulls (following pages) by its smaller size. Adult Herring Gull has pink legs and a yellow bill with a red spot. Adult California Gull is darker gray above and has greenish legs, a yellow bill with black and red spots, and dark eyes. First-winter Herring and California Gulls are overall much browner.
■ **voice** Calls include a plaintive, mewing *kee-ew* and a sharper *kyow*.

RANGE Widespread species. Most backyard birders see these gulls in winter, but small numbers of immature birds remain in southern locations during the summer. Spring **migration:** February–April; fall migration: September–October.

FOOD In winter, scavenges along beaches, harbors, lakeshores, and garbage dumps for refuse but also catches fish and consumes insects, earthworms, and grain.

NESTING *Location:* Ring-billed Gulls breed in colonies, mostly on low, sparsely vegetated islands in lakes—not typical backyard locations. Seventy percent of the world population breeds in Canada.

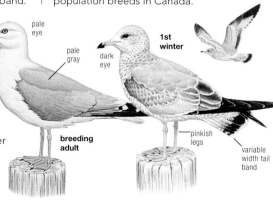

pale eye

black subterminal band

pale gray

dark eye

1st winter

breeding adult

pinkish legs

variable width tail band

Sightings

JAN	FEB	MAR	APR	MAY	JUN	JUL	AUG	SEP	OCT	NOV	DEC

California Gull
Larus californicus, L 21" (53 cm)

The California Gull is increasing its numbers along the Pacific Coast, where it is the most common gull on the coastal slope. State bird of Utah.

IDENTIFICATION Common. Intermediate in size between the smaller Ring-billed Gull and larger Herring Gull, and with a fairly long, straight-sided bill and a lanky look.

■ **plumage** Takes almost four years to reach adult plumage. **Winter adult** is medium gray above; importantly, its bill is yellow with red and black spots near the tip and it has dark eyes and greenish yellow legs. In flight from below, note the smoky gray secondaries. **First-winter** bird has mottled, brownish-gray plumage, a pinkish bill with a black tip, and pink legs.

■ **similar species** Resembles Ring-billed and Herring Gulls (opposite and next pages). Adult Ring-billed is lighter gray above and has pale eyes and a yellow bill with a prominent black ring, while the adult Herring is bigger with pink legs and has no black on its bill. First-winter Herring and California Gulls both have mottled brown backs (not pale gray, like first-winter Ring-billed); the Herring Gull's bill is heavier and blacker, and its head is usually paler.

■ **voice** **Calls** include a throaty *kyow* and a higher pitched *kier*.

RANGE Western species. Breeds mainly in the arid interior West, and migrates primarily to the Pacific Coast in winter.

In spring, adults **migrate** away from coastal areas as early as late February; fall migrants leave breeding colonies in July.

FOOD Summer diet consists mainly of insects, supplemented with worms, small rodents, and carrion. Along the coast in winter, they eat marine life and scavenge around harbors and garbage dumps.

NESTING *Location:* Breeds in colonies on islands in rivers and lakes, areas located well away from most backyards.

slender pinkish bill with blackish tip

dark eye

heavy brownish wash

black and red spots

darker gray than Ring-billed or Herring

pinkish legs

1st winter

dark secondaries

no obvious pale window

winter adult

yellowish green legs

Sightings

JAN	FEB	MAR	APR	MAY	JUN	JUL	AUG	SEP	OCT	NOV	DEC

Herring Gull
Larus argentatus, L 25" (64 cm)

Distributed around the Northern Hemisphere. Extremely adaptable, the Herring Gull is an opportunistic feeder around human activities and is able to survive in almost any climate.

IDENTIFICATION Common. A large gull with pink legs at all ages and a fairly stout bill.

■ **plumage** Takes almost four years to reach adult plumage. **Winter adult** is pale gray above, white below; white head is flecked with brown (pure white in summer); and it has a yellow bill with a red spot near the tip, pale yellow eyes, and pink legs. **First-winter** is a mottled brown overall, often looking pale headed by midwinter; bill is dark with variable pink at base.

■ **similar species** See Ring-billed (page 70) and California Gulls (previous page). Gray mantle colors of adult Herring and Ring-billed Gulls are almost identical; the California Gull is noticeably darker gray.

■ **voice** Variety of **calls,** including a trumpeting *keeyow, kyow-kyow-kyow.*

RANGE Widespread species. Breeds along the Atlantic coast of the U.S. and Canada, throughout the Great Lakes region, and in the far north. It is especially abundant in the Northeast, where it both breeds and winters. Herring and Ring-billed Gulls winter together across large sections of the U.S. Usually arrives in wintering areas by October and departs by May.

FOOD Generalist predator. Feeds on fish, marine invertebrates (shellfish, sea urchins, crabs, etc.), insects, other birds (and their eggs and young) and is an opportunistic

scavenger of dead fish, carrion, and human refuse.

NESTING *Location:* On the ground; prefers to breed on islands. *Nest:* Scraped indentation. *Eggs:* Usually 3; incubated by both parents for 27–30 days. *Fledging:* Leaves nest in a day or two, but remains nearby; able to fly at about 6 weeks.

pale window

dark tail

1st winter

often pale headed

striking pale eye

extensive streaking

pale gray upperparts

pink legs

winter adult

Pigeons & Doves
Family Columbidae

A large family with over 300 species worldwide. The larger species of these birds are usually called pigeons, the smaller ones doves. They feed their young a regurgitated liquid "pigeon's milk" for the first few days of life.

color variations

Rock Pigeon
Columba livia, L 12½" (32 cm)

Non-native species. Introduced from Europe to eastern North America in the early 17th century. The adaptable "city pigeon" spread across the continent and remains closely tied to human-dominated landscapes.

IDENTIFICATION Common to abundant. Highly variable plumage, but usually instantly recognizable by structure and behavior. Found in small to large flocks, these tame birds strut, bob, and peck their way around most city parks and squares.
■ **plumage** The ancestral—and most prevalent—type is gray (darker on head, with iridescent neck) with two blackish wing bars, white rump, and blackish tail band. Many color variants exist. Variants often retain the two dark wing bars and whitish rump of the ancestral type, but solidly colored birds do not. All birds have pinkish red legs and feet.

■ **similar species** The larger, shyer Band-tailed Pigeon (next page) of the West has similar plumage coloration. Note the Band-tail's yellow-based bill, yellow feet, white crescent on the nape, and broad, pale gray (not black) tail band.
■ **voice** Soft **call** *coo-cuk-cuk-cuk-cooo.*

RANGE Widespread species; year-round resident. Found in cities, towns, and farms; able to survive in the most urbanized landscapes.

FOOD Seeds, waste grain, and fruits. Park birds greedily gather around anyone handing out bread crumbs. Visits bird feeders, but is usually an unwelcome guest.

ancestral natural coloration

white rump

NESTING *Location:* Usually on or in a man-made structure—a bridge, apartment windowsill, farm building, and so forth. *Nest:* Loose construction of twigs and debris. *Eggs:* Usually 2; incubated by both parents for 17–19 days. *Fledging:* Leaves nest at 25–32 days. *Broods:* Breeds year-round in most areas and may raise 5 or more broods per year.

Sightings

JAN	FEB	MAR	APR	MAY	JUN	JUL	AUG	SEP	OCT	NOV	DEC

Band-tailed Pigeon
Patagioenas fasciata, L 14½" (37 cm)

A big, sociable pigeon of the Pacific states. It can be common in urban parks and suburban neighborhoods, including at backyard bird feeders.

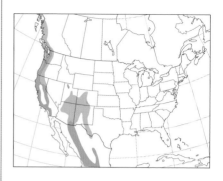

white band

yellow-based bill

IDENTIFICATION Fairly common. Larger and shier than the Rock Pigeon, but both species are usually found in flocks.

■ **plumage** Grayish overall with purplish tint on head and breast. Nape is iridescent with a white crescent above; tail has a broad pale band at tip. Bill is yellow with a black tip; feet are also yellow. **Juvenile** is similar, but lacks white nape crescent.

■ **similar species** Compare to Rock Pigeon (previous page), which lacks white nape crescent and has a dark tail tip, reddish feet, and often a white rump (Band-tailed never has a white rump). Band-taileds perch in trees, a location usually avoided by Rock Pigeons. In Band-tailed flocks, birds look uniform;

rather long tail with broad pale tail band

in most Rock Pigeon flocks, there is lots of variation from bird to bird.

■ **voice** Often silent; **call** is an owl-like, low-pitched *whoo-whoo*.

RANGE Western species. Two separate populations: mountains of the interior West, and West Coast (see map). Year-round resident in some areas (including some northern cities, such as Vancouver, Seattle, and Portland). Nomadic winter flocks wander in search of food, and northernmost breeders move south for the winter. Spring **migration:** February–late May; fall migration: mid-August–November.

FOOD Seeds, berries, grain, acorns, pine nuts, and tree buds. Fruit and nut orchards are also visited. Feeds on the ground on spilled or waste grain, but more often feeds in trees.

■ **feeding** Comes to platform feeders and grain scattered on ground; also eats berries of holly and other fruiting residential trees and shrubs.

NESTING *Location:* In a tree or shrub, 8–20 feet up. *Nest:* Shallow twiggy platform. *Eggs:* 1; incubated by both parents for 18–20 days. *Fledging:* Leaves nest at 25–30 days.

Sightings

JAN	FEB	MAR	APR	MAY	JUN	JUL	AUG	SEP	OCT	NOV	DEC

Eurasian Collared-Dove

Streptopelia decaocto, L 12½" (32 cm)

Non-native species. Accidentally introduced to the Bahamas and spread to Florida in 1978. Now found across much of the U.S. and into southern Canada, a colonization of North America astonishing for its speed and success.

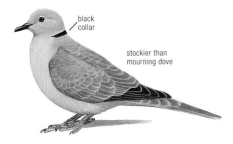

black collar

stockier than mourning dove

IDENTIFICATION Common. Large, pale dove; conspicuous and vocal. Feeds on the ground, but often perches on buildings and overhead wires. Flaps on broad, black-tipped wings, sometimes soars briefly, and floats down to a landing with tail spread.
■ **plumage** Light grayish tan overall with black hindneck collar; squared-off tail with large white tip and black base (most noticeable from below). **Juvenile** similar; black collar obscured or missing.
■ **similar species** Often occurs with Mourning Dove (next page), a darker and slimmer dove with a long pointed tail. White-winged Dove (page 77) is also darker overall; it has white wing patches, but a similar tail pattern and shape.
■ **voice** Three-syllable **call** *coo-COO-cup* is repeated monotonously.

RANGE Widespread species; year-round resident. Continues to colonize new areas, but is not migratory. Notably absent from New England,

although that is changing. Found in towns, suburbs, and farms; seems to avoid city centers and heavily forested areas.

FOOD Seeds, waste grain, and some berries and insects. Feeds on the ground; takes handouts from humans.
■ **feeding** Frequents platform feeders and grain scattered on ground. Rapidly becoming a well-known backyard bird in many areas.

NESTING *Location:* In tree, shrub, or sheltered building ledge, at mid-level. *Nest:* Flimsy platform of sticks and twigs. *Eggs:* Usually 2; incubated by both parents for 14–19 days. *Fledging:* Leaves nest at 16–20 days. *Broods:* 2 or more per year; probably breeds throughout the year in southern areas.

three-toned wing

grayish

large white tip

JAN	FEB	MAR	APR	MAY	JUN	JUL	AUG	SEP	OCT	NOV	DEC

Mourning Dove
Zenaida macroura, L 12" (31 cm)

One of the most abundant land birds in North America, with a population of about 350 million. Its mournful cooing (hence its name) is recognized by many people, although some mistake it for an owl.

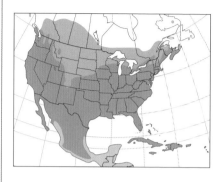

long tail

pointed

Present year-round in most of the U.S., but northern breeders are **migratory**. In winter, large flocks congregate around abundant food sources, such as stubble fields or feed lots.

IDENTIFICATION Common to abundant. Medium-size dove; long slender body, tiny head, and long pointed tail. Bursts into flight, the wind whistling through its wings and its tail spread (showing large amounts of white).
■ **plumage** Brown with tan head and underparts (slightly pinkish). Black-and-white tail pattern is hidden on perched birds. **Male** has purplish iridescence on neck. **Juvenile** is darker with pale feather fringes that give it a scaly look.
■ **similar species** Larger, heavier White-winged Dove (opposite) has a shorter, square-tipped tail and white wing patches (partially hidden when perched). See also Eurasian Collared-Dove (previous page). "Scaly" juvenile can be confused with Inca Dove (page 78).
■ **voice** Slow, mournful **call** *oowoo-woo-woo-woo*. Wings make a loud whistling sound in flight, especially during takeoff.

RANGE Widespread species. Prefers open locations, including rural and residential areas, deserts, and weedy fields; avoids thick forests.

FOOD Seeds of cultivated and wild plants. Feeds on the ground.
■ **feeding** Very common feeder bird. Can land on a hanging feeder, but normally feeds on seed scattered below or at a platform feeder.

NESTING *Location:* In a tree or shrub, 10–25 feet up; rarely on a building ledge. *Nest:* Flimsy platform of sticks and twigs. *Eggs:* 2; incubated by both parents for 14–15 days. *Fledging:* Leaves nest at 13–15 days. *Broods:* Up to 6 per year in southern areas.

tapered tail with white tips

♂

juvenile

scaly

black spotting

Sightings

JAN	FEB	MAR	APR	MAY	JUN	JUL	AUG	SEP	OCT	NOV	DEC

White-winged Dove

Zenaida asiatica, L 11½" (29 cm)

Flocks of these doves are a common sight in summer in areas near the Mexican border. The adaptable White-wing is increasing in numbers, and its range on the Great Plains is expanding northward.

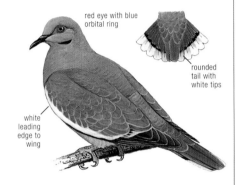

red eye with blue orbital ring

rounded tail with white tips

white leading edge to wing

IDENTIFICATION Common. Medium-large dove with a bulky body, square-tipped tail, and broad wings. The bill appears long (for a dove) and slightly downcurved. Its orange-red eyes are surrounded by blue skin.
■ **plumage** Brownish gray upperparts, grayer below. Large white wing patch, conspicuous in flight; appears as a white stripe when wing is folded. Blackish tail with white terminal band, prominent when spread, mostly hidden when perched.
■ **similar species** Similar in color and overall length to Mourning Dove (opposite). Mourning Dove lacks the white wing patches and has a slender body and long, pointed tail. Eurasian Collared-Dove (page 75) is much paler, has a black band across the hindneck, and also lacks white wing patches.
■ **voice** Very vocal; its drawn-out cooing **call**, *who-cooks-for-you*, has many variations.

RANGE Southwestern and Texas species. Inhabits mesquite woodlands, riparian woodlands, citrus groves, cactus-paloverde desert, and wooded residential areas. Present year-round in its southern range, but western birds are strongly migratory (wintering in Mexico). Spring **migration** peaks in March–April, fall migration in early August–mid-September.

FOOD Seeds, nuts, and fruits. Forages on the ground, perched in trees and cacti (an important pollinator of giant saguaro cactus), or clinging to seed stalks.
■ **feeding** Common feeder bird. Comes to seed scattered on the ground or to an elevated feeder. Occasionally wanders far to the north, and many of those rare sightings have occurred at bird feeders.

crescent-shaped white patch

NESTING *Location:* In a medium-height tree, shrub, or cactus. Nests singly or in large colonies. *Nest:* Flimsy platform of twigs. *Eggs:* Usually 2; incubated by both parents for 14–20 days. *Fledging:* Leaves nest at 13–18 days. *Broods:* 2–3 per year.

Sightings

JAN	FEB	MAR	APR	MAY	JUN	JUL	AUG	SEP	OCT	NOV	DEC

Inca Dove

Columbina inca, L 8¼" (21 cm)

These dainty little doves are closely associated with towns, suburbs, and cities and are slowly spreading to the north and east. The repetitive, melancholy call sounds like no hope, *earning it the nickname "Doomsday Dove."*

IDENTIFICATION Common. Small and slender, with a long tail. Small groups of these tame doves sometimes huddle tightly together on a single perch. The wing and tail patterns are best seen on stretching or flying birds. Flight is direct, and takeoffs from the ground are explosive, often from nearly underfoot. Forages on open ground and lawns; moves around with a shuffling gait.

scaly pattern on head and body

■ **plumage** Grayish overall, paler below; black fringes on feathers create a scaly pattern. Bright chestnut on wings and white outer tail feathers (features mostly hidden on perched birds). **Juvenile** is browner and less scaly.

■ **similar species** Shape recalls a miniature Mourning Dove (page 76), but Mourning Dove lacks "scaly" plumage and chestnut in wings. Common Ground-Dove (not illustrated) has chestnut in wing and overlaps in range, but is slightly smaller; it has a scaly pattern only on head and breast (not on back), and a short tail.

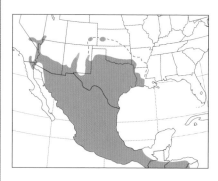

■ **voice** Low-pitched, two-syllable **call** *kooo-poo* ("no hope"), given repeatedly throughout the day.

RANGE Southwestern and Texas species; year-round resident. Closely associated with human development—cities, towns, suburbs, parks, farms, and feedlots; avoids extensive forest and dense brush.

FOOD Weed and grass seeds, grains, and birdseed.

■ **feeding** Common feeder bird. Comes to seed scattered on the ground or to an elevated platform feeder. Needs a source of water.

NESTING *Location:* In a medium-height tree, shrub, or cactus; often exposed to direct sun. *Nest:* Small, compact platform of twigs and weed stalks. *Eggs:* 2; incubated by both parents for 13–15 days. *Fledging:* Leaves nest at 12–16 days. *Broods:* Up to 5 per year.

rufous primary patches

long tail with white edges

Sightings

JAN	FEB	MAR	APR	MAY	JUN	JUL	AUG	SEP	OCT	NOV	DEC

Cuckoos
Family Cuculidae

A large family with more than 140 species worldwide, but only six species breed in North America.

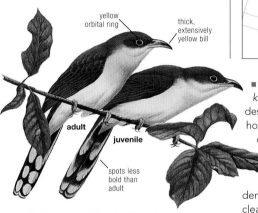

yellow orbital ring

thick, extensively yellow bill

adult

juvenile

spots less bold than adult

Yellow-billed Cuckoo
Coccyzus americanus, L 12" (31 cm)

The Yellow-billed Cuckoo is a summer resident in most of the East, but rare in the West. Local numbers fluctuate in response to insect populations.

IDENTIFICATION Fairly common. Medium in size, with a slender body and long tail. Tends to stay hidden in thickets and leafy treetops, where its presence is most often revealed by its loud vocalizations.
■ **plumage** The wings have reddish primaries, most noticeable in flight; black-and-white tail pattern is best seen from below. Yellow color on the bill is usually easy to see. **Juvenile** has muted tail pattern and buff undertail coverts.
■ **similar species** Much less common Black-billed Cuckoo (not illustrated) has an all-dark bill, less white in the tail, and lacks reddish color in the wings.

■ **voice** **Calls** include a rapid staccato *kuk-kuk-kuk* that usually slows and descends into *kakakowlp-kowlp;* sounds hollow and wooden, but carries long distances.

RANGE Widespread species; summer resident. Favors deciduous woodland with clearings or bordering rivers and streams. Winters in South America. Spring **migration:** mid-April–mid-June; fall migration: August–October.

FOOD Large insects, especially caterpillars. Forages in treetops and shrubbery, where it moves slowly and deliberately.

NESTING *Location:* At low to medium height in a tree, shrub, or vines. *Nest:* Loose platform of twigs. *Eggs:* Usually 2–3; incubated by both parents for 9–11 days. *Fledging:* Leaves nest at 7–19 days.

adult

rufous primaries striking in flight

Sightings

JAN	FEB	MAR	APR	MAY	JUN	JUL	AUG	SEP	OCT	NOV	DEC

Typical Owls
Family Strigidae

A large family with more than 180 species worldwide—18 of which breed in North America. Most owls hunt at night and roost by day. Some species give familiar hooting calls, others do not.

prominent broad ear tufts on side of head

large yellow eyes

bulky body shape

barred below

Great Horned Owl
Bubo virginianus, L 22" (56 cm)

This powerful nighttime predator can take prey larger than itself. Roosts during the day, when the raucous cawing of mobbing crows may lead you to the bird. Provincial bird of Alberta.

IDENTIFICATION Fairly common. At dusk or dawn, can be identified by its silhouette: a large, barrel-shaped body with prominent, wide-set ear tufts (ornamental feathers, not ears).
■ **plumage** Mostly brown with a multitude of bars and speckling, white throat, and large yellow eyes. Overall plumage varies regionally—dark along the Pacific coast,

paler and grayer in the interior West.
■ **similar species** Only the rarer Long-eared Owl (not illustrated) also has large ear tufts, but it is a smaller and much more slender bird with close-set ear tufts.
■ **voice** Deep, muffled **hoots** given in rhythmic sets of three to eight (often five) syllables: *hoo hoo-HOO hoooo hoo.*

RANGE Widespread species; year-round resident. Lives just about everywhere but prefers woodlands with open areas and edge habitat.

FOOD Preys on mammals (up to the size of a large hare) and lesser numbers of large birds, snakes, and large insects. City and suburban birds catch large numbers of rats. Small prey are swallowed whole. Occasionally hunts during the day, but most active after sunset and just before dawn.

NESTING Begins as early as January. *Location:* Often reuses the nest of another large bird; other locations include broken-off tree trunks, cliff ledges, deserted buildings, and artificial platforms. *Nest:* Material already present. *Eggs:* Usually 2–3; incubated mostly by female for 30–37 days. *Fledging:* Leaves nest at 30–45 days; able to fly well at 60–70 days.

Sightings

JAN	FEB	MAR	APR	MAY	JUN	JUL	AUG	SEP	OCT	NOV	DEC

HOW DO OWLS HUNT IN THE DARK?

When we look at an owl's face, we are first drawn straight to the eyes. In most owl species, they are huge relative to the size of the face, with a light-gathering capability said to be three to six times greater than that of humans. Further, the eyes are set to focus straight ahead from the flat face, which provides better binocular vision for estimating the distance to an object.

■Ears Experiments have shown that owls can locate their prey by ear with pinpoint accuracy. First, the rim of raised feathers around its face, the "facial disk," channels sounds into the ears with such precision that the owl can tell exactly which direction to face. Second, an owl's ears are able to hear sound at much lower frequencies than human ears can, sensing the soft, low-pitched footfalls of small mammals. Third, night-hunting owls' ears are situated asymmetrically on the sides of the face, and the ear openings differ in width. These anatomical features enable the owl to sense an unseen object's precise position vertically and horizontally, as well as its exact distance away.

■Feathers Apart from the owl's own senses, its success depends first on an ability to prevent prey from hearing it coming. Owls' flight feathers are serrated aerodynamically at the edges in a way that disturbs airflow over the wing and eliminates noise that normal friction over smoothly edged feathers would create.

Most owl species hunt mainly at night, but the Barred Owl sometimes seeks small mammals, birds, amphibians, and even fish during the day.

Barred Owl
Strix varia, L 21″ (53 cm)

This woodland owl dozes by day on a well-hidden perch. It flies off when disturbed, seldom tolerating close approach except where accustomed to heavy foot traffic.

dark eyes

barred breast

vertical streaks

IDENTIFICATION Fairly common. Large, chunky owl with dark eyes and a large, round head lacking ear tufts.

■ **plumage** Mostly brown plumage is spotted with white on the upperparts, pale buff below with dark, vertical streaks. Its name refers to the horizontal barring on its breast.

■ **similar species** The much rarer Spotted Owl (not illustrated) of the West is similar, but has white spots below (not heavy, dark streaks), and the Great Horned Owl (page 80) is larger, with prominent ear tufts.

■ **voice** Known colloquially as the "eight-hooter" for its most common **call:** *who-cooks-for-you, who-cooks-for-YOU-ALL?* Highly vocal, with a wide range of calls that include a shorter *you-all* and maniacal laughter exchanged between courting

birds. More likely than most other owls to be heard in the daytime. Responds to imitations of its call.

RANGE Widespread species; year-round resident. Lives in mature forest; especially common in river bottoms and southern swamps. Also resides in wooded residential areas and large city parks. Range is expanding in Pacific Northwest, where it overlaps with the Spotted Owl.

FOOD Mostly a nocturnal hunter, but also active at dusk and dawn. Searches for prey from an elevated perch and then swoops down on it. Preys mostly on small mammals, but also birds, reptiles, amphibians, fish, and large insects.

NESTING *Location:* In a natural tree cavity, the reused nest of another large bird such as a hawk, or an old squirrel nest. *Nest:* Material already present. *Eggs:* Usually 2–3; incubated by female for 28–33 days. Laid as early as December in the South, but typically March–April. *Fledging:* Leaves nest at 28–35 days; able to fly at about 70 days.

■ **housing** Will use a nest box located at a height of 15–30 feet.

	JAN	FEB	MAR	APR	MAY	JUN	JUL	AUG	SEP	OCT	NOV	DEC

Eastern Screech-Owl

Megascops asio, L 8½" (22 cm)

A small woodland owl with an extensive range. If you learn to whistle the Eastern Screech-Owl's tremolo call, it will attract a host of woodland songbirds that come to investigate the location of their mortal enemy—just don't overdo it.

rufous morph

gray morph juvenile

rufous morph more numerous in Southeast

IDENTIFICATION Fairly common. Robin-size owl with a big head, ear tufts (sometimes flattened), and yellow eyes. Roosting bird often assumes a very cryptic, elongated pose that mimics tree bark or a dead stick.

■ **plumage** Two color morphs—rufous and gray; mixed pairs not uncommon. Darker above with white spots and fine barring; underparts marked with vertical dark streaks and fainter cross-hatching (like tree bark). **Fledgling** is finely barred overall with tiny ear tufts.

■ **similar species** If you are in the West and see a very similar bird, it will most likely be a Western Screech-Owl (not illustrated); the ranges of the two species scarcely overlap.

■ **voice** Two typical **calls**: a long trill or tremolo on one pitch, and a series of quavering

whistles that descend in pitch ("horse whinny"). Despite its name, this owl rarely screeches.

RANGE Eastern and Great Plains species; year-round resident. Lives in a variety of wooded habitats: forests, woodlots, suburban backyards, large city parks.

FOOD Nocturnal hunter. Varied diet; preys mostly on songbirds and rodents, but also large insects, earthworms, snakes, lizards, frogs, and crayfish.

NESTING *Location:* In an old woodpecker hole or natural tree cavity. *Nest:* Material already present. *Eggs:* Usually 4–5; incubated by female for 27–30 days. Laid as early as December in the South. *Fledging:* Young leave the nest at about 28 days, clamber to a tree roost, and are able to fly about 2 weeks later.

■ **housing** Will use a nest box. Since nest cavities can be scarce, a nest box of the correct size may entice a pair of owls to take up residence in a woodsy backyard. Fasten nest box to a sturdy tree at a height of 10–15 feet. Often uses its nest box as a winter roost.

overall pale

yellow eyes

pale-greenish bill

gray morph

Sightings

JAN	FEB	MAR	APR	MAY	JUN	JUL	AUG	SEP	OCT	NOV	DEC

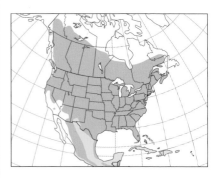

Goatsuckers
Family Caprimulgidae

A family of insect-eaters, active mainly at dusk and night, that includes nighthawks, nightjars, Whip-poor-wills, and others. They capture their food in flight with gaping mouths.

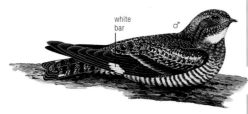

white bar ♂

Common Nighthawk
Chordeiles minor, L 9½" (24 cm)

Despite its name, the Common Nighthawk is often seen in flight during the day and is not related to hawks. Nighttime foragers seek insects over brightly lit playing fields and parking lots, but most backyard birders will see them flying overhead on warm summer evenings. Its population appears to be declining.

IDENTIFICATION Fairly common. In flight, its long pointed wings and tail recall those of a falcon. Flight is graceful, but with a bouncy, bat-like quality (a folksy name is "Bullbat"). Roosts on the ground or lengthwise on a branch, where its cryptic plumage makes it difficult to spot. Also perches in the open on fence posts.

■ **plumage** Mottled and speckled upperparts; tightly barred underparts. Only the **adult male** has a white throat and tail band, but all birds have a prominent white wing bar visible in flight. Varies geographically—Eastern birds are the darkest.

■ **similar species** Lesser Nighthawk (next page) of the Southwest, which overlaps a bit in range, is very similar, distinguished by the white wing bar closer to the wing-tip, buff underparts, and its trilling call.

■ **voice** **Call** is a nasal *peent* given in flight. During courtship flight—a U-shaped swooping dive—the male's vibrating primary feathers produce a booming sound.

RANGE Widespread species; summer resident. No strong habitat preferences, as long as food and nesting habitat are available. Migrates to South America for winter. Spring **migration:** April–early June; fall migration: late August–mid-September.

FOOD Captures insects—moths, mayflies, flying ants, beetles—in flight, mostly at dusk and dawn. Feeds from low to high in the sky, sometimes in loose flocks of up to 100 birds. Drinks on the wing as well, by skimming the water's surface.

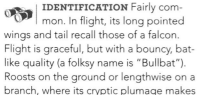

long pointed wings

♂

white bar on primaries

NESTING *Location:* On the ground or flat gravel roofs in urban areas. *Nest:* None. *Eggs:* 2; incubated by female for 16–20 days. *Fledging:* Able to fly at 17–18 days.

Sightings

JAN	FEB	MAR	APR	MAY	JUN	JUL	AUG	SEP	OCT	NOV	DEC

Lesser Nighthawk
Chordeiles acutipennis, L 8½" (22 cm)

The Lesser Nighthawk's trilling twilight call is a familiar spring sound of the desert Southwest. They often congregate near a water source at dusk and are rarely active during midday.

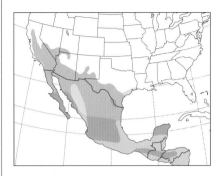

buffy primary markings

IDENTIFICATION Fairly com-
mon. Resembles the Common Nighthawk in lifestyle and plumage, but the two species are rarely seen together.
■ plumage Mottled and speckled upperparts; buff underparts with faint barring. The **adult male** has a prominent white wing bar (buff in **female**), white throat (buff in female), and white tail band (lacking in female). **Juvenile male**'s wing bar is small; juvenile female's is indistinct.
■ similar species Common Nighthawk (opposite) is very similar, but habitats of the two species have little overlap: its white wing bar is closer to the body, wings more pointed, underparts whiter, and *peent* call very different. Lesser Nighthawk flies with a looser, fluttery wingbeat and closer to the ground.
■ voice Distinctive **call** is a rapid, tremulous trill.

RANGE Southwestern species; summer resident. Found in dry, open country, scrubland, and desert, but also frequents lush suburban areas, cities, and open areas with nighttime lighting.

Where its range overlaps with Common Nighthawk in the Southwest, Common Nighthawk is found at higher elevations. Vacates the U.S. in winter, moving as far south as Colombia. Spring **migration:** early March–early May; fall migration: early August–October.

FOOD Captures insects—flying ants, swarming termites, mosquitoes—in flight, mostly at dusk and dawn, though sometimes at midday on overcast days. Roams far and wide in search of food, often attracted to insects gathered over bodies of water or around outdoor lighting.

NESTING *Location:* On the ground, sometimes shaded by a shrub, but often fully exposed. Also nests on flat gravel roofs in urban areas. *Nest:* None. *Eggs:* 2; incubated by female for 18–19 days. *Fledging:* Able to fly at about 21 days.

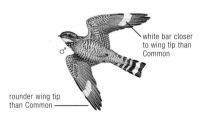

white bar closer to wing tip than Common

rounder wing tip than Common

Sightings

JAN	FEB	MAR	APR	MAY	JUN	JUL	AUG	SEP	OCT	NOV	DEC

Hummingbirds
Family Trochilidae

Hummingbirds are the smallest of birds. Their glittering plumage, remarkable powers of flight, and attraction to hummingbird feeders offer endless entertainment.

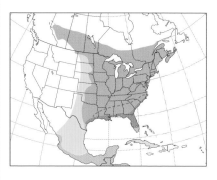

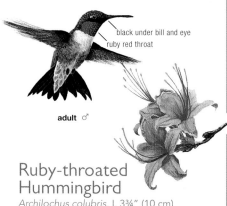

black under bill and eye
ruby red throat

adult ♂

Ruby-throated Hummingbird
Archilochus colubris, L 3¾" (10 cm)

The only hummingbird seen regularly in the East, where it is common at sugar water feeders.

IDENTIFICATION Common. The Ruby-throated has a feisty personality and aggressively defends its nectar source from others.
■ **plumage** Metallic green above. Only the **adult male** has an iridescent ruby red gorget (throat) with small black chin and blackish, forked tail. **Adult female** and **juvenile** have a whitish throat, rarely with a few red spots, and a tail with large white tips.
■ **similar species** None in the East. Any hummer that shows up at an Eastern feeder after early October should be scrutinized; it could be a Rufous Hummingbird (page 90) or another rarity.
■ **voice** Slightly twangy chips—*tchew* or *chih*. Chase notes given in rapid series.

RANGE Eastern species; summer resident. Inhabits open woodlands, woodland edges, and flowering gardens. Despite tiny size, most fly nonstop across the Gulf of Mexico to winter in Mexico and Central America. Spring **migration:** March–May; fall migration: August–September.

FOOD Hover-feeds on flower nectar or at feeders; also captures small insects and spiders, the main foods fed to nestlings.
■ **feeding** Hummingbird feeders and backyard flower gardens.

NESTING *Location:* In a tree or shrub, usually 10–20 feet up. *Nest:* Tiny cuplike bowl of plant down and spiderweb, the exterior decorated with lichen and dead leaves. *Eggs:* 2; incubated by female for 11–16 days. *Fledging:* Leaves nest at 18–20 days.

immature males often develop a few red throat spots by Sept.

white throat

♀

immature ♂

Sightings

	JAN	FEB	MAR	APR	MAY	JUN	JUL	AUG	SEP	OCT	NOV	DEC

ATTRACTING HUMMINGBIRDS

Many hummingbird feeder designs are available, from simple hanging bottles to large multiport models. Be sure to buy a feeder that is easy to take apart for cleaning—*an essential feature*. Basin-type feeders are easiest.

■Installation Hang your feeder from a window frame or overhanging eave or use a five- to six-foot-long metal pole with a hook. Note: hummingbirds will not delay migration if you leave your feeder up in fall.

■Sugar-water mixture Stick to this recipe: 1 part refined white sugar to 4 parts water. If you're mixing a small batch to use immediately, you can skip boiling it—just use hot water. Do *not* use red food coloring or any sweetener other than refined white sugar.

■Maintenance Replace the sugar solution every three to four days—otherwise it will ferment (becoming cloudy). Clean your feeder whenever you fill it. Use hot water (no soap) and a bottle brush to clean the feeding ports.

This popular feeder has two species of hummingbird in attendance: Broad-tailed and Rufous. Can you tell them apart?

■Hummingbird plants This is a great way to provide natural food for hummers. Some favorite hummingbird plants are cardinal flower, scarlet sage, honeysuckle, trumpet vine, bee balm, and fuchsia. To find out more online, visit www.hummingbirds.net and www.hummingbirdsplus.org.

Black-chinned Hummingbird

Archilochus alexandri, L 3¾" (10 cm)

The Black-chinned is one of the most widespread hummers in the West, ranging north to British Columbia and particularly common at low elevations in the Southwest.

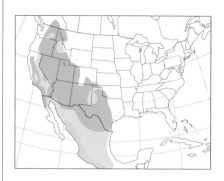

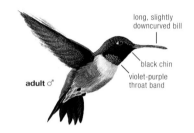

long, slightly downcurved bill

black chin

adult ♂

violet-purple throat band

IDENTIFICATION Common. Slender with a medium-to-long bill. When feeding, habitually wags its tail. The male's wings create a dry buzzing in flight, softer in females and juveniles.
■ **plumage** Metallic green above. **Adult male**'s gorget is matte black above and violet below (often appears all black); it has a white breast band below the gorget and a black, slightly forked tail. **Adult female** has grayish white face, throat, and underparts; a longer bill; and a shorter tail with white tips. **Immature male** is similar to female, usually with a few violet feathers on its throat.

immature ♂

crown has a dusky cast

♀

■ **similar species** Larger female Anna's Hummingbird (page 91) has a shorter bill, is duskier below with green on the flanks, and usually has some red feathers on the throat.
■ **voice** Slightly twangy or nasal chips—*tchew* or *chih*—nearly identical to the Ruby-throated.

RANGE Western species; summer resident. Found in open woodlands, streamside groves, shady canyons, suburban gardens, and parks—it's partial to sycamores and oaks. Winters primarily in western Mexico. Spring **migration:** March–mid-May; fall migration: August–late September.

FOOD Hover-feeds on flower nectar or at feeders; also captures small insects and spiders, the main foods fed to nestlings.
■ **feeding** Hummingbird feeders and backyard flower gardens.

NESTING *Location:* In a shrub or tree, usually 4–10 feet up. *Nest:* Distinctive, straw-colored cup often built of fuzz from sycamore leaves (looks like felt). *Eggs:* 2; incubated by female for 11–16 days. *Fledging:* Leaves nest at about 21 days.

Sightings

JAN	FEB	MAR	APR	MAY	JUN	JUL	AUG	SEP	OCT	NOV	DEC

Broad-tailed Hummingbird
Selasphorus platycercus, L 4" (10 cm)

The Broad-tailed is a hummingbird of Western mountains, where the adult male's cricket-like wing trill is a signature sound of summer. Separating a female Broad-tailed from a female Rufous Hummingbird is challenging even for experts.

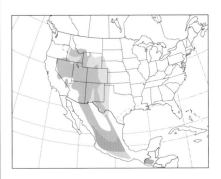

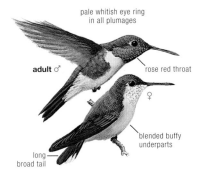

pale whitish eye ring in all plumages

adult ♂

rose red throat

♀

blended buffy underparts

long broad tail

IDENTIFICATION Common. Average in size and structure, but the tail is impressively large. The narrow tips of the male's outer primary feathers produce a trilling noise in flight, often the first indication of its presence.

■ **plumage** Metallic green above. **Adult male's** gorget is rose red with a thin white stripe under the bill, extending around and behind the eye; white breast band contrasts with green flanks and a black tail with thin rufous edging. **Adult female** has a white throat with tiny green spots, sometimes rose red feathers at center, underparts washed with cinnamon, and a broad tail with rufous base and white tips.

■ **similar species** Female and immature birds can be confused with female Rufous (next page). Here are the basics: the female Rufous is smaller, is more intensely rufous on its flanks and smaller

tail, and has a whiter forecollar. The Rufous's call—a hard, sharp *tewk*—is very different from the Broad-tailed's metallic *chip*.

■ **voice** Calls include a metallic *chip*, often doubled as *ch-chip* or repeated in a series. Males' impressive courtship dives are accompanied by loud wing trilling.

RANGE Western species; summer resident. From foothill canyons to high mountain meadows of southern and central Rockies (but not in Canada). Winters mainly in Mexico. Spring **migration:** March–mid-May; fall migration: August–late September.

FOOD Hover-feeds on flower nectar or at feeders; also captures small insects and spiders, the main foods fed to nestlings.

■ **feeding** Hummingbird feeders and backyard flower gardens.

♀ **tail**

longer than Rufous and has more restricted rufous

NESTING *Location:* In a tree or shrub, usually 4–20 feet up. *Nest:* Neat cup of plant down and spiderweb, decorated on the outside with lichen, moss, and bits of bark. *Eggs:* 2; incubated by female for 16–19 days. *Fledging:* Leaves nest at 21–26 days.

Sightings

JAN	FEB	MAR	APR	MAY	JUN	JUL	AUG	SEP	OCT	NOV	DEC

Rufous Hummingbird
Selasphorus rufus, L 3¾" (10 cm)

The Rufous Hummingbird is a pugnacious species that breeds farther north than any other hummer. In migration, it is common at feeders throughout the West.

rufous back

adult ♂

green-flecked ♂

IDENTIFICATION Common. Small in size but large in personality, it often chases off other hummers at feeding locations.

■ **plumage** **Adult male** is bright, coppery rufous on the upperparts, flanks, and spiky tail; sometimes with green flecks on the back; the gorget is red with orange highlights. **Adult female** has metallic green upperparts; a white throat with bronzy green spots, usually with red at the center; white underparts with rufous flanks; and a tail with rufous base and white tips. **Immature male** is similar to female, but with red spots on its white throat, and green on the back. Immature female has a white throat.

■ **similar species** Male Allen's Hummingbird (not illustrated) along the West Coast has a solid green back, but is very similar to male Rufous (some male Rufous have green-flecked backs); female Allen's is almost identical to female Rufous. Female and immature Rufous Hummingbirds have more rufous flanks and tail than other species detailed in this book.

slight golden cast

white collar

adult ♀

immature ♂

♀ tail

extensive rufous

■ **voice** Hard, sharp **call** *tewk;* chase note *zee-chuppity-chuppity.*

RANGE Western species; summer resident. Breeds in open forests, clearings, and streamside groves. Winters in Mexico; small numbers along Gulf Coast, strays to East. Spring **migration** (mainly through Pacific lowlands): early February–May; fall migration (mainly through Rockies): late June–mid-October.

FOOD Hover-feeds on flower nectar or at feeders; also captures small insects and spiders.
■ **feeding** Hummingbird feeders and flower gardens.

NESTING *Location:* In a tree or shrub, 4–30 feet up. *Nest:* Neat cup of plant down and spiderweb. *Eggs:* 2; incubated by female for 15–17 days. *Fledging:* Leaves nest at about 21 days.

Sightings

JAN	FEB	MAR	APR	MAY	JUN	JUL	AUG	SEP	OCT	NOV	DEC

Anna's Hummingbird
Calypte anna, L 4" (10 cm)

*Unlike other North American humming-
birds, Anna's is nonmigratory. It is a familiar
and welcome resident of West Coast
backyards from southern California to
southern British Columbia.*

rose red
head and
throat

adult ♂

IDENTIFICATION Common.
Medium-size hummer with a
chunky look. Male "sings" a wiry, scratchy
song, often for prolonged periods.
■ **plumage** Metallic green upperparts;
dingy grayish white and green below.
Flashy **adult male** has brilliant rose red
gorget *and* crown ("helmeted") and a
blackish tail. **Adult female** has a white
throat with green spots and blotched with
red in center; tail has white tips. **Immature
male** similar to adult female, but with
more red on throat and a few red feathers
on crown; **immature female** lacks any red
and is paler below.
■ **similar species** Compare female
and immature Anna's to female Black-
chinned (page 88), a slender
hummer with paler underparts
that never has red on throat.
■ **voice** Common **call** is a sharp *tewk*,
chase call a scratchy twittering *chicka-
chicka-chicka* series, and male's **song**
a rhythmic series of scratchy notes.
The male's breakneck, 100-foot display
dive creates an explosive pop as it pulls up
just short of the perched female.

RANGE West Coast species; year-
round resident. Originally lived
in riparian thickets, chaparral, and coastal
scrub, but now abundant in backyard
gardens and city parks. Colonized southern Arizona and southern Nevada in the
mid-20th century.

FOOD Hover-feeds on flower nectar or at feeders; also captures
small insects and spiders.
■ **feeding** Hummingbird feeders and
backyard flower gardens.

NESTING *Location:* In a tree or
shrub, 4–30 feet up. *Nest:* Neat
cup of plant down and spiderweb. *Eggs:*
2; incubated by female for 14–19 days.
Fledging: Leaves nest at 18–23 days.

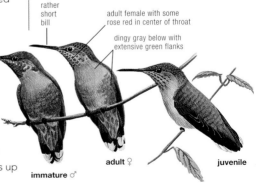

rather
short
bill

adult female with some
rose red in center of throat

dingy gray below with
extensive green flanks

immature ♂

adult ♀

juvenile

Sightings ───

JAN	FEB	MAR	APR	MAY	JUN	JUL	AUG	SEP	OCT	NOV	DEC

Swifts
Family Apodidae

A family of superb aerialists almost always seen roaming the sky in search of insects. They are unable to perch, but can cling to vertical surfaces with tiny, sharp-clawed feet.

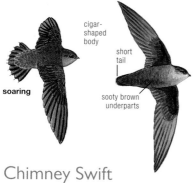

cigar-shaped body

short tail

soaring

sooty brown underparts

Chimney Swift
Chaetura pelagica, L 5¼" (13 cm)

The only swift in the East. In many residential and city locations, they are seen coursing overhead and often nest in chimneys. Tiny spine-like projections at the tips of the tail feathers help it cling to a vertical surface. If you suspect your chimney has nesting swifts, don't light a fire during the nesting season!

IDENTIFICATION Common. Flies with stiff, fluttering wing beats; when soaring, the wings look more rounded and the tail is often spread. Displaying pairs glide in tandem with their wings held in a V.

■ **plumage** Often described as "a cigar with wings." The plumage is dark overall, slightly paler (grayish brown) on the throat.

■ **similar species** Sometimes mistaken for a martin or swallow. By comparison, Chimney Swift has longer, more pointed, and swept-back wings and flies faster with stiffer ("twinkling") wing beats. See Purple

Martin (pages 132–133). Vaux's Swift (not illustrated) is a very similar swift—smaller and slightly paler on the throat and rump—that is fairly common in the Pacific region. If you see a look-alike swift in that region, chances are it's a Vaux's.

■ **voice** Quite vocal in flight. **Call** is a series of chippering notes, sometimes run together into a rapid twitter.

RANGE Eastern species; summer resident. Most abundant around cities and towns. Migrating birds assemble at dusk in large flocks to roost for the night in building shafts, church steeples, and large chimneys. At high speed, hundreds of swirling birds disappear one by one into a dark shaft—a memorable sight. Winters in South America. Spring **migration:** late March–mid-May; fall migration: late September–mid-October.

FOOD Captures small insects in flight. Usually forages high and descends to drink, skimming the water's surface with its bill.

NESTING *Location:* In a chimney or building shaft. *Nest:* Half cup of short twigs, adhered to a vertical surface with sticky saliva. *Eggs:* Usually 4–5; incubated by both parents for 19–20 days. *Fledging:* Able to fly at about 30 days.

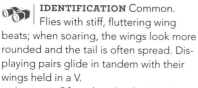

Sightings

JAN	FEB	MAR	APR	MAY	JUN	JUL	AUG	SEP	OCT	NOV	DEC

Woodpeckers
Family Picidae

Sharp claws and stiff tail feathers enable woodpeckers to climb tree trunks; sharp bill is used to chisel out insect food and nest holes and to drum a territorial signal.

female has black forecrown bar ♀

clown head pattern

♂

Acorn Woodpecker
Melanerpes formicivorus, L 9" (23 cm)

The clown-faced Acorn Woodpecker lives in communal groups that maintain impressive granaries—thousands of acorns are stored in holes drilled in tree trunks (granary trees).

IDENTIFICATION Fairly common. A sturdy, midsize woodpecker. Often flycatches for insects, but rarely descends to the ground.
■ **plumage** Boldly patterned: striking head plumage is an ornate combination of red, white, and black. White wing patch and rump are most visible in flight. **Male** has red crown bordering white forehead;

female has red crown with black band in front.
■ **similar species** None.
■ **voice** Calls given by noisy family groups include *ja-cob ja-cob* and a raucous *wack-a wack-a wack-a* that inspired the creator of Woody Woodpecker.

RANGE Western species; year-round resident. Inhabits oak woodlands and mixed oak-conifer or oak-riparian woodlands.

FOOD Despite its name and habit of storing thousands of acorns, nuts make up only about half of its diet (mostly in fall and winter). Their preferred food is insects—particularly ants—supplemented in spring and summer with sugary tree sap.

NESTING Cooperative breeder—lives in family groups of a dozen or more birds that assist each other. *Location:* Cavity excavated in a large tree and reused for many years. *Nest:* No material added. *Eggs:* Usually 3–7; incubated by both parents for about 11 days. *Fledging:* Leaves nest at about 30 days.

♂

white primary patch

Sightings

JAN	FEB	MAR	APR	MAY	JUN	JUL	AUG	SEP	OCT	NOV	DEC

Red-bellied Woodpecker
Melanerpes carolinus, L 9¼" (24 cm)

The Red-bellied is the familiar zebra-striped woodpecker of the East. Its "red belly" amounts to little more than a hard-to-see pinkish blush, but its crown and nape are vibrantly red.

solid red crown and nape

♂

♀

red nape

pink on lower belly

white rump

♂

whitish primary patch

 **IDENTIFICATION** Common. A lanky, midsize woodpecker—smaller than a flicker.
■ **plumage** Only zebra-striped woodpecker in the East. White wing patch and rump are visible only in flight. **Male** has red extending from bill to nape; **female** has red only on nape.
■ **similar species** Overlaps in Texas with similar Golden-fronted Woodpecker (not illustrated), which has golden orange feathers on the nape and above the bill and black (not barred) tail.
■ **voice** **Song** is a loud volley of churring notes. **Call** is a conversational *chiv-chiv*.

RANGE Eastern species; year-round resident. Inhabits open woodlands, suburbs, and parks. Abundant in the Southeast, particularly along watercourses and in swamp country. Northern range continues to expand, for example, from central Pennsylvania (1960s) to southern Vermont (2000), but it is uncommon in northernmost areas.

FOOD Seldom excavates wood in search of food, but forages opportunistically for insects, nuts, fruits, seeds, and sometimes catches flying insects in the air. Stores food in tree bark crevices.
■ **feeding** Suet, peanuts, and sunflower seeds are all relished. Dominates Downy and Hairy Woodpeckers and smaller birds at feeders, about equal with Blue Jay. Usually shy and wary around people, but feeder visitors eventually become more trusting.

NESTING *Location:* Cavity excavated in a dead tree, stump, or telephone pole. *Nest:* No material added. *Eggs:* Usually 4–5; incubated by both parents for 12–14 days. *Fledging:* Leaves nest at 22–27 days. Parents accompany and often feed young birds for about 6 weeks after they leave the nest.
■ **housing** Will use a nest box mounted on a tree or pole.

Sightings

JAN	FEB	MAR	APR	MAY	JUN	JUL	AUG	SEP	OCT	NOV	DEC

Yellow-bellied Sapsucker
Sphyrapicus varius, L 8½" (22 cm)

These woodpeckers drill evenly spaced rows of holes in living trees and then visit these "wells" for the sap and the insects attracted to it. Other birds also feed at these sugary seeps, especially hummingbirds. Three closely related species, with different ranges, are covered on the following pages.

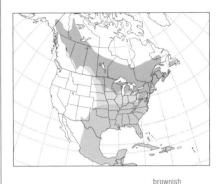

brownish

juvenile

IDENTIFICATION Fairly common. Medium-size woodpecker. Although often noisy and conspicuous when breeding, most backyard birders will encounter the Yellow-bellied Sapsucker on its migration or in winter when it is quiet and secretive.

■ **plumage** Striped face pattern and longitudinal white slash on the wing are good field marks. **Male** has red throat and forecrown; **female** has white throat and red forecrown. **Juvenile** differs from adult until about March—head is brownish, body mottled brown, wings like adult.

■ **similar species** See Red-naped Sapsucker (next page), a Western relative whose range overlaps somewhat.

■ **voice** Unusual **calls** that are worth learning— a nasal squeal *weeah* and catlike *meeww*— are often the first indication that a sapsucker is nearby.

RANGE Eastern species. Breeds in open forests in Appalachians, north through New England, and extensively in Canada, then spends October–March throughout the South and Mid-Atlantic. Spring **migration:** mid-April–early May; fall migration: mid-September–October.

FOOD Sap and insects at freshly drilled sap wells. Also flycatches for insects and eats some fruit and seeds.

■ **feeding** Irregular at feeders, but will take suet and sunflower seeds.

NESTING *Location:* Cavity excavated in a tree, often an aspen, poplar, or birch. *Nest:* No material added. *Eggs:* Usually 3–7; incubated by both parents for 12–13 days. *Fledging:* Leaves nest at 25–29 days. Parents feed their young for an additional 1–2 weeks and teach them the sapsucking technique.

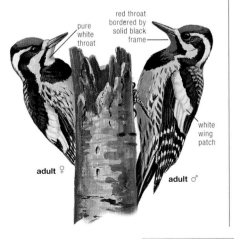

pure white throat

red throat bordered by solid black frame

white wing patch

adult ♀

adult ♂

Sightings

	JAN	FEB	MAR	APR	MAY	JUN	JUL	AUG	SEP	OCT	NOV	DEC

Red-naped Sapsucker

Sphyrapicus nuchalis, L 8½" (22 cm)

For most of the 20th century, this species was considered a Western subspecies of the Yellow-bellied Sapsucker. The two species look almost identical, but there are subtle differences. Read the Yellow-bellied Sapsucker account (previous page) to find out more about the sapsucker's lifestyle.

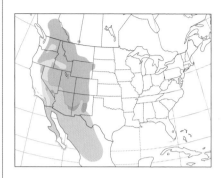

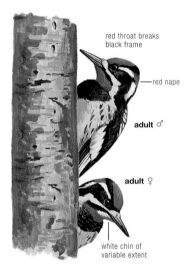

red throat breaks black frame

red nape

adult ♂

adult ♀

white chin of variable extent

IDENTIFICATION Fairly common. Medium-size woodpecker that is easy to overlook.

■ **plumage** Striped face pattern and longitudinal white slash on the wing are good field marks. Named for the spot of red on the nape of both sexes. **Male** and **female** both have red throat and forecrown, but female also has some white feathering under the chin. **Juvenile** resembles Yellow-bellied juvenile (previous page), but unlike Yellow-bellied, Red-naped looks similar to the adult by fall migration.

■ **similar species** Yellow-bellied Sapsucker (previous page) is a close Eastern relative that lacks the red nape spot and has a heavier black border around the throat. Ranges of the two species barely overlap.

■ **voice** **Calls** include a nasal squeal *weeah* and catlike *meeww*.

RANGE Interior West species. Breeds in aspen parklands and leafy groves within coniferous forests; favors groves along mountain streams and rivers. Migrates south to winter at lower elevations; often found in shady parks and suburban neighborhoods. Some birds winter in southern California. Spring **migration**: mid-March–early May; fall migration: late August–October.

FOOD Sap and insects at freshly drilled sap wells—conifers, quaking aspen, alder, and willow are often tapped. Also flycatches for insects and eats some seeds and fruit.

■ **feeding** Irregular at feeders, but will take suet and sunflower seeds.

NESTING *Location:* Cavity excavated in a tree, often a quaking aspen. *Nest:* No material added. *Eggs:* Usually 4–7; incubated by both parents for 11–15 days. *Fledging:* Leaves nest at 23–32 days. Parents feed their young for an additional 1–2 weeks and teach them the sapsucking technique.

Sightings

JAN	FEB	MAR	APR	MAY	JUN	JUL	AUG	SEP	OCT	NOV	DEC

Red-breasted Sapsucker
Sphyrapicus ruber, L 8½" (22 cm)

The Red-breasted Sapsucker is a more colorful West Coast version of the closely related Red-naped Sapsucker. Where the ranges of the two species come into contact, they frequently interbreed.

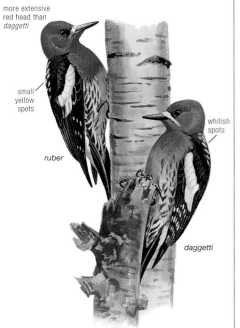

more extensive
red head than
daggetti

small
yellow
spots

ruber

whitish
spots

daggetti

■ **similar species** None. Full red head of adult makes it easy to identify.
■ **voice** **Calls** include a nasal squeal *weeah* and catlike *meeww*.

RANGE West Coast species. Breeds in a variety of habitats, from moist coniferous forests to streamside woodlands and from near sea level up to 8,000 feet. Some birds are resident; others migrate south or move to lower elevations for the winter. Wintering birds can be found in shady parks and suburban neighborhoods as far south as southern California (where it is more numerous than Red-naped). Spring **migration:** not apparent; fall migration: late September–early October.

IDENTIFICATION Fairly common. Medium-size woodpecker, often quiet and retiring. The northern breeding subspecies (*ruber,* from southern Oregon northward) is deeper red above and more solidly yellow below; the paler, but still colorful, *daggetti* subspecies occupies the rest of the range.
■ **plumage** Vivid red head and breast, and white wing patch like other sapsuckers. **Male** and **female** are alike. **Juvenile** (see illustration of similar, but paler, Yellow-bellied juvenile on page 95) differs from adult until about September.

FOOD Sap and insects at freshly drilled sap wells. Also flycatches for insects and eats some fruit and seeds.
■ **feeding** Irregular at feeders, but will take suet and sunflower seeds.

NESTING *Location:* Cavity excavated in a tree, often dead or dying. *Nest:* No material added. *Eggs:* Usually 4–7; incubated by both parents for 11–15 days. *Fledging:* Leaves nest at 23–32 days. Parents feed their young for an additional 1–2 weeks and teach them the sapsucking technique.

Sightings

JAN	FEB	MAR	APR	MAY	JUN	JUL	AUG	SEP	OCT	NOV	DEC

Ladder-backed Woodpecker

Picoides scalaris, L 7¼" (18 cm)

The Ladder-backed Woodpecker scratches out a living in desert areas across a wide swath of the Southwest. An alternate name was "Cactus Woodpecker."

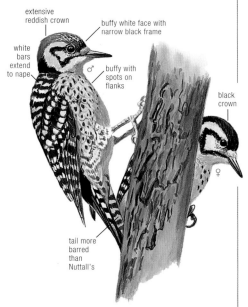

extensive reddish crown

buffy white face with narrow black frame

white bars extend to nape

♂ buffy with spots on flanks

black crown

♀

tail more barred than Nuttall's

IDENTIFICATION Fairly common. A small, active woodpecker that presents a somewhat disheveled appearance. Fairly tame and often quite vocal.
■ **plumage** Black-and-white, ladder-like bars evenly spaced on the back and similar pattern on wings; underparts buff with small dark spots; pale face with black stripes. **Male** has red crown with black and white speckles near the bill; **female** has black crown, and **juvenile's** crown is red with white flecking.
■ **similar species** Nuttall's Woodpecker (next page) is blacker above, with a heavy black bar on the upper back, and whiter below; their ranges meet only on the western fringes of the Mojave Desert. Downy and Hairy Woodpeckers—not often seen in the desert Southwest—have a white stripe (not bars) up the back.
■ **voice** Most common **call** is a fairly high, sharp *pik* (like the Downy's); also has a descending whinny.

RANGE Southwestern species; year-round resident. Inhabits desert scrub, mesquite woodlands, and arroyos; piñon-juniper woodlands and oaks are favored in Texas. Often seen in residential areas near desert habitat.

FOOD Seldom drills into wood, but probes and gleans insects (especially beetle larvae) from trees, cacti, agaves, yuccas, and weed stems. Also eats cactus fruit and some seeds.
■ **feeding** Suet, peanuts, and sunflower seeds; able to cling to hanging feeders. Visits birdbaths.

NESTING *Location:* Cavity excavated in a desert tree, large agave, or yucca (Joshua tree). *Nest:* No material added. *Eggs:* Usually 4–7; incubated by both parents for 12–14 days. *Fledging:* Age at first flight unknown.
■ **housing** Will use a nest box mounted on a tree or pole.

Sightings

JAN	FEB	MAR	APR	MAY	JUN	JUL	AUG	SEP	OCT	NOV	DEC

Nuttall's Woodpecker
Picoides nuttalli, L 7½" (19 cm)

Nuttall's Woodpecker is found only California and nearby Baja California. It occurs over a large portion of the state, but shuns the desert habitat favored by the similar-looking Ladder-backed Woodpecker.

IDENTIFICATION Common. This moderately small, chunky woodpecker forages actively, but can be hard to spot. Its loud calls often announce its presence before it is seen.

■ **plumage** Crisp black-and-white plumage; mostly black back with narrow white bars and a wide black bar at base of the neck; underparts white with black spots and bars on the sides; black face with white stripes. **Male** has a red patch at rear of crown; **female** has black crown.

■ **similar species** Downy (smaller; page 100) and Hairy (larger; page 101) Woodpeckers look similar from a distance, but have a white stripe up the back, not horizontal bars. Also see Ladder-backed Woodpecker (opposite).

■ **voice** Most common **call** is a short, staccato *p-r-r-t*; also makes a longer rattle and loud *kweek-kweek-kweek* when birds interact.

RANGE California species; year-round resident. Favors oak groves and riparian forests, but also occurs in residential suburbs and wooded parks. Sometimes wanders after the nesting season is over.

FOOD Seldom drills into wood, but scales off bark, probes, and gleans insects from tree trunks and branches. Occasionally eats acorns, seeds, and fruit.

■ **feeding** Suet and sunflower seeds.

NESTING *Location:* Cavity excavated in a tree, or sometimes a fence post or utility pole. *Nest:* No material added. *Eggs:* Usually 3–6; incubated by both parents for about 14 days. *Fledging:* Leaves nest at about 14 days.

■ **housing** Will use a nest box mounted on a tree or pole.

black face with white borders

red restricted to rear crown

♂

black bar at base of neck

white underparts

black crown

♀

outer tail feathers with fewer bars than Ladder-backed

Sightings

JAN	FEB	MAR	APR	MAY	JUN	JUL	AUG	SEP	OCT	NOV	DEC

Downy Woodpecker
Picoides pubescens, L 6¾" (17 cm)

The Downy is the smallest and the best known woodpecker in North America. It seems content to live anywhere there are trees, except in the arid Southwest.

IDENTIFICATION Very common. The Downy, with its petite bill and tubular body, has a toylike quality, enhanced by its jerky, stop-and-go movements. At feeders, it gives way to the larger, look-alike Hairy Woodpecker.
■ **plumage** Crisp black-and-white plumage; black back with white stripe up the middle; underparts unmarked white; white outer tail feathers barred. **Male** has a small red patch at rear of crown; **female**'s crown is black, and **juvenile**'s has patchy red at the front.
■ **similar species** Only the larger Hairy Woodpecker (opposite) also has a white stripe up the back. Size can be difficult to judge on a lone bird, so focus on proportions: the Hairy's bill is nearly as long as its head; the Downy's is about half as long as its head. Also useful: Hairy has pure white outer tail feathers; Downy has black bars on those feathers. Hairy is less common and more restricted to forested areas, and has a louder, slightly longer, more emphatic call.
■ **voice** **Call** is a sharp, high-pitched *pik!* Rattle call descends in pitch and trails off.

RANGE Widespread species; year-round resident. Inhabits most types of woodland, including backyards and city parks; avoids desert areas.

FOOD Actively probes, gleans, and drills into wood for insects. Forages on branches and sometimes descends to large weed stalks; female is more likely to forage on tree trunks.
■ **feeding** Favors suet, but also consumes peanuts, peanut butter, sunflower seeds.

NESTING *Location:* Cavity excavated in a tree trunk or limb. *Nest:* No material added. *Eggs:* Usually 3–6; incubated by both parents for about 12 days. *Fledging:* Leaves nest at 20–25 days.
■ **housing** Will use a nest box mounted on a tree or pole.

male has red hindcrown spot

white back stripe

short, stubby bill

♂

barred outer tail feathers

♀

♂

Hairy Woodpecker
Picoides villosus, L 9¼" (24 cm)

The Hairy Woodpecker inhabits forested areas from coast to coast. Its name derives from the "hairy" quality of the white feathers in the middle of its back.

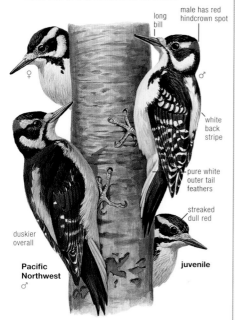

long bill

male has red hindcrown spot

white back stripe

pure white outer tail feathers

streaked dull red

duskier overall

Pacific Northwest ♂

juvenile

IDENTIFICATION Fairly common. The Hairy is a typical, well-proportioned, medium-size woodpecker. Its longish bill gives the head a wedge-shaped look that differs from the round-headed look of the smaller Downy Woodpecker.

■ **plumage** Crisp black-and-white plumage; black back with white stripe up the middle; pure white outer tail feathers. **Male** has a small red patch at rear of crown, **female** has black crown, and **juvenile** has patchy red on top of crown. Birds in the Pacific Northwest have smoky brown underparts and less white on the wings.

■ **similar species** Downy Woodpecker is much smaller, but almost identical in plumage (see "similar species" section opposite).
■ **voice** Call is a loud, emphatic, high-pitched *PEEK!* Rattle call is a loud series of *peek* calls.

RANGE Widespread species; year-round resident. Inhabits a variety of forests and woodlands, but prefers mature forest with large trees. Also resides in well-wooded suburbs and urban parks.

FOOD Actively probes, scales off bark, and drills into wood for insects. Works over tree trunks and larger limbs, chiseling out chunks of dead or diseased wood to get to insect larvae. Also eats some fruits and seeds.
■ **feeding** Visits suet feeders; shier around people than Downy Woodpecker. Also consumes peanuts, peanut butter, and sunflower seeds.

NESTING *Location:* Cavity excavated in a tree. *Nest:* No material added. *Eggs:* Usually 3–6; incubated by both parents for about 14 days. *Fledging:* Leaves nest at 28–30 days.
■ **housing** Will use a nest box mounted on a tree or pole.

Sightings

	JAN	FEB	MAR	APR	MAY	JUN	JUL	AUG	SEP	OCT	NOV	DEC

Northern Flicker
Colaptes auratus, L 12½" (32 cm)

The Northern Flicker breaks the woodpecker mold—it is mostly brown and spends much of its time on the ground. There are two different color groups: "Yellow-shafted" in the East and far north and "Red-shafted" in the West, with interbreeding on the Great Plains where the two ranges overlap. The two groups were considered two separate species until 1973, when scientists "lumped" them (classified them as a single species). Even so, most birders continue to use their more colorful group names. State bird of Alabama (referred to as the Yellowhammer).

all North American flickers have white rumps

"Yellow-shafted" ♀

female lacks whisker

yellow underwing

red nape and pale brown face

male has black whisker

"Yellow-shafted" ♂

underparts. In flight, the white rump is very conspicuous. The **"Yellow-shafted"** has bright yellow underwings and undertail, tan face, and gray crown with red patch on nape; **male** has a black whisker mark on the face, absent in **female**. The **"Red-shafted"** has salmon pink underwings and undertail, gray face, and brown crown and nape (no red nape patch); **male** has a red whisker mark on the face, lacking in **female.** Intergrades between the two subtypes show a mix of characteristics.

IDENTIFICATION Common. Large woodpecker. When foraging on the ground, hops from place to place. It also spends time in trees, clinging vertically to tree trunks (like a normal woodpecker) or perched high up on small branches looking very alert with lots of head jerking and bowing.

■ **plumage** All Northern Flickers have a brown back with black bars, a bold black crescent on the chest, and spotted

The golden yellow underwings of the "Yellow-shafted" Flicker are completely hidden when the wings are closed.

With the temperature outside at -20°F, this male "Red-shafted" Flicker has fluffed its body feathers to conserve heat.

■ **similar species** Similar Gilded Flicker (not illustrated) is restricted to desert areas of southern Arizona and near the Colorado River—not typical backyard habitat.
■ **voice** Highly vocal. Single, piercing *klee-yer!* or *keeew!* call is given year-round. Long, loud *wick-a-wick-a-wick-a* call is heard in breeding season (can be confused with Pileated Woodpecker's call).

RANGE Widespread species. Found in open woodlands, forest edges, woodlots, shelterbelts, suburban areas, and city parks. Avoids deep forest with thick undergrowth, but needs trees for nesting. Overall population is declining, possibly due to nest hole competition with European Starlings, fewer available dead trees (overmanaged forests), or pesticide application to agricultural fields and suburban lawns. Conserving the flicker is important because it's a keystone forest species, providing nest holes and roosting sites for many animals that can't excavate their own. Northern breeders migrate south in fall. Spring **migration:** late March–April; fall migration: late September–October.

FOOD Specializes in foraging on the ground for ants, picking them from the surface or vigorously digging out their underground nests ("ground-pecker"). Rarely forages on tree trunks or branches. Many birds shift to berries and other fruits in late fall and winter.
■ **feeding** Visits suet feeders, where it is usually the dominant woodpecker. Also consumes peanuts, peanut butter, and sunflower seeds.

NESTING *Location:* Cavity excavated in a tree, usually dead or diseased. *Nest:* No material added. *Eggs:* Usually 5–8; incubated by both parents for 11–13 days. *Fledging:* Leaves nest at 24–27 days.
■ **housing** Will use a nest box mounted on a tree or pole at least 6 feet off the ground.

"Red-shafted" ♂

male has red whisker

brown nape and gray face

salmon pink underwing

"Red-shafted" ♀

Sightings

JAN	FEB	MAR	APR	MAY	JUN	JUL	AUG	SEP	OCT	NOV	DEC

EXCAVATIONS AND DRUMMING

Woodpeckers are the carpenters of the bird world. Their chisel-like bills and reinforced skulls and necks allow them to hammer into both live and dead wood with great effectiveness—without damaging their brains. Their stiff tails and strong feet allow them to perch vertically on a tree trunk while working.

■Food excavations Some species, like the Red-bellied Woodpecker, don't do much wood excavating for food, but for most woodpeckers this is an important activity. The tiny Downy Woodpecker works on smaller dead branches, drilling shallow holes. Our largest species, the Pileated Woodpecker, sometimes chisels out huge oval holes. To reach deep into an excavated hole, the woodpecker has an exceptionally long tongue. Additionally, the tip of the tongue is barbed and coated with sticky saliva to help extract its prey.

■Nest excavations The woodpecker's nest is a cavity excavated in a tree trunk or large branch—usually a dead or diseased one. Most nest holes go straight in and then down about the length of the bird's body. Old woodpecker holes are used by many other birds and mammals for nesting and shelter.

■Drumming Although most woodpeckers have loud calls, they have no territorial songs—rhythmic drumming takes its place. Most species search out a resonant substrate to drum on. With experience, you can learn the different patterns and speeds that make a drum roll unique to a species.

Three young Pileated Woodpeckers crowd their nest hole entrance waiting to be fed *(left)*; notice the oval shape and larger size of the adult's food-excavation holes *(right)*.

Pileated Woodpecker
Dryocopus pileatus, L 16½" (42 cm)

Spectacular, crow-size woodpecker with a flaming crimson crest. Pairs defend a large forested territory (100+ acres) year-round. Its numerous excavations are crucial assets of the forest ecosystem, used for shelter and nesting by a diverse array of animals.

female has black forecrown and whisker

♂ white wing patch

♀ extensive white underwing

♂

IDENTIFICATION Fairly common. Big, rangy woodpecker with a long neck and tail. For such a dramatic species, it is surprisingly inconspicuous and shy. Its presence is most often revealed as it flies from tree to tree or by its loud, ringing call.
■ **plumage** Mostly black. Head has a red crest and black-and-white pattern. In flight, wings flash black and white. **Male** has complete red crest and red whisker; **female** has red crest with black forecrown and black whisker.

■ **similar species** None.
■ **voice** Loud, echoing series of *kuk* notes with a laughing quality, similar to a Northern Flicker, or a loud *wuck* note or series of notes. Often calls in flight.

RANGE Widespread species; year-round resident. Prefers mature forest with large trees, but is also found in woodlots, wooded suburbs, and large wooded parks. Uncommon in its western range; most common in the South.

FOOD Chisels vigorously into dead, diseased, or live trees for insects, primarily carpenter ants and beetle larvae, making unique large oval or rectangular excavations. Often descends to forage on fallen logs. Also eats fruits, nuts, and berries.
■ **feeding** Occasionally visits suet feeders.

NESTING *Location:* Cavity excavated in a tree; also excavates night-roosting cavities with multiple entrances. *Nest:* No material added. *Eggs:* Usually 4; incubated by both parents for 15–18 days. *Fledging:* Leaves nest at 24–31 days, but dependent on parents for several months (until fall).
■ **housing** Will use a nest box mounted on a tree.

	JAN	FEB	MAR	APR	MAY	JUN	JUL	AUG	SEP	OCT	NOV	DEC

Tyrant Flycatchers
Family Tyrannidae

A family of small to medium-size birds that specialize in capturing insects in flight. Most species sit upright on exposed perches from where they launch their attacks. In general, they have drab plumage, large heads with broad-based bills, tiny legs and feet, and simple songs.

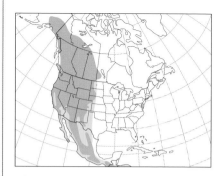

averages darker than Eastern, but identification safely done only by voice

long wings

paler adult　　　**darker adult**

Western Wood-Pewee
Contopus sordidulus, L 6¼" (16 cm)

The name pewee derives from the song of the closely related Eastern Wood-Pewee, not the "peewee" size of these birds.

 IDENTIFICATION Fairly common. Small, drab flycatcher with a large head and a distinctive voice.

■ **plumage** Dark, grayish olive above, with two thin wing bars; olive color washes across the breast (like a vest). Base of bill is yellow or orange.

■ **similar species** Different range and voice than the almost identical Eastern Wood-Pewee (opposite). Easily mistaken for an *Empidonax* flycatcher, a confusing group of small greenish flycatchers that also have two wing bars (their specific identification is beyond the scope of this book); in general, "empids" are smaller, often flick their longer tails (something pewees don't do), and have whitish eye rings.

■ **voice** Most common **song** is a harsh, burry, descending whistle *PEEeeer* given throughout the day. **Calls** include a clear, descending *peeer*.

RANGE Western species; summer resident. Common in open Western woodlands, forest edges, and riparian groves. In suburban backyards, most often seen during migration. Winters mostly in South America. Spring **migration:** late April–mid-June; fall migration: August–September.

FOOD Captures insects in flight. Flies out (sallies) from an exposed perch to capture flies, flying ants, bees, and wasps. An audible snap of the bill usually signifies a miss. Often returns to the same perch.

NESTING *Location:* Straddling a tree branch, usually 15–30 feet up. *Nest:* Neat cup of fine fibers and plant down, bound together with spiderweb; outside decorated with moss or lichen. *Eggs:* Usually 3; incubated by female for 12–15 days. *Fledging:* Leaves nest at 14–18 days.

Sightings

JAN	FEB	MAR	APR	MAY	JUN	JUL	AUG	SEP	OCT	NOV	DEC

Eastern Wood-Pewee
Contopus virens, L 6¼" (16 cm)

The wing length of many birds is tied to the length of their migrations—long wings for long-distance migrants. On pewees (which winter in South America), the wing tip is prominent; on Eastern Phoebe (next page), a short-distance migrant, it is mostly hidden.

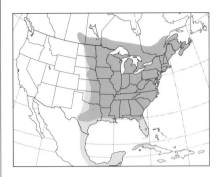

 IDENTIFICATION Fairly common. Small, drab flycatcher with a large head and a distinctive voice. It perches quietly, often for an extended period—then suddenly darts out to snatch an airborne insect, sometimes in a lengthy, twisting pursuit. It usually returns to the same perch and starts the process over.
■ **plumage** Dark, grayish olive above with two thin wing bars; olive color washes onto sides of breast (like a vest). Base of bill is yellow or orange.
■ **similar species** Eastern Phoebe (next page) is darker above, somewhat bulkier, lacks wing bars, has shorter wings, and—importantly—constantly pumps its tail (pewees never do). Easily mistaken for an *Empidonax* flycatcher (see the "similar species" section opposite). Different range and voice than the almost-identical Western Wood-Pewee.
■ **voice** Most common **song** is a slow, plaintive, whistled *pee-a-WEE*, with the second note lower; this phrase often

alternates with a down-slurred *PEE-yeer*. **Call** is an up-slurred *pewee*.

 RANGE Eastern species; summer resident. Common in a variety of woodland habitats; frequents forest edges and clearings. In suburban backyards, it is most often seen and heard during migration. Winters mostly in South America. Long wings—notice the prominent wing tip that extends well beyond the white-edged tertials—are usually a feature of species that have long migrations. Spring **migration**: mid-April–May; fall migration: mid-September–October.

 FOOD See Western Wood-Pewee (opposite).

 NESTING See Western Wood-Pewee (opposite).

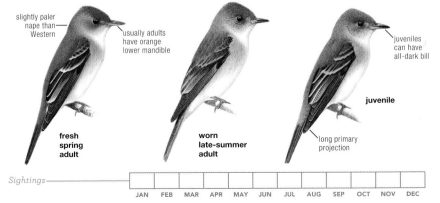

slightly paler nape than Western

usually adults have orange lower mandible

juveniles can have all-dark bill

juvenile

fresh spring adult

worn late-summer adult

long primary projection

Sightings

JAN	FEB	MAR	APR	MAY	JUN	JUL	AUG	SEP	OCT	NOV	DEC

Eastern Phoebe
Sayornis phoebe, L 7" (18 cm)

The Eastern Phoebe is a flycatcher with a penchant for nesting under bridges and around outbuildings and homes—often constructing a nest and raising a family under a porch roof near a busy door. Although drably colored and unobtrusive, its endearing acceptance of people has made it one of the most familiar summer birds in eastern North America.

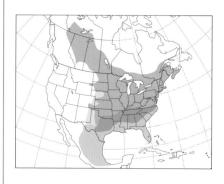

 IDENTIFICATION Common. Medium-size flycatcher (bigger than a pewee) with the habit of constantly pumping—rapidly down and slowly up—and spreading its long tail. Usually perches at low to middle levels around open areas or near the forest edge.

■ **plumage** Brownish gray above, darker on the wings (no wing bars or one faint one) and tail. White throat contrasts strongly with the dark, almost blackish head. Underparts are mostly white, with pale olive wash on sides and breast. Molts in the fall before migrating. The fresh fall feathers on the underparts are tinted pale yellow, and the wing feathers have noticeable, pale edges that can form a faint lower wing bar. **Juvenile** is very similar to the adult but has two cinnamon wing bars and cinnamon tips to the feathers of the upperparts.

■ **similar species** Eastern Wood-Pewee (previous page) has greenish olive plumage, two white wing bars, and longer wings but is most easily separated from phoebe by the phoebe's distinctive tail wagging. Pewees are shier forest birds that usually select a higher perch and have a different song. An *Empidonax* flycatcher (or empid) is smaller, has two strong wing bars and a white eye ring, and usually flicks its tail upward (not up and down).

■ **voice** Distinctive **song** is a harsh, emphatic *fee-bee*, often alternated with a longer *fee-b-be-bee*. Both songs are given throughout the day by the male. Typical **call** is a sharp *chip*, given by both sexes.

RANGE Eastern species. Common around homes, but needs some wooded habitat nearby and prefers

worn summer adult

dark cap and face

fresh fall

pale yellow belly in fresh plumage

Eastern Phoebes are one of the first spring migrants to arrive in many parts of the East.

locations in the vicinity of water. More common in rural backyards than suburban ones. One of the earliest migrants to arrive in spring. Northern breeders move south in fall, and most spend the winter months in the southeastern U.S., although some continue on to Mexico. Spring **migration:** March–late April; fall migration: October–November.

FOOD Captures flying insects, including many wasps and bees, occasionally descending to the ground while in pursuit. Sallies from an exposed perch and frequently moves from perch to perch. Small fruits are an important food source from fall to early spring.

NESTING *Location:* In a sheltered niche on a building, bridge, culvert, or, rarely, rock crevice. *Nest:* Cup of mud pellets, grass, moss, and other fibers. *Eggs:* Usually 5; incubated by female for 14–16 days. *Fledging:* Leaves nest at 15–17 days, but fed by parents for an additional 2–3 weeks.

■ **housing** Phoebes adapt to many artificial sites, but you can encourage them by adding a nest shelf to a sheltered location such as a porch or under a deck.

A fledgling Eastern Phoebe waits patiently for food. The colorful, fleshy gape of its mouth is a feature of many young birds.

Sightings

JAN	FEB	MAR	APR	MAY	JUN	JUL	AUG	SEP	OCT	NOV	DEC

Black Phoebe

Sayornis nigricans, L 6¾" (17 cm)

The only black-and-white flycatcher in North America, elegantly attired in "black topcoat and white pants." This charming bird goes about its business—invariably in the vicinity of water—paying scant attention to anyone nearby.

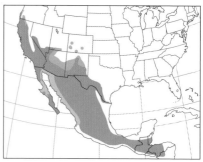

blackish

sharply contrasting white belly

phoebes drop their tail down

rusty wing bars

juvenile

RANGE West Coast and Southwestern species; year-round resident. Strongly associated with water: rivers, creeks, ponds, seaside cliffs—even backyard pools, park fountains, and cattle troughs. Prime habitat is a stream with overhanging branches and a nearby bridge or sheltered structure for nesting. Most birds are permanent residents, but in winter vacate highest breeding locations and northern edge of range in Southwest.

IDENTIFICATION Common. Medium-size flycatcher with a large, slightly crested head and a rather long tail that give it a front-heavy appearance. This active bird's energy extends to its tail, which is pumped up and down, especially after alighting.
■ **plumage** Black and white. Matte black above, with thin silvery edges on the wings and outer tail feathers; black breast, flanks, and tail contrast abruptly with the snow white belly. Dark eyes and bill blend into the black head. **Juvenile** has rusty wing bars.
■ **similar species** None. Sometimes seen with Say's Phoebe (opposite), mostly in winter.
■ **voice** **Song** alternates between two high, thin, whistled phases: *pi-tsee* and *pi-tsew*. **Call** is a sharp, high *tsip*.

FOOD Insects captured during darting flights from a low branch or creekside rock. Occasionally descends to the ground or snatches prey from the water's surface; known to catch small minnows.

NESTING *Location:* Attached to a sheltered vertical wall or in a niche; often uses a man-made structure such as a bridge, culvert, or building eave. Pairs often return to the same nest site year after year. *Nest:* Mud-and-grass cup lined with plant fiber. *Eggs:* Usually 4–5; incubated by female for 15–17 days. *Fledging:* Leaves nest at about 18 days.
■ **housing** Will use a nesting shelf placed in a sheltered location, for example, under a porch roof or eave.

Sightings

JAN	FEB	MAR	APR	MAY	JUN	JUL	AUG	SEP	OCT	NOV	DEC

Say's Phoebe

Sayornis saya, L 7½" (19 cm)

Say's Phoebe is the northernmost breeding flycatcher in the world—almost reaching the Arctic Ocean. Needless to say, it is highly migratory there. Its population center is in the arid interior West.

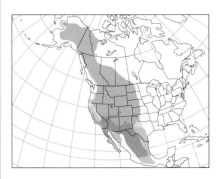

IDENTIFICATION Common. Medium-size flycatcher with large head, but well proportioned overall. Like other phoebes, often pumps and fans its tail. Buoyant flight, with noticeably dark tail and pale underwings.

■ **plumage** Dusty grayish brown above, with slightly paler throat and breast. Cinnamon underparts and blackish tail are eye-catching field marks. **Juvenile** is paler with buff wing bars.

■ **similar species** Slightly overlaps in range with Eastern Phoebe (pages 108–109), which is about the same size and shape but has white (not cinnamon) belly and white throat.

■ **voice** **Song** is a fast *pit-tsee-eur*, often given in fluttering flight. Typical **call** is a plaintive, down-slurred whistle: *pee-ee*.

RANGE Western species; mostly a summer resident. Favors arid country of all kinds—dry grasslands, parched foothills, rocky canyons, sagebrush flats, ranchlands, rimrock country, and tundra (in northern Alaska). Unlike other phoebes, avoids forested areas and well-watered land. Migrates south in fall, except in the southernmost part of its breeding range, where it is present year-round. Spring **migration:** late February–mid-May; fall migration: late September–October.

FOOD Mostly flying insects— often bees and wasps—captured during darting flights from a low perch on a boulder, bush, or fence post. In cold weather or when flying insects are scarce, hovers overhead to spot prey on the ground.

NESTING *Location:* In a sheltered rocky niche or cliff overhang; often uses a man-made structure such as a porch, abandoned farm building, or mine shaft. *Nest:* Grass-and-fiber cup. *Eggs:* Usually 4–5; incubated by female for 12–18 days. *Fledging:* Leaves nest at 17–21 days.

■ **housing** Will use a nest shelf placed in a sheltered location like a porch or house eave.

grayish back

tawny belly

blackish tail

Sightings ————

JAN	FEB	MAR	APR	MAY	JUN	JUL	AUG	SEP	OCT	NOV	DEC

Eastern Kingbird
Tyrannus tyrannus, L 8½" (22 cm)

The kingbirds—this species and the following two—are flycatchers found in open or broken country. The group name refers both to their brazen behavior of chasing off larger birds and their hidden "crowns" of red feathers, seen only when a bird is highly agitated.

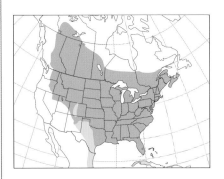

IDENTIFICATION Common. Moderately large, white-bellied flycatcher. Like other kingbirds, often perches high up on dead branches and power lines, or much lower on fences and shrubs.

■ **plumage** Slate gray above, head almost black, and wings edged with white; underparts are snow white with a pale gray wash across the breast. Black tail with white tip. **Juvenile** is browner above with an indistinct pale tip to the tail.

■ **similar species** Gray Kingbird (not illustrated) of coastal Florida, which is larger, paler, larger billed, and has a forked tail without a white tip.

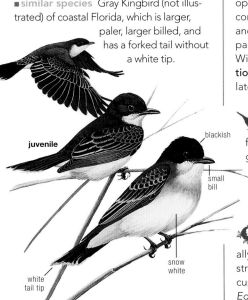

juvenile

blackish

small bill

snow white

white tail tip

■ **voice** Call is single buzzy *dzeet*. Also gives a stuttering series of notes: *kip-kip-kipper-kipper* or *dzee-dzee-dzee*.

RANGE Widespread species; summer resident. The only kingbird in the East, it overlaps with the Western Kingbird in many Midwestern and Western locales (see range maps). Favors open country with scattered trees and is common around farms, along roadsides, and in streamside thickets, suburban parks, golf courses, and athletic fields. Winters in South America. Spring **migration:** late March–mid-June; fall migration: late July–late September.

FOOD Mostly flying insects. Prey is captured during sallying flight from a perch, but also glides to the ground, gleans insects from bushes, and hovers over fields. Diet also includes wild fruits and berries, especially during fall migration and in winter.

NESTING *Location:* In a tree away from the trunk; occasionally on a utility tower or other man-made structure. *Nest:* Disheveled but sturdy cup of small twigs and weed stems. *Eggs:* Usually 3–4; incubated by female for 14–17 days. *Fledging:* Leaves nest at 16–17 days.

Sightings

JAN	FEB	MAR	APR	MAY	JUN	JUL	AUG	SEP	OCT	NOV	DEC

MOBBING BEHAVIOR

Strength in numbers is the strategy of a "mob" of birds harassing a potential predator. An enemy that a single bird could never overpower alone can be annoyed and confused by a flashing, fluttering horde to the point that it gives up whatever attack it may have planned. If you track a screeching, cawing flock of jays and crows, you may find that their objective is to pester a hawk or an owl until it leaves the premises.

MOBBED OR MOBBING?

Rather than being the mobbers, crows often become the targets for Red-winged Blackbirds and Common Grackles, because crows are notorious nest robbers. A Red-tailed Hawk sometimes attracts a mob of smaller birds even though it is not usually a predator of either the adults or their nests. The behavior may be an ingrained hawk-equals-danger response.

A particular type of mobbing is directed at two species that would not ordinarily target nests or nestlings, but instead seek out the adults as prey. These are the bird-eating Sharp-shinned Hawk and Cooper's Hawk. One bird among a feeding flock of chickadees, titmice, and nuthatches may happen to see one of those hawks coming. It gives a signal that every other bird understands, and rather than darting for cover, the flock springs into action as a harassment squad. Not only do the birds hassle the hawk, they warn every other bird in the vicinity that a predator is present.

This encounter is not so scary as it might seem. A Baltimore Oriole harasses a Red-tailed Hawk, but the big bird is too slow to capture the annoying oriole.

CROSS TALK

Experimenters have discovered that different species know details of each other's language. For example, Red-breasted Nuthatches can understand from Black-capped Chickadees' various calls not only that a predator is present but also what kind of predator, how far away it is, and how dangerous it may be.

Western Kingbird
Tyrannus verticalis, L 8¾" (22 cm)

The Western Kingbird is a conspicuous summer bird over large areas of the Great Plains and West. Pairs don't tolerate larger birds getting too close to their nest tree—passing predators are chased and briskly escorted out of the area.

darker wings contrast with gray back

white edge

adults

 | **IDENTIFICATION** Common. Moderately large, yellow-bellied flycatcher. Perches high or low. Buoyant flight; sometimes hovers briefly.
■ **plumage** Soft, pale gray above and on chest (slightly olive on back). White throat blends into gray chest, which blends into yellow belly. Faint, dark face mask. Black tail contrasts sharply with pale gray back; the tail has white edges, which can wear off by fall.
■ **similar species** Cassin's Kingbird (next page) is darker gray above and on chest,

pale gray head and back

black tail with white edge

spring adult ♂

has a white chin surrounded by dark gray, and has a pale tip (not white edges) to the tail. Also compare to Say's Phoebe (page 111).
■ **voice** Song is a fast *pik pik peek PEEK-a-loo.* Common **call** is a sharp *kip,* given singly or in a stuttering series.

| **RANGE** Great Plains and Western species; summer resident. Favors dry country interspersed with trees as well as towns and urban parks. Winters in Mexico and Central America, with small numbers in southern Florida. Spring **migration:** mid-March– mid-May; fall migration: late July–September.

adult ♂

| **FOOD** Insects. Most prey are captured during sallying flights from a perch, but also from the ground or gleaned from bushes.

| **NESTING** *Location:* On the outer branches of a tree or shrub, or on man-made structures such as a building, a utility pole, or even a city lamppost. *Nest:* Untidy cup mostly of grasses and weed stems. *Eggs:* Usually 4; incubated by female for 12–18 days. *Fledging:* Leaves nest at 16–17 days.

Sightings

	JAN	FEB	MAR	APR	MAY	JUN	JUL	AUG	SEP	OCT	NOV	DEC

Cassin's Kingbird
Tyrannus vociferans, L 9" (23 cm)

Cassin's Kingbird is a loud, boisterous summer bird of western North America. Not as widespread or common as the Western Kingbird (the "default" yellow-bellied kingbird), but the two species overlap in range and habitat. They sometimes even nest in the same tree.

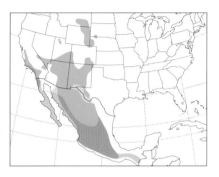

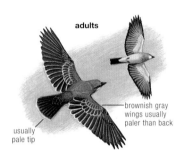

adults

brownish gray wings usually paler than back

usually pale tip

 IDENTIFICATION Fairly common. Moderately large, stocky, yellow-bellied flycatcher.
■ **plumage** Dark gray above and on chest. White chin contrasts with dark gray throat; paler wings do not contrast with the upperparts. Dark tail is tipped in buff, with faint, pale edges.
■ **similar species** Western **adult ♂** Kingbird (opposite page) is paler overall, but its darker wings contrast with its pale gray body; its white throat blends into a paler gray breast and black tail is edged in white. Also compare to Say's Phoebe (page 111).
■ **voice** Very vocal. **Call** is a strident, burry *chi-BEER* or *CHE-brrr*, given singly or run into a stuttering series.

RANGE Western species; summer resident. Most common in the Southwest and southern California. Favors parklike areas interspersed with trees—cottonwood, juniper, eucalyptus. Some winter in southern California (sometimes in small flocks), but most move to Mexico. Spring **migration:** mid-March–May; fall migration: late July–October.

FOOD Mostly flying insects. Most prey are captured during sallying flights from a perch; also glides to the ground or gleans insects from bushes. Winter diet includes wild fruits and berries.

NESTING *Location:* Outer branches of a tall tree. *Nest:* Substantial cup of small twigs and weed stems. *Eggs:* Usually 3–4; incubated by female for 12–14 days. *Fledging:* Leaves nest at 16–17 days.

dark gray head, back, and breast

white chin

adult ♂

pale tip

Scissor-tailed Flycatcher

Tyrannus forficatus, L 13" (33 cm)

If you live in the southern Great Plains, you may have the "Prairie Kingbird" as a summer neighbor. State bird of Oklahoma.

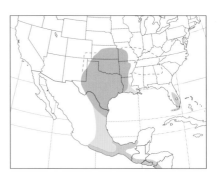

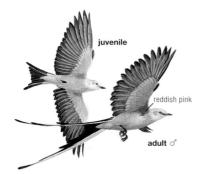

juvenile

reddish pink

adult ♂

 IDENTIFICATION Common. Medium-large, long-tailed flycatcher. The Scissortail is a common roadside bird, often seen perched on a barbed-wire fence or low shrub.

■ **plumage** Very pale gray upperparts; dark wings edged in white; salmon pink belly and underwings; scarlet red where the wings meet the body; and a very long, black-and-white tail. **Males** have a longer tail than females; **juvenile** has an even shorter tail and is yellowish pink on belly.

■ **similar species** Western Kingbird (page 114) resembles juvenile Scissortail, but has a pure yellow belly and an even shorter, unforked tail.

■ **voice** **Song** is similar to Western Kingbird's. Common **call** is a sharp *kip* or *pup* given singly or in a stuttering series.

RANGE Texas and southern Great Plains species; summer resident. Favors prairies, savannas, and open country with scattered trees; common around farms and along roadsides, but also near urban shelterbelts and golf courses. Most winter in Mexico or Central America, with small numbers in southern Florida. Spring **migration:** mid-March–early May; fall migration: late September–early November.

FOOD Insects, especially grasshoppers, crickets, and beetles.

NESTING *Location:* In an isolated tree or shrub. *Nest:* Sturdy cup of small twigs and weed stems. *Eggs:* Usually 4–5; incubated by female for 13–16 days. *Fledging:* Leaves nest at 14–17 days.

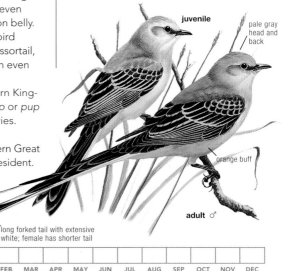

juvenile

pale gray head and back

orange buff

adult ♂

long forked tail with extensive white; female has shorter tail

Sightings

JAN	FEB	MAR	APR	MAY	JUN	JUL	AUG	SEP	OCT	NOV	DEC

Great Crested Flycatcher
Myiarchus crinitus, L 8½" (21 cm)

The Great Crested Flycatcher's penchant for adding a shed snakeskin to its nest was noted by early naturalists. The assumption was that it scared away potential predators. Nowadays, these flycatchers are as likely to substitute a piece of crinkly cellophane or plastic wrap—possibly seeking a decorative effect rather than protective one.

IDENTIFICATION Common. Medium-large, lanky flycatcher with a moderate crest and a heavy bill. Much of its time is spent high up in leafy trees, where it would go unnoticed except for its loud and regular vocalizing.
■ **plumage** Dark olive brown upperparts; gray throat and breast; and bright lemon yellow belly. Wings have rufous primaries, most visible in flight; tail has rufous inner webs, best seen from below.
■ **similar species** None in the East.
■ **voice** Distinctive **call** is a loud, hoarse, ascending *wheep!*

RANGE Eastern species; summer resident. Inhabits open deciduous forest, including woodlots, second-growth woodlands, and suburban and urban areas with numerous large shade trees. It has probably benefited from forest fragmentation. Winters in Central and South America and in southern Florida. Spring **migration:** mid-March–May; fall migration: late August–October.

FOOD Mostly insects. Hunts from a perch, sallying out to capture insects in flight, sometimes involving a lengthy pursuit, or hovering briefly to pick insects off a leaf or branch; occasionally pursues insects on the ground. Supplements diet with small wild fruits.

NESTING *Location:* In an old woodpecker hole or natural cavity. *Nest:* Bulky cup of leaves, fur, and other found objects, including snakeskins and plastic wrap. *Eggs:* Usually 4–5; incubated by female for 13–15 days. *Fledging:* Leaves nest at 14–15 days.
■ **housing** Will use a nest box.

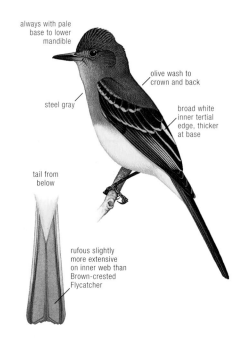

always with pale base to lower mandible

olive wash to crown and back

steel gray

broad white inner tertial edge, thicker at base

tail from below

rufous slightly more extensive on inner web than Brown-crested Flycatcher

Sightings

	JAN	FEB	MAR	APR	MAY	JUN	JUL	AUG	SEP	OCT	NOV	DEC

Ash-throated Flycatcher
Myiarchus cinerascens, L 7¾" (19 cm)

The Ash-throated Flycatcher is a common summer resident across a large swath of western North America.

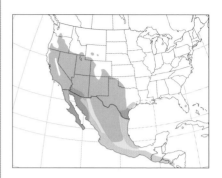

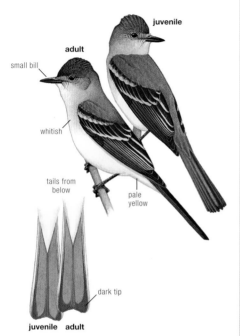

juvenile

adult

small bill

whitish

tails from below

pale yellow

dark tip

juvenile **adult**

IDENTIFICATION Common. Medium-large, slender, bushy-crested flycatcher. Usually perches within the tree canopy, but territorial birds sing from more open perches. Does not pump its tail.

■ plumage Grayish brown upperparts, with pale gray throat and breast that blends into pale yellow belly. Wings have rufous primaries, most visible in flight; tail has rufous inner webs, best seen from below.

■ similar species Brown-crested Flycatcher (next page) is larger, with brighter yellow underparts that are more sharply contrasted and a different undertail pattern. Say's Phoebe (page 111) lacks rufous color in wings and tail, has cinnamon (not yellow) underparts, and frequently pumps its tail.

■ voice Song is a series of *ka-brick* notes. Distinctive **call** is a rough *prrrt*.

RANGE Western species; summer resident. A habitat generalist that is found from sea level to about 8,000 feet in a variety of open woodlands and arid scrub—but avoids humid, densely forested areas. Winters from extreme southwestern U.S. to Central America. Spring **migration:** mid-March–mid-May; fall migration: August–mid-September.

FOOD Mostly insects. Hunts by moving from perch to perch, then hovering briefly to pick an insect off a leaf or branch; aerial pursuits are uncommon. Supplements its diet with wild fruits and small reptiles.

NESTING *Location:* In a natural cavity or old woodpecker hole in a tree or cactus. *Nest:* Bulky cup of weeds, fur, and other found objects. *Eggs:* Usually 4–5; incubated by female for 14–16 days. *Fledging:* Leaves nest at 13–17 days.

■ housing Will use a nest box—or even a tin can nailed to a fence post.

Sightings

JAN	FEB	MAR	APR	MAY	JUN	JUL	AUG	SEP	OCT	NOV	DEC

Brown-crested Flycatcher
Myiarchus tyrannulus, L 8¾" (22 cm)

The Brown-crested Flycatcher has a much smaller North American range than the Ash-throated, but the two species occur together and are difficult to tell apart.

IDENTIFICATION Fairly common. Large, robust, bushy-crested flycatcher with a large bill. The subspecies in Texas is smaller. Does not pump its tail.

■ **plumage** Grayish-brown upperparts; gray throat and breast contrast with yellow belly. Wings have rufous primaries, most visible in flight; tail has rufous inner webs, best seen from below.

■ **similar species** Ash-throated Flycatcher (previous page) is a smaller, lankier bird with paler yellow underparts that blend into the pale gray breast and with a different undertail pattern and voice. In southern Texas (during migration), compare to the similar-size Great Crested Flycatcher (page 117).

■ **voice** Song is a clear musical whistle, a rolling *whit-will-do*. **Call** is a sharp, emphatic *whit*.

RANGE Southwestern and South Texas species; summer resident. Inhabits riverside groves of sycamore, cottonwood, and willow in the Southwest or mesquite, hackberry, and ash in Texas, as well as towns and suburbs with large shade trees; also common around saguaro cacti of Southwestern deserts. Seldom seen on **migration,** but is present in the U.S. from late April to mid-August, wintering in Mexico and Central America.

FOOD Mostly insects. Hunts by hovering briefly to pick an insect off a leaf or branch; aerial pursuits are less common. Supplements its diet with wild fruits (including cactus fruit) and small reptiles.

NESTING *Location:* In a natural cavity or old woodpecker hole in a tree or cactus. *Nest:* Bulky cup of weeds, fur, and other found objects. *Eggs:* Usually 4–5; incubated by female for 14–15 days. *Fledging:* Leaves nest at 12–18 days.

■ **housing** Will use a nest box or even an open pipe of a suitable dimension.

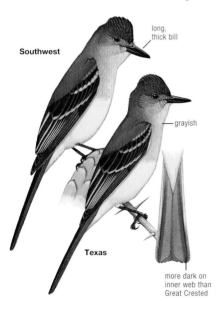

Southwest

long, thick bill

grayish

Texas

more dark on inner web than Great Crested

Sightings

JAN	FEB	MAR	APR	MAY	JUN	JUL	AUG	SEP	OCT	NOV	DEC

Vireos
Family Vireonidae

The vireos are a family of small song-birds with short, sturdy bills slightly hooked at the tip. They are generally chunkier and less active than warblers.

olive above, white below

black lateral crown stripe

breeding

pale yellow

1st fall

Red-eyed Vireo
Vireo olivaceus, L 6" (15 cm)

This vireo is probably the most common summer bird in Eastern woods, and its range extends far to the west. Its persistent singing earned it the nickname "preacher bird" in the 19th century.

IDENTIFICATION Very common. This small songbird moves sluggishly through the leafy treetops and would be hard to detect if not for its incessant singing—heard throughout the summer, from dawn till dusk. Its signature red eyes are revealed only with a very close look.

■ **plumage** Boldly striped head pattern with white eyebrows, bordered above and below with black, and a gray crown. Olive green upperparts; white underparts. No wing bars. **First-fall** has dark eyes; extensive yellowish wash on undertail coverts and flanks, which may extend up to the bend of the wing.

■ **similar species** Warbling Vireo (next page) lacks dark stripes on face.

■ **voice** **Song** is a series of sweet, singsong phrases: *chit-a-wit, de-o, cher-ee, cheer-o-wit* ("Here I am, over here, see me, where are you?"). **Call** is a nasal, whiny *queee*.

RANGE Widespread species; summer resident. Most common in mature deciduous forests, but also lives in mixed pine-hardwood forests and in residential areas and urban parks with large trees. Winters in South America. Spring **migration:** April–May; fall migration: late August–mid-October.

FOOD Gleans insects, particularly caterpillars, from leaves and twigs, or plucks them from leaves while hovering. Active, but methodical, as it moves about the canopy or mid-levels of the forest. Also eats small fruits, mostly in late summer and fall.

NESTING *Location:* In a shrub or low tree, usually 5–10 feet up. *Nest:* Open cup of papery bark, grasses, and rootlets, suspended from a forked branch. *Eggs:* Usually 3–5; incubated by both parents for 11–14 days. *Fledging:* Leaves nest at 10–12 days.

Sightings

JAN	FEB	MAR	APR	MAY	JUN	JUL	AUG	SEP	OCT	NOV	DEC

Warbling Vireo
Vireo gilvus, L 5½" (14 cm)

Plain and pale, the Warbling Vireo is most appreciated for its rapid, warbling song that emanates from the forest canopy in spring and summer.

 IDENTIFICATION Common. Compact and nicely proportioned, with a relatively slender bill. Its dark eye stands out on a pale face. Recent research has shown that there are likely two species of Warbling Vireo—an eastern one and a considerably smaller western one.
■ **plumage** There are not many field marks on this plain bird: brownish olive upperparts, whitish underparts, no wing bars. Face pattern is ill defined: pale eyebrow and dusky line through the eye. In fall, birds have a yellow wash on the underparts.
■ **similar species** Red-eyed Vireo (opposite), discernible by its boldly striped face pattern.

■ **voice** Persistent singer. **Song** is a complex series of rambling warbles; as a memory aid, try this ode to a caterpillar that approximates the song's cadence: "If I sees you, I will squeeze you, and I'll squeeze you till you squirt." **Call** is a nasal *eahh*.

RANGE Widespread species; summer resident. Most common in mature deciduous forests, especially near water; also lives in residential areas and urban parks with large trees. Winters in Mexico and Central America. Spring **migration:** mid-April–early May in the East, early March–late May in the West; fall migration: mid-August–early September in East, late July–mid-October in West.

FOOD Gleans insects, particularly caterpillars, from leaves and twigs, or plucks them from leaves while hovering. Active, but methodical, as it moves about the canopy or mid-levels of the forest.

NESTING *Location:* In a tree, usually 20–60 feet up. *Nest:* Open cup of bark strips, grasses, hair, rootlets, and so forth, woven into the crotch of a forked twig. *Eggs:* Usually 3–4; incubated by both parents for 12–14 days. *Fledging:* Leaves nest at about 14 days.

eastern
fall

pale
lores

smaller and
paler than
Red-eyed Vireo

yellow
brightest
on sides

western
fall

eastern
spring

western birds
are smaller with
slighter bill

Sightings

	JAN	FEB	MAR	APR	MAY	JUN	JUL	AUG	SEP	OCT	NOV	DEC

Yellow-throated Vireo
Vireo flavifrons, L 5½" (14 cm)

The Yellow-throated Vireo is a colorful species, but its combination of yellow, olive, and gray is very good camouflage in the leafy treetops it frequents. The first clue to its presence is usually its distinctive song.

IDENTIFICATION Uncommon. Large vireo with a stocky body, heavy bill, short tail, and typical, sluggish vireo movements as it forages methodically through the forest canopy. Often cocks its head as it surveys its surroundings.

■ **plumage** Clean, bright colors. Yellow spectacles, throat, and breast are distinctive. Olive green upperparts, bold white wing bars, gray rump, and white belly.

■ **similar species** Pine Warbler (page 180) has similar pattern and color, but has a yellowish rump, streaked sides that look dingy, a thinner bill, a more active lifestyle, and different vocalizations.

■ **voice** Persistent singer throughout the breeding season. **Song** is series of lazy, slurred phrases separated by fairly long pauses: *de-a-ree, three-eight*. **Calls** include a rapid, harsh series of *cheh* notes.

RANGE Eastern species; summer resident. Breeds in open deciduous forests with mature trees (oaks and maples are favorites), preferring wooded edges with water nearby; also lives in old orchards, woodsy suburbs, and urban parks with tall shade trees. Unevenly distributed and may be scarce in large areas of its mapped breeding range. Winters from southern Mexico to northern South America, and in the Caribbean. Spring **migration:** mid-March–May; fall migration: September–mid-October.

FOOD Methodically gleans insects—caterpillars, moths, butterflies, and a variety of small bugs—from leaves and twigs; sometimes hovers briefly. Supplements its diet with small fruits, mostly in fall.

NESTING *Location:* In a tree, usually 20–60 feet up. *Nest:* Deep, rounded cup of plant fibers and spiderweb, with flakes of lichen covering the outside, woven into the crotch of a forked twig. *Eggs:* Usually 4; incubated by both parents for about 13 days. *Fledging:* Leaves nest at about 13 days.

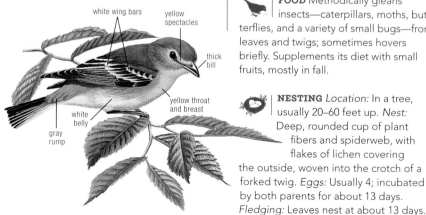

white wing bars

yellow spectacles

thick bill

yellow throat and breast

white belly

gray rump

Sightings

JAN	FEB	MAR	APR	MAY	JUN	JUL	AUG	SEP	OCT	NOV	DEC

BOOKS·A·MILLION

shop online at booksamillion.com

Store # 134
7000 Arundel Mills Circle Spac
Hanover   MD 21076
443-755-0210

KU	Description	QTY	PRICE	TOTAL
78947156	SMITHSON HDBK BIRDS	1	$30.00	$30.00
02676408	NGEO BACKYARD GUIDE	1	$18.95	$18.95

	Sub Total	$48.95
	Tax	$2.94
	Total	$51.89
	Debit Card	$51.89

cct# ***********4391   Auth# 585102

Take our survey for a chance to win
a $350 Gift Card good at any location!
Go to booksamillion.com/storesurvey
Buy our Discount Card & Save - $4.90

ssociate: Jeff   ID: 2623

rx 106   Str 134 Reg 003 Till 22   10/11/11 20:50

or returns, bring the item and this receipt back on or
efore 10/25/2011. Some items cannot be returned if
pened.

For returns with valid receipts (within 14 days), we will refund:

Cash if your purchase was made with cash,

Cash if your purchase was made with a check over 7 days ago,

Credit to your credit card if your purchase was made with a credit card,

Credit to a gift card if your purchase was made with a gift card.

After 14 days, merchandise cannot be returned or exchanged.

BOOKS·A·MILLION
shop online at booksamillion.com

Bookland   books&co.   JOE MUGGS

Return Policy

If you are not completely satisfied with your purchase, simply return it along with your original receipt within 14 days of purchase.

For returns with valid receipts (within 14 days), we will refund:

Cash if your purchase was made with cash,

Cash if your purchase was made with a check over 7 days ago,

Credit to your credit card if your purchase was made with a credit card,

Credit to a gift card if your purchase was made with a gift card.

After 14 days, merchandise cannot be returned or exchanged.

BOOKS·A·MILLION
shop online at booksamillion.com

SLEEPING BIRDS

Shortly after sunset, but before it's fully dark, your backyard birds have a decision to make: where to sleep. Most species slink quietly away, trying to avoid the eyes of possible predators. Unlike predatory mammals—which have a developed sense of smell and good night vision and move confidently at night—most birds settle in for the night and prefer not to move.

■Posture A popular misconception is that birds sleep with their heads under their wings. In truth, the most typical sleep posture is with the head turned rearward, resting on the back and the bill tucked under the scapular feathers to one side. Perching birds have a foot structure that makes grasping less of a muscular activity, but there's still restless shifting of weight throughout the night.

■Safety Safety relies on location. Waterfowl may sleep while floating or fly to a predator-free island. Cavity nesters, such as woodpeckers, chickadees, nuthatches, and bluebirds tend to sleep in their nest holes. Large communal roosts of crows, swallows, starlings, and blackbirds might seem vulnerable, but there are always some watchful individuals that can alert the entire flock.

■Warmth Staying warm at night when temperatures are coldest can challenge many species. Some species that are otherwise solitary are known to form nighttime sleeping roosts and huddle close together. This includes swifts, chickadees, titmice, bluebirds, and Brown Creepers. Other species seek out crevices and dense conifers— some grouse even burrow under the snow. Hummingbirds are able to lower their body temperature overnight to conserve energy. Individually, feathers are wonderful insulation and birds can fluff their body feathers to further trap body heat while asleep.

This rufous-morph Eastern Screech-Owl will sleep through the daylight hours, relying on its camouflaged plumage to keep it hidden.

Crows & Jays
Family Corvidae

Harsh voices and an aggressive manner draw attention to these large, often gregarious birds. Their powerful, all-purpose bills efficiently handle a varied diet. The jays are long-tailed and colorful; crows and ravens are entirely black.

bluish crest

extensive white in wings

blackish throat band

white tail tips

Blue Jay
Cyanocitta cristata, L 11" (28 cm)

Blue Jays have personality to spare. A partial list of descriptive adjectives would include: conspicuous, colorful, boisterous, brassy, loud, domineering, raucous, adaptable, intelligent, inquisitive, thieving, handsome, and unmistakable. They are the only jay in the East (except in Florida), and one of the most well-known backyard birds. Provincial bird of Prince Edward Island.

IDENTIFICATION Common. Large, easily recognized, crested jay. Hops from limb to limb or on the ground when foraging, and often perches up high when less active. Lands at feeders with an assertive flourish of wings, but also glides quietly through the forest. Loose flocks of migrating jays fly with steady wing beats well above the treetops. Jays are shy and secretive when nesting, except when mobbing a predator such as an owl, hawk, snake, or cat.

■ **plumage** Bright blue upperparts, crest (sometimes flattened), wings, and tail; wings with a bold, white wing bar and spots; tail with a broad white tip; white face encircled with a black necklace; and white underparts, often shaded buff gray on the breast and flanks.

■ **similar species** None. Range barely overlaps with two other species of western "blue jays": crested Steller's Jay (page 126), which is much darker and has no white in its wings or tail; and Western Scrub-Jay (page 127), which lacks a crest and has a dark face. The Florida Scrub-Jay (very similar to the Western Scrub-Jay) is restricted to central Florida, lacks a crest, has no white in its wings and tail, and has a dark face.

■ **voice** Wonderfully diverse array of **calls:** piercing *jay, jay, jay*; musical *wheedle-wheedle*; liquid, whistled *tooli*; and quiet, low-pitched rattle, as well as a very convincing mimic of Red-shouldered and Red-tailed Hawk calls.

RANGE Eastern and Midwestern species. Inhabits a variety of forested areas and mixed woodlands (especially with oaks). Locally abundant in suburbs and urban areas, probably as a result of bird-feeding activity. A permanent resident in many locations, but northern breeders (and others?) move south in fall and many spend the winter months in the Southeast. Large numbers of Blue Jays are sometimes seen migrating in loose flocks, but numbers vary from year to year. Spring **migration**: late April–late May; fall migration: mid-September–late October.

FOOD Omnivorous—a varied diet including acorns and other nuts, fruits, seeds, insects, bird eggs and nestlings (infrequently), and other small animals. Feeds in trees, on the ground, and at bird feeders. Caches acorns and other seeds by burying them in the ground. Since many nuts are not retrieved, this activity disperses acorns throughout the forest and results in the propagation of many new oak trees.

■ **feeding** Very common at feeders. Whole peanuts, sunflower seeds, and cracked

During aggressive confrontations, most birds, like these Blue Jays, try to look as large as possible.

corn are favorites. Dominates smaller birds; feeders that restrict the access of jays and other large birds are available.

NESTING *Location:* On a horizontal tree branch, usually 5–50 feet up. *Nest:* Bulky, open cup of twigs, grass, and bark, sometimes cemented with mud. *Eggs:* Usually 4–5; incubated by female for 16–18 days. *Fledging:* Leaves nest at 17–21 days.

The Blue Jay's crest is often held flattened against the top of its head.

Sightings

JAN	FEB	MAR	APR	MAY	JUN	JUL	AUG	SEP	OCT	NOV	DEC

Steller's Jay
Cyanocitta stelleri, L 11½" (29 cm)

Steller's Jays are raucous, inquisitive jays of Western forests. They frequently interact with people in backyards, campgrounds, picnic areas, and anywhere else they can expect (or demand) a handout. Provincial bird of British Columbia.

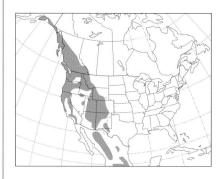

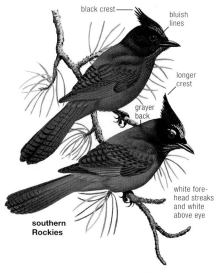

black crest
bluish lines
longer crest
grayer back
white fore-head streaks and white above eye
southern Rockies

■ **voice** Diverse array of **calls:** piercing *SHECK, SHECK, SHECK*; harsh, descending *SHHHHKK!*; and a variety of rattles and whistles. Frequently mimics hawks.

RANGE Western species; year-round resident. Inhabits coniferous and mixed coniferous-deciduous forests, from sea level to high elevations. Very common in the Pacific Northwest and in areas, including suburban backyards, where it is accustomed to being fed. Though nonmigratory, may move to lower elevations in winter.

FOOD Omnivorous, with a varied diet of nuts, seeds, fruits, insects, bird eggs and nestlings, and other small animals. Feeds in trees, on the ground, and at bird feeders.
■ **feeding** Common at feeders. Whole peanuts, sunflower seeds, and suet are favorites.

NESTING *Location:* Typically, high in a conifer, but often much lower when nesting near houses. *Nest:* Bulky, open cup of twigs, grass, and bark, sometimes cemented with mud. *Eggs:* Usually 4–5; incubated by female for 16–18 days. *Fledging:* Able to fly well at about 30 days.

IDENTIFICATION Common. Large, dark, shaggy-crested jay. Flies on broad wings; a descent to the ground from a high perch is often accomplished with a series of undulating glides. Although bold and aggressive around campgrounds and picnic areas, it is often shy in wilder places. When not breeding, mated pairs band together in small flocks.
■ **plumage** Blackish head and crest. Birds from the central and southern Rockies have white lines on the crown and a white arc over the eye; birds from the rest of the range have bluish lines just on the crown. **Juveniles** are browner with a short crest.
■ **similar species** None. No other jay in North America is both all dark and crested.

	JAN	FEB	MAR	APR	MAY	JUN	JUL	AUG	SEP	OCT	NOV	DEC

Western Scrub-Jay
Aphelocoma californica, L 11" (28 cm)

The most familiar "blue" jay in many parts of the West, the Western Scrub-Jay has successfully adapted to a variety of suburban and urban habitats, where it is a frequent and conspicuous backyard bird.

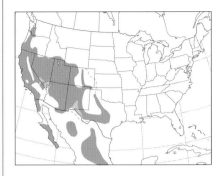

IDENTIFICATION Common. Large, but slender, long-tailed jay without a crest. Hops from branch to branch and frequently descends to the ground. In flight, it swoops and glides across open spaces, often calling harshly and loudly, as if protesting. Birds of the interior West are less common and rather shy compared to their boisterous coastal cousins.

■**plumage** Coastal birds have deep blue upperparts, a brownish patch on the back, a partial blue collar, and pale gray underparts. Inland birds (also known as **"Woodhouse's Jay"**) are paler blue above, with a less contrasting (more blended) brown back, an indistinct collar, and browner flanks. **Juvenile** is mostly grayish brown on head.

■**similar species** None. Other jays have conspicuous crests.

■**voice** Its most common **calls** are a harsh, up-slurred *jaaay?* or *jreeee?* and a rapid series of raspy *shreep* notes.

RANGE Western species; year-round resident. Inhabits chaparral and brushy areas, scrubby woodlands, and suburban and city backyards.

FOOD Omnivorous—nuts, seeds, fruits, insects, bird eggs and nestlings, and other small animals. Feeds on the ground and in trees. As with the Blue Jay in the East, the Scrub-Jay's habit of caching acorns plays an important role in the propagation of oaks; both jays have excellent spatial memory, but many acorns are never retrieved and some end up sprouting.

■**feeding** Common at feeders. Whole peanuts, sunflower seeds, and suet are favorites.

NESTING *Location:* In a tree or bush, usually 3–10 feet up. *Nest:* Bulky, open cup of twigs, grass, bark, and hair. *Eggs:* Usually 2–3; incubated by female for 15–17 days. *Fledging:* Leaves nest at 18–23 days.

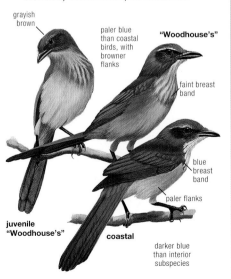

grayish brown

paler blue than coastal birds, with browner flanks

"Woodhouse's"

faint breast band

blue breast band

paler flanks

juvenile "Woodhouse's"

coastal

darker blue than interior subspecies

Sightings

JAN	FEB	MAR	APR	MAY	JUN	JUL	AUG	SEP	OCT	NOV	DEC

Fish Crow
Corvus ossifragus, L 15½″ (39 cm)

If you live in Fish Crow country, you're faced with an identification challenge—telling it apart from the ubiquitous American Crow. The two species look almost identical, but thankfully, they sound completely different. If you're wondering about a silent crow, simply wait until it calls.

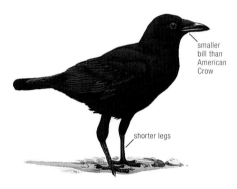

smaller bill than American Crow

shorter legs

IDENTIFICATION Common. Structure is very similar to the American Crow, but Fish Crow is a bit smaller, has slightly shorter legs, and more pointed wings.
- **plumage** All black. **Juvenile** has duller, sooty plumage.
- **similar species** American Crow (opposite) is slightly larger, less glossy, and longer legged, but looks almost identical—the two are best separated by voice. Grackles (pages 216–217) are smaller, slender birds with much longer tails.
- **voice** Distinctive, nasal **call** of *kah-uhh* or *uh-uhh* is very different from American Crow's cawing.

RANGE Eastern and Southern species. Inhabits coastal and tidewater areas, as well as inland areas, mostly along main river valleys; also common in suburbs and cities throughout its range. Forms large flocks in fall and winter that congregate around dependable food sources such as garbage dumps and shopping centers. Flocks disperse and individuals return (migrate) to their breeding areas in mid-March–April.

FOOD Omnivorous. Insects, shrimp, crayfish, crabs, eggs of birds, nestling birds, carrion, garbage, grain, seeds, and fruit are the main items.

NESTING *Location:* In a tree, usually 20–80 feet up. *Nest:* Bulky basket of sticks, twigs, grass, and sometimes mud. *Eggs:* Usually 4–5; incubated by female for 16–19 days. *Fledging:* Leaves nest at 32–40 days.

To confirm the identity of a Fish Crow, listen for its distinctive *uh-uhh* call, very different from the cawing of an American Crow.

Sightings

JAN	FEB	MAR	APR	MAY	JUN	JUL	AUG	SEP	OCT	NOV	DEC

American Crow

Corvus brachyrhynchos, L 17½" (45 cm)

There are other black birds, even other crows, but the abundant and widespread American Crow is the one that everybody knows. Crows are bold, inquisitive birds that are also very intelligent and surprisingly well organized. Cohesive family groups include immature and adult helpers that act as sentinels or scouts, help feed nestlings, and can communicate among themselves with a large vocabulary of sounds.

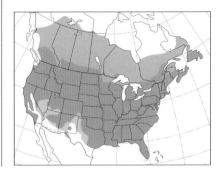

IDENTIFICATION Common to abundant. The American Crow is a large, sturdy bird with a heavy bill and strong legs for walking (strutting, really) and hopping on the ground. Its flight is strong and direct ("as the crow flies") on broad wings and a slightly rounded tail.

slightly rounded tail

■ **plumage** All black, including legs, feet, bill, and eyes. **Juvenile** has duller, sooty plumage; **just fledged young** has pink skin at the base of the bill.

■ **similar species** Fish Crow (opposite) is almost identical and best separated by voice. Common Raven (page 130) is larger; has a heavier bill, shaggy throat feathers, a wedge-shaped tail, and deeper call; and often soars (crows never soar). Male Great-tailed Grackle (page 214) has a much longer tail and pale eyes.

■ **voice** Familiar *caw, caw, caw* that changes depending on its context.

RANGE Widespread species. Inhabits a variety of habitats, particularly open areas with scattered trees. Northern breeders migrate south in fall, and family groups band together into large, noisy flocks. Nighttime roosts at favored locations can number in the thousands. Spring **migration:** mid-February–early April; fall migration: late October–December.

FOOD Omnivorous and opportunistic—insects, earthworms, bird eggs and young, rodents, snakes, carrion, garbage, grain, seeds (including birdseed), fruit, and more.

NESTING *Location:* In a tree or large bush, 10–70 feet up. *Nest:* Large, bulky basket of sticks, twigs, grass, and sometimes mud. *Eggs:* Usually 4–6; incubated by female for about 18 days. *Fledging:* Leaves nest at about 35 days.

smaller bill than ravens

long legs

Sightings

	JAN	FEB	MAR	APR	MAY	JUN	JUL	AUG	SEP	OCT	NOV	DEC

Common Raven
Corvus corax, L 24" (61 cm)

The majestic Common Raven is distributed around the globe in the Northern Hemisphere and has entered the folklore of many cultures. If you live in the West, chances are good that these intelligent and opportunistic birds are somewhere nearby. Provincial bird of Yukon Territory.

long, heavy bill

IDENTIFICATION Common to uncommon. Weighing about 2½ pounds, the Common Raven is heavier than a Red-tailed Hawk. When perched, the raven's feathers often look shaggy or ruffled, and the long, thin throat feathers (hackles) flare out when it croaks. The raven is a consummate flier, with long wings and a wedge-shaped tail, soaring with ease and even engaging in aerial acrobatics.
■ **plumage** All black (glossy, in some light), including legs, feet, bill, and eyes.
■ **similar species** American Crow (previous page) is much smaller and lighter. A crow never soars and has shorter, more rounded wings and a slightly rounded (rather than wedge-shaped) tail.
■ **voice** Extremely varied. Most common **call** is a low, drawn-out, croaked *kraaah;*

another is a deep, nasal, and hollow *broooonk.*

RANGE Widespread species. Most abundant in the West, uncommon in the East (south through the Appalachians), and largely absent from the Midwest (except in the northern states) and Southeast. Lives in a multitude of habitats, including mountains, seacoasts, tundra, deserts, farmland, towns, and suburbs.

FOOD Omnivorous. The majority of its diet is animal matter, either from scavenged carrion and human garbage or from animals caught and killed—rodents, reptiles, large insects, adult and fledgling birds, bird eggs. Also consumes grain and fruit. Does most of its feeding on the ground.

long wings

NESTING *Location:* On a sheltered rock ledge or large fork of a tree. *Nest:* Large construction of sticks and twigs, often lined with animal hair. *Eggs:* Usually 4–6; incubated by female for 18–21 days. *Fledging:* Leaves nest at 4–7 weeks.

long, wedge-shaped tail

Sightings

JAN	FEB	MAR	APR	MAY	JUN	JUL	AUG	SEP	OCT	NOV	DEC

Black-billed Magpie
Pica hudsonia, L 19" (48 cm)

The striking, long-tailed magpie graces many of the open spaces of the West. Some of the magpie's fascinating behaviors include following coyotes and foxes to steal food from them and conducting "funerals"—poorly understood, noisy gatherings of up to 40 birds around a dead magpie that last for 10–15 minutes before they all fly off in silence.

white primaries

IDENTIFICATION Fairly common. Relatively tame and inquisitive. Magpies hop and walk on the ground with a confident, swaggering gait, perch conspicuously on fence posts and tall shrubs, and fly with steady, rowing wing beats often ending with a swooping glide to a perch. Sometimes gather in large flocks.
■ **plumage** Showy black-and-white plumage with glossy blue, green, and violet highlights on the wings and extremely long tail.
■ **similar species** Yellow-billed Magpie (not illustrated) is found primarily in California's Central Valley, where the Black-billed does not occur.
■ **voice** Quite varied **calls** include a quick series *mag, mag, mag* (like a Steller's Jay, but less piercing) and a whining, rising *mee-aaah.*

RANGE Western species; year-round resident. Inhabits open woodlands, forest edges, scrublands, and rangelands, often near watercourses; is also at home in suburbs, towns, and urban parks.

FOOD Omnivorous and opportunistic. Eats animal matter, either from scavenged carrion and human garbage or from animals caught and killed—rodents, reptiles, insects, ticks (from live deer and moose), fledgling birds, bird eggs. Also consumes quantities of grain and fruit. Foraging takes place on the ground, rarely in trees. Magpies often cache food in scattered locations.

NESTING *Location:* In a tree or tall shrub; nests are often quite noticeable. *Nest:* Bulky, ball-shaped construction of sticks with an interior cup lined with mud, dung, and animal hair. *Eggs:* Usually 6–7; incubated by female for about 18 days. *Fledging:* Leaves nest at 22–29 days.

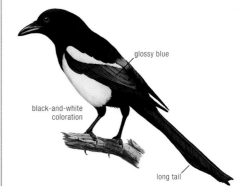
glossy blue
black-and-white coloration
long tail

Sightings

JAN	FEB	MAR	APR	MAY	JUN	JUL	AUG	SEP	OCT	NOV	DEC

Swallows
Family Hirundinidae

Adept aerialists, swallows dart and swoop in pursuit of flying insects. They all have very similar shapes, with slender bodies and long wings. North American species are highly migratory, some flying as far as southern South America for the winter.

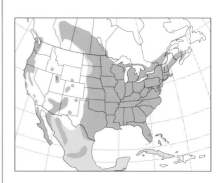

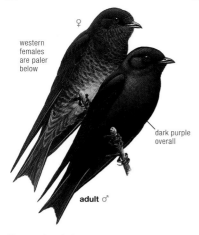

♀

western females are paler below

dark purple overall

adult ♂

Purple Martin
Progne subis, L 8" (20 cm)

In late winter, male martins leave their winter home in the Amazon and head north for the coming breeding season, arriving as early as January on the Gulf Coast and early March in the Mid-Atlantic. Competition is fierce at their colonial nest sites. Females follow several weeks later, and pair with males that have been successful in staking a claim to a favorable nest hole. In the East, their nests are almost exclusively located in housing provided by people—large martin apartment houses are typical, but suspended hollow gourds are also used. Martins are much less numerous in the West, where they nest primarily in tree or cactus cavities.

IDENTIFICATION Common to uncommon. North America's largest, most popular swallow, the colonial-nesting Purple Martin is noticeably larger when seen perched next to other swallows. In flight, which includes more soaring and gliding than swallows do, note the triangular wings and relatively short, forked tail.

■ **plumage** Distinctive **adult male** is all dark, with a purplish blue gloss. **Female** and **juvenile** are streaky or grayish below; **first-spring male** has some purple feathering on the underparts.

■ **similar species** All other swallows are smaller and have paler, cleaner underparts. (Note: Many female and juvenile martins have lighter, streakier underparts than illustrated.) Compare the adult male martin to the Chimney Swift (page 92) and European Starling (page 210): the swift has narrow wings and flickering wing beats; the starling doesn't swoop through the air and spends most of its time on or near the ground.

■ **voice** Common **call** is a sharp *churr*. **Song**, alternating between rough and liquid phrases, is composed of chortles, warbles, twitters, and croaks.

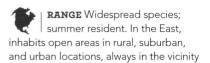

RANGE Widespread species; summer resident. In the East, inhabits open areas in rural, suburban, and urban locations, always in the vicinity of nest boxes offered by people. Avoids dense forest and wooded residential areas without surrounding fields. Absent from many areas of the West. Winters in South America. Spring **migration:** mid-January–early May (early April–mid-May in the West); fall migration: July–early October. After nesting, Eastern birds gather (mostly in August) in pre-migration flocks of thousands of birds at favored locations.

FOOD Flying insects, both large (dragonflies, hornets, butterflies) and small (midges, flies), but contrary to popular belief, mosquitoes are rarely captured because they fly too low.

NESTING *Location:* In a hollow gourd or martin apartment; in the West, a cavity (usually a woodpecker hole) in a tree or saguaro cactus. *Nest:* Twigs, plant material, and sometimes mud, filling the available space. *Eggs:* Usually 3–6; incubated by female for 15–18 days. *Fledging:* Leaves nest at 28–29 days.

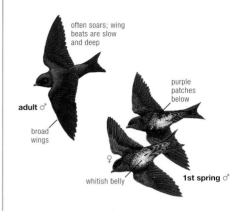

often soars; wing beats are slow and deep

purple patches below

adult ♂

broad wings

whitish belly

♀

1st spring ♂

■ housing Apartment houses come in many sizes and designs, but hanging gourds painted white (or plastic alternatives) seem to be favored by the martins and are less attractive to starlings and House Sparrows. If you're considering becoming a Purple Martin landlord, check the Purple Martin Conservation Organization website (www.purplemartin.org) for detailed information.

Although Purple Martins nest colonially, they are even more sociable after breeding, when they gather in large flocks for their fall migration to South America.

Sightings

JAN	FEB	MAR	APR	MAY	JUN	JUL	AUG	SEP	OCT	NOV	DEC

Tree Swallow
Tachycineta bicolor, L 5¾" (15 cm)

Tree Swallows nest in cavities—which are scarce commodities, and competition for them is intense. Starlings and House Sparrows take control of many sites.

1st spring ♀

adult

bluish patches on upperparts

adult

America. Spring **migration**: February–April; fall migration: July–early November.

FOOD Flying insects and small fruits. Tree Swallows can survive on a fruit diet, which allows them to linger in fall and to winter farther north than any other swallow.

NESTING *Location:* In a natural tree cavity or old woodpecker hole. *Nest:* Dry grasses and other plant material. *Eggs:* Usually 4–6; incubated by female for 13–16 days. *Fledging:* Leaves nest at 18–22 days.
■ housing Will use a nest box identical to the ones bluebirds use.

IDENTIFICATION Very common. In flight, adds a graceful glide after a series of energetic flapping. The wing has a triangular shape.
■ plumage **Adult** plumage is crisply bicolored: dark, metallic blue or blue-green above, snow white below. The **juvenile** is grayish brown above and has a diffuse grayish band across the chest. By October, most juveniles look like adults.
■ similar species Violet-green Swallow (opposite) is smaller, has more white in the face, and has large white patches that almost meet across the lower back.
■ voice **Calls** include liquid twittering and short chirping notes.

RANGE Widespread species. Needs open habitat—fields, large lawns, marshes—and prefers to nest and forage near water. Winters from the East Coast and southern U.S. to Central

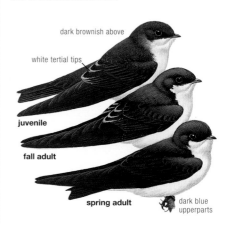

dark brownish above

white tertial tips

juvenile

fall adult

spring adult

dark blue upperparts

Sightings

JAN	FEB	MAR	APR	MAY	JUN	JUL	AUG	SEP	OCT	NOV	DEC

Violet-green Swallow
Tachycineta thalassina, L 5¼" (13 cm)

Well before the dawn of a summer day, Violet-green Swallows start their liquid twittering in coniferous forests throughout the West. Later in the heat of the day, they forage high over the pine forests, at a height more typical of swifts and soaring raptors.

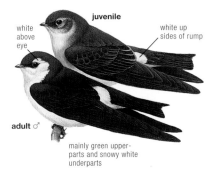

juvenile

white above eye

white up sides of rump

adult ♂

mainly green upperparts and snowy white underparts

 IDENTIFICATION Common. Small, compact swallow with a short tail.

■ **plumage** Adult male is green backed, with snow white underparts. The white extends onto the face and almost encircles the dark eye. Two white flank patches almost meet across the lower back. Females are duller. Juvenile has a similar pattern, but is brownish above and has less white on the face.

■ **similar species** Tree Swallow (opposite) has bluish plumage, a longer tail, eyes hidden in a dark face, and lacks big white flank patches.

■ **voice** Calls include twittering and short chirping notes, like the Tree Swallow's but higher pitched and buzzier.

RANGE Western species; summer resident. Principally found in mountain forests (at lower elevations farther north), where it forages above the forest and over bodies of water. Winters from California (scarce in lowland areas) to Mexico. Early spring migrant: early February–early May; fall **migration:** late September–late October.

FOOD Flying insects. Feeds singly or in small loose flocks, often foraging higher in the sky than other species of swallows.

NESTING *Location:* In an old woodpecker hole or natural cavity in a dead tree, commonly in small colonies of up to 25 nests. *Nest:* Dry grasses and other plant material, lined with feathers (usually white). *Eggs:* Usually 4–6; incubated by female for 14–15 days. *Fledging:* Leaves nest at 23–25 days.

■ **housing** Will use a nest box located under a building eave or on a tree 10–15 feet up.

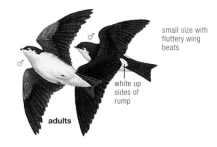

small size with fluttery wing beats

♂

♂

white up sides of rump

adults

Sightings

JAN	FEB	MAR	APR	MAY	JUN	JUL	AUG	SEP	OCT	NOV	DEC

Barn Swallow
Hirundo rustica, L 6¾" (17 cm)

The graceful Barn Swallow swoops over fields and pastures across North America, where it is one of the most popular birds of summer. Its range extends well beyond North America; in fact, it is the most widely distributed and abundant swallow in the world—breeding throughout the Northern Hemisphere and wintering in much of the Southern Hemisphere.

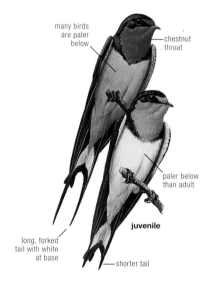

many birds are paler below

chestnut throat

paler below than adult

juvenile

long, forked tail with white at base

shorter tail

IDENTIFICATION Common. Its long, forked tail—it's our only swallow with a "swallowtail"—and slender body present an elegant appearance. In flight, the tail can be either spread (when banking or landing) or, more often, folded in a long point. Like other swallows, it's often seen perched on overhead wires.
■ **plumage** Glossy, steel blue above; chestnut forehead and throat; orangish underparts; white spots visible when tail is spread. **Male** has a longer tail and deeper

orange underparts than **female** (females prefer to mate with the males that have the longest and most symmetrical tails). **Juvenile** has a much shorter forked tail and whitish buff underparts.
■ **similar species** None. The adult's orangish underparts and very long tail are unique. Shorter tailed juveniles resemble Cliff Swallows (page 138) but have a dark rump and a forked tail.
■ **voice Song** is a long series of scratchy, warbling phrases, interspersed with a grating rattle. Flight **call** is a high-pitched *chee-jit.*

RANGE Widespread species; summer resident. Has three basic habitat requirements: open areas for

Barn Swallows are sociable birds that often nest in small colonies.

Sticky mud pellets allow the Barn Swallow to adhere its nest directly to a vertical wall.

foraging (fields, pastures, golf courses, large yards); a man-made structure to shelter its nest (barn, culvert, bridge, pier, porch); and a body of water that provides mud for nest building. Avoids deserts and dense forest, but as human development continues to spread into new areas, the Barn Swallow will surely follow. Most birds winter in South America. Spring **migration:** late January–mid-May; fall migration: August–early November. After nesting, gathers in large, pre-migration flocks with other swallows.

FOOD Flying insects. Pursues insects lower to the ground than other swallow species. Drinks on the wing by skimming the water's surface with its bill.

NESTING Location: Rarely nests anywhere other than in or on a man-made

structure. Nests in small colonies where nesting sites are plentiful and good habitat is available. Ancestral Barn Swallows used mostly caves as nesting sites. *Nest:* Cup of mud and dried grass, lined with feathers. *Eggs:* Usually 4–5; incubated by both parents for 12–17 days. *Fledging:* Leaves nest at 15–24 days.

■ **housing** Will use a nesting platform added to a porch or open garage.

bluish above

JAN	FEB	MAR	APR	MAY	JUN	JUL	AUG	SEP	OCT	NOV	DEC

Cliff Swallow
Petrochelidon pyrrhonota, L 5½" (14 cm)

Eastward ho! Unlike the westward expansion of modern human settlement across North America, the colonial Cliff Swallow has ventured east. The construction of bridges, culverts, and buildings offered suitable nest sites, and over the past 150 years Cliff Swallows have pushed across the Great Plains and into New England.

in Southwest has cinnamon forehead like Cave

Southwest

IDENTIFICATION Common. The compact Cliff Swallow has a chunky body; a short, square-tipped tail; and broad, relatively short wings. Being a colonial nester, it is often found in flocks.
■ **plumage** Most have a white forehead, chestnut cheeks and throat, and significantly, a buff rump patch. **Juvenile** has a darker, less patterned face, but paler throat.
■ **similar species** Cave Swallow (not illustrated), found mostly in Texas, has dark chestnut forehead and much paler throat and face.
■ **voice** **Song** is a series of squeaking and grating notes. **Calls** include rough *chrrr* and more musical *veeew* notes.

RANGE Widespread species; summer resident. Common to abundant in the West, scarcer and local in the East. Needs open habitat for foraging, overhanging cliffs or man-made structures

for nesting, and a supply of mud for nest construction. Winters in South America. Spring **migration:** late February–mid-May; fall migration: July–late September.

FOOD Flying insects. Aerial flocks often gather around swarming insects.

NESTING *Location:* Plastered to a sheltered rock wall or building (typically under the eaves); often in large colonies with tightly packed nests touching each other. *Nest:* Gourd-shaped with a tubular entrance, built completely of mud pellets. *Eggs:* Usually 4–6; incubated by both parents for 12–16 days. *Fledging:* Leaves nest at 20–26 days.

white forehead

dark throat

dusky throat and forehead on juvenile, often with some whitish feathers

juvenile

buffy rump

	JAN	FEB	MAR	APR	MAY	JUN	JUL	AUG	SEP	OCT	NOV	DEC

SEX, EGGS, AND INCUBATION

You may not have considered the intimate lives of your backyard birds, but their sex lives and the production of eggs and young are fascinating bird behaviors that you can observe . . . with some patience and luck. A reminder: never get so close to an active nest that you flush an incubating or brooding bird.

■**Sex** The sex act (copulation) is very brief in birds. Birds have an all-purpose opening (cloaca), located above the undertail coverts, which passes waste and is also where sexual contact is made. In the male, sperm collects at the opening, ready to be passed to the female's cloaca. The male usually stands on the female's back and the actual passing of sperm happens quickly, when the cloacae of the two birds touch.

■**Eggs** In the female, the fertilized egg (ovum) usually takes about 24 hours to be transformed into an egg ready to be laid. The egg's shell is deposited in the uterus, near the end of the egg's journey down the oviduct. The markings on an egg's shell are deposited as it moves and rotates in the uterus. Swirls and lines record periods of rapid movement; spots and blotches record periods of slow or little movement.

During copulation, the male Killdeer stands on the female's back. The two sexes look almost identical, but the female usually has less black on the face.

■**Laying and Incubation** Laying takes place as soon as the egg's shell is complete. Since there is no room in a bird's body for more than one fully formed egg at a time, the 24-hour process of egg formation repeats until a full clutch of eggs is laid. Most, but not all, birds wait until the last egg is laid before starting to incubate. In that way, all the eggs hatch at about the same time.

Chickadees & Titmice
Family Paridae

Grays and blacks predominate in this small family of small birds: chickadees have dark caps and throats; titmice are crested. What they lack in color and size, they make up for with their endearing acceptance of people, bird feeders, and nest boxes.

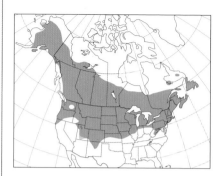

worn summer

less buffy when worn

cheeks uniformly white

prominent white-edged secondaries

fresh fall

Black-capped Chickadee
Poecile atricapillus, L 5¼" (13 cm)

Active and energetic, the Black-capped Chickadee seems immune to the harshest winter weather—no small feat for a bird weighing less than half an ounce. It copes by eating high-calorie foods (like black-oil sunflower seeds), roosting in a tree cavity at night (sometimes in small groups), fluffing out its insulating body feathers, and even lowering its body temperature. State bird of Maine and Massachusetts; provincial bird of New Brunswick.

IDENTIFICATION Common. Like all chickadees, the Black-capped is small and "cute," with a big, "no-neck" head. Acrobatic and restless, it is able to cling upside down using its strong feet. Joins roaming flocks of other small woodland birds in fall and winter.

■ **plumage** Has a black cap and throat and white cheek; otherwise, grayish olive above and white below with buff flanks. The wing coverts and tertials are brightly edged in white, but these edges are usually worn off by late summer.

■ **similar species** Carolina Chickadee (page 142) is very similar and its range overlaps in a narrow zone (see the range map). In fall and winter, the Black-capped has broad white edges on its wing coverts; these are dull, grayish white on the Carolina. The Black-capped *chick-a-dee* calls are slower and lower pitched. The two species sometimes interbreed (hybridize).

■ **voice** Less vocal in summer, when nesting. **Song** is a clear, whistled *fee-bee* or *fee-bee-ee*, the first note higher. **Call** is a slow, harsh *chick-a-dee-dee-dee*.

RANGE Widespread species; year-round resident. Inhabits woodlands and wooded edges, suburbs, towns, and tree-filled urban parks. In some winters, numbers of Black-capped birds move south into the northern part of the Carolina Chickadee's range.

FOOD Insects, spiders, seeds, and small fruits. In breeding season, about 90 percent of its diet is animal (mostly caterpillars); in winter, that changes to about half animal (insects and spiders, often their eggs and pupae) and half seeds and berries.

■ feeding Very common at feeders. Black-oil sunflower seeds and suet are preferred. Makes back-and-forth trips throughout the day. Large quantities of seeds are cached in bark crevices for later consumption (chickadees have excellent spatial memory); others are taken to a perch, hammered open, and eaten.

NESTING *Location:* An existing cavity in rotted wood or sometimes an old woodpecker hole in a tree. *Nest:* Cavity is enlarged and lined with moss, weed stems, and animal fur.

The short, rounded wings of the Black-capped Chickadee allow it to maneuver in tight spaces.

Eggs: Usually 4–5; incubated by female for 12–13 days. *Fledging:* Leaves nest at about 16 days.

■ housing Will use a nest box, especially if bottom is covered with sawdust. You can encourage chickadees (and some other cavity nesters) to excavate their own nest holes by using a cordless drill to bore a 1⅛" hole into the dead wood of a tree, at least 5 feet off the ground.

The Black-capped Chickadee and a few other species can be hand-tamed, but it usually takes a period of weeks working patiently with the same bird to gain its trust.

Sightings

	JAN	FEB	MAR	APR	MAY	JUN	JUL	AUG	SEP	OCT	NOV	DEC

Carolina Chickadee
Poecile carolinensis, L 4¾" (12 cm)

The Carolina Chickadee looks almost identical to the Black-capped Chickadee (pages 140–141), but has a more southern distribution. Chickadees of all species have many similarities—see the Black-capped Chickadee description for more information about the behavior, feeding, and housing of chickadees.

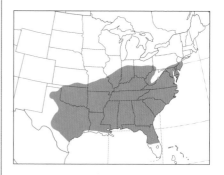

grayish tinge to rear cheek

fresh fall

slightly duller flanks than Black-capped

worn summer

slightly shorter tail than Black-capped

 IDENTIFICATION Common. Similar to Black-capped Chickadee.

■ **plumage** Has a black cap and throat and white cheek that becomes grayer toward the back; otherwise, gray above and white below with light buff flanks. The wing coverts and tertials have thin, grayish white edges that are almost completely worn off from by late summer.

■ **similar species** Black-capped Chickadee (previous page), in the narrow zone along the Carolina Chickadee's northern border where the two species overlap. Throughout the South (except in the Appalachians above about 4,000 feet), the Carolina is the *only* chickadee.

■ **voice** Less vocal in summer, when nesting. **Song** is a clear, four-note whistle:

fee-bee fee-bay. **Call** is *chick-a-dee-dee-dee*, higher and faster than the Black-capped's.

RANGE Mid-Atlantic, Midwestern, and Southern species; year-round resident. Inhabits woodlands and wooded edges, suburbs, towns, and tree-filled urban parks. In winter, flocks roam over a wider area and are concentrated around bird feeders.

FOOD Insects, spiders, seeds, and small fruits. In breeding season, about 90 percent of its diet is animal (mostly caterpillars); in winter, that changes to about half animal (insects and spiders, often their eggs and pupae) and half seeds and berries.

■ **feeding** Very common at feeders. Black-oil sunflower seeds and suet are preferred.

NESTING *Location:* An existing cavity in rotted wood or sometimes an old woodpecker hole in a tree. *Nest:* Cavity is enlarged and lined with moss, weed stems, and animal fur. *Eggs:* Usually 5–8; incubated by female for 12–15 days. *Fledging:* Leaves nest at 16–19 days.

■ **housing** Will use a nest box located at least 5 feet above the ground.

Sightings

JAN	FEB	MAR	APR	MAY	JUN	JUL	AUG	SEP	OCT	NOV	DEC

Mountain Chickadee
Poecile gambeli, L 5¼" (13 cm)

When an autumn chill is in the air and conifer seeds have ripened in the western mountains, the tiny Mountain Chickadee is hard at work caching and defending stores of seeds. The insects that made up the bulk of its summer diet will soon be much harder to find.

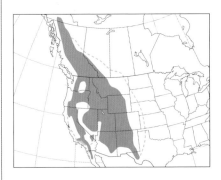

 IDENTIFICATION Common. Chickadees of all species have many similarities.

■ **plumage** White eyebrow and a slash of black through the eye that resembles a "bandit's mask." Otherwise, quite similar to Black-capped Chickadee (pages 140–141).

■ **similar species** None; the white eyebrow is unique. Juveniles often have a broken or messy eyebrow stripe, but the white is there if you look closely.

■ **voice** Less vocal in summer, when nesting. **Song** is a three- or four-note descending whistle: *fee-bee-bay* or *fee-bee fee-bee*. **Call** is a hoarse *chick-adee-adee-adee*.

RANGE Western species; year-round resident. Inhabits montane evergreen and mixed forests, as well as residential areas, towns, and parks with similar wooded habitat. In winter, some birds descend to lower elevations. Exceptionally, many birds may move out of the mountains (irrupt), and some turn up in unexpected places.

FOOD Gleans insects—especially caterpillars and insect eggs and larvae—and spiders from foliage, often involving acrobatic hanging from branch tips. During fall and winter, turns to a diet based on conifer seeds.

■ **feeding** Attracted to feeders. Black-oil sunflower seeds and suet are preferred.

NESTING *Location:* In an old woodpecker hole or natural cranny; not known to excavate its own cavity. *Nest:* Cavity is lined with moss, weed stems, and animal fur. *Eggs:* Usually 6–12; incubated by female for 12–15 days. *Fledging:* Leaves nest at 17–23 days.

■ **housing** Will use a nest box located at least 5 feet above the ground.

white eyebrow

California

broader white eyebrow in Rockies

Rockies

warmer colored flanks

Sightings

JAN	FEB	MAR	APR	MAY	JUN	JUL	AUG	SEP	OCT	NOV	DEC

Chestnut-backed Chickadee

Poecile rufescens, L 4¾" (12 cm)

From Santa Barbara County to almost as far north as Anchorage, the colorful Chestnut-backed Chickadee's range traces a narrow ribbon up the West Coast and into the Sierra Nevada and Cascades. The chickadees likely expanded north with the advancing forests as the last Pleistocene glaciers retreated between 15,000 and 10,000 years ago.

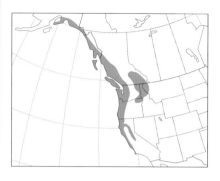

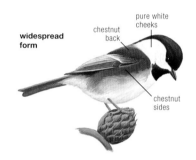

widespread form

pure white cheeks

chestnut back

chestnut sides

chestnut back

coastal central California

gray sides

| **IDENTIFICATION** Common. Smallest and shortest tailed of the chickadees. Tends to forage in the tops of conifers, but also comes to feeders. Chickadees of all species have many similarities.

■ **plumage** Back, rump, and flanks are rich chestnut; has a sooty brown cap and black bib. The chestnut plumage may be hard to discern in dark, shadowy forests. Birds on the central California coast show almost no chestnut below.

■ **similar species** None. Separated from all other chickadees by chestnut back and rump.

■ **voice** **Call** is a high, scratchy *tseek-a-dee-dee* given rapidly. Does not have a *fee-bee* song like other chickadees.

RANGE Western species; year-round resident. Inhabits humid coastal and interior forests, and riparian habitats; also found in residential areas, towns, and parks with similar wooded areas. During the past half century, the species has colonized the central Sierra Nevada and suburban areas around eastern San Francisco Bay.

FOOD Gleans insects and spiders from foliage. Diet is supplemented with conifer seeds, berries, and other small fruits.

■ **feeding** Attracted to feeders, mostly in winter. Black-oil sunflower seeds and suet are preferred.

NESTING *Location:* Enlarges a cavity in rotted wood or may use an old woodpecker hole. *Nest:* Cavity is lined with moss, weed stems, and animal fur. *Eggs:* Usually 6–7; incubated by female for 12–14 days. *Fledging:* Leaves nest at 18–21 days.

■ **housing** Will use a nest box.

FEEDER PECKING ORDER

With 30, 50, or more individual birds under your feeders, it may be surprising that so few skirmishes occur. An exception is when a jay or other large bird zooms in and scatters the small ones; otherwise, a behavioral trait called the "pecking order" keeps the peace. Also called the "peck order," this is a hierarchy of dominance and submission with two benefits: It enables birds to save energy and injury by avoiding conflict and affords them more time to eat undisturbed.

Dominance and submission arises when a bird consistently wins aggressive pecking encounters with its flock mates of the same species. The most consistent loser winds up as the most subordinate. Between them is a series of birds whose proportions of wins and losses give them relatively high or low status in the hierarchy. As these relationships are established more firmly, the losers give up challenging birds that are higher in rank.

Physical strength is not always the most important factor in the peck order. Researchers have demonstrated that a "badge of status"—the size of the black bib on a Harris's Sparrow or the brightness of a White-crowned Sparrow's crown stripes—may be sufficient to establish dominance within its group.

The result, however, is a relatively stable social structure in which even weaker flock members can eventually feed—unless, of course, the food runs out, in which case the higher ranking birds survive to propagate the species.

Different species—such as the Northern Cardinal, Black-capped Chickadee, and House Finch—may dine together peacefully, but sometimes large birds chase smaller ones away.

Oak Titmouse

Baeolophus inornatus, L 5" (13 cm)

The Oak Titmouse is a plain-looking bird with a short crest and beady black eyes. Of greater interest, particularly to any out-of-state visitors: the Oak Titmouse is nearly endemic to California and a vocal backyard feeder visitor in many areas.

slight brownish tint above

worn

short grayish crest

fresh

IDENTIFICATION Common. Larger than a chickadee, but not by much, with a short crest that is can be raised and lowered depending on the bird's state of agitation. Pairs mate for life. Often joins mixed-species flocks in winter.
■ **plumage** Plain grayish brown overall, with slightly paler underparts.
■ **similar species** Bushtit (page 149) is smaller and has a long tail. Juniper Titmouse (not illustrated) is a look-alike species that lives in relatively unpopulated areas of piñon-juniper woodland east of the Sierra Nevada.
■ **voice** A variety of simple, cheery **songs,** such as *pee-doo, pee-doo, pee-doo* or *tu-wee, tu-wee, tu-wee.* **Call** is a hoarse *tsicka-dee-dee.*

RANGE West Coast species; year-round resident. Prefers live-oak woodlands and where oaks mix with chaparral, streamside groves, and low-elevation conifers. Also found in residential areas, towns, and parks with similar wooded habitat.

FOOD Diet is equal parts animal and plant food. Gleans insects from bark and foliage, often pecking into bark crevices or chipping away bark to reach a beetle or bug; sometimes hangs upside down. Main plant foods are seeds (primarily acorns), leaf buds, berries, and fruits, including cultivated varieties.
■ **feeding** Common visitor to bird feeders in wooded areas. Prefers larger, striped sunflower seeds to smaller black-oil types; also relishes whole peanuts, peanut butter, and suet.

NESTING *Location:* In an old woodpecker hole or natural cavity; sometimes a pair will enlarge an existing cavity in a rotted wood. *Nest:* Cavity is lined with moss, weed stems, and animal fur. *Eggs:* Usually 6–7; incubated by female for 14–16 days. *Fledging:* Leaves nest at 16–21 days.
■ **housing** Will use a nest box or sheltered building crevice.

Sightings

	JAN	FEB	MAR	APR	MAY	JUN	JUL	AUG	SEP	OCT	NOV	DEC

Tufted Titmouse
Baeolophus bicolor, L 6¼" (16 cm)

Peter-peter-peter, the simple, cheerful song of the Tufted Titmouse, is often heard in woodsy backyards throughout the East. Pairs are monogamous, and families often stay together through the winter. The following spring, one of the young birds may help the mated pair raise the next generation.

IDENTIFICATION Common. Larger than a chickadee, with an obvious crest that can be raised and lowered. Regularly descends to the ground, unlike chickadees.
■ **plumage** Crested head with a small black forehead and large, dark eyes. Buff flanks, but otherwise gray above and whitish below. **Juvenile** lacks the black forehead.
■ **similar species** Chickadees have black-and-white heads and no crest. Black-crested Titmouse (not illustrated) has a black crest and pale forehead and occurs in the western half of Texas.

■ **voice** Noisy and vocal, except when nesting. **Song** is a loud, whistled *peter-peter-peter,* repeated over and over. **Call** is a hoarse, chickadee-like *tsicka-dee-dee.*

RANGE Eastern species; year-round resident. Inhabits deciduous woods, generally below 2,000 feet, and is also common in wooded suburbs, orchards, towns, and parks. Over the past 50 years, Tufted Titmice have expanded northward, probably in response to the warming climate and the proliferation of bird feeders.

FOOD Gleans insects from bark and foliage, sometimes pecking into bark crevices or chipping away bark to reach a beetle or bug. Main plant food is seeds (primarily acorns and birdseed); also consumes some wild fruits and berries.
■ **feeding** Common feeder visitor. Enjoys sunflower seeds, shelled peanuts, peanut butter, and suet. Like chickadees, caches food in winter.

NESTING *Location:* In an old woodpecker hole or natural cavity. *Nest:* Cavity is filled with moss or dried grass, often lined with animal fur. *Eggs:* Usually 5–6; incubated by female for 12–14 days. *Fledging:* Leaves nest at 15–18 days.
■ **housing** Will use a nest box.

gray forehead

juvenile

dark forehead

pinkish flank patch

adult

Sightings

JAN	FEB	MAR	APR	MAY	JUN	JUL	AUG	SEP	OCT	NOV	DEC

[
Verdin
Family Remizidae
The Verdin is the only New World representative of this small Old World family of tiny birds known as penduline tits.
]

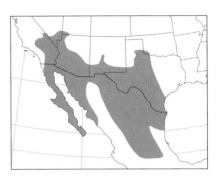

yellow head, black eye line

sharply pointed bill

chestnut lesser coverts

very plain, lacks yellow head

juvenile

Verdin
Auriparus flaviceps, L 4½" (11 cm)

If you live in the desert Southwest, you may have seen this tiny bird's conspicuous, ball-shaped nest of twigs, even if you've never focused on the bird itself.

IDENTIFICATION Common. Tiny songbird, among the smallest in North America. Restless and nimble as it forages in desert trees and scrub, hanging from small branches or probing into flowers with its short, sharp bill.
■ **plumage** Yellow head and throat; chestnut shoulder patch, though often hard to see. The rest of the bird is gray, paler below. **Juvenile** is confusingly plain; it has

brownish plumage and lacks the yellow head and rusty wing patch, but is usually attended by adults.
■ **similar species** Juvenile resembles a Bushtit (next page), but the Bushtit has a much longer tail and is seen in small flocks.
■ **voice** Very vocal, even when foraging. **Song** is a three-note whistle: *sweet sweet sweet.* **Calls** include sharp, piercing *tschep* and rapid series of *chip* notes.

RANGE Southwest species; year-round resident. Mainly found in thorny desert scrub—acacia, paloverde, smoketree, mesquite—chiefly around washes; also at the edges of desert riparian corridors and in residential neighborhoods and some urban parks.

FOOD Mostly insects, but also pierces flowers for nectar and sometimes visits hummingbird feeders.

NESTING *Location:* Near the outer edge of a shrub, low tree, or cactus. *Nest:* Unusual ball-shaped nest of thorny twigs about 6–8 inches in diameter; also builds smaller roosting nests that are used year-round. *Eggs:* Usually 4; incubated by female for 14–18 days. *Fledging:* Leaves nest at about 18 days.

Sightings

JAN	FEB	MAR	APR	MAY	JUN	JUL	AUG	SEP	OCT	NOV	DEC

Bushtit
Family Aegithalidae
Members of this small family of tiny, long-tailed birds live in social groups and build hanging nests. The Bushtit's closest relative lives in Eurasia.

female with pale eye

long tail

interior ♀

gray crown

black ear coverts

"Black-eared Bushtit" juvenile ♂

Bushtit
Psaltriparus minimus, L 4½" (11 cm)

When not nesting, Bushtits band together in small, noisy flocks that move frenetically through the shrubbery. Sometimes the entire flock emits a shrill, trilling alarm—a good clue that a hawk is flying overhead.

 | **IDENTIFICATION** Common. Tiny songbird with a plump, loosely feathered body and a long tail. Very tame. Busy flocks of 10–40 birds forage together. They can land on the tiniest branches, and often hang upside down to reach a hidden insect.

■ **plumage** Drab gray above, paler below. Coastal birds have a brown crown; interior birds, a brown mask and gray crown. **Male** has dark eyes; **female** has pale eyes. **Juvenile males** and some adult males in the Southwest have a black mask (this "Black-eared Bushtit" was formerly considered a separate species).

■ **similar species** Blue-gray Gnatcatcher (page 159) has a black-and-white tail and is never in flocks. Also similar to a juvenile Verdin (opposite).

■ **voice** Very vocal. Flock members **call** constantly—a rapid, twittering *pit pit pit* or *tsee tsee tsee*. Calls of interior birds are slower and sharper.

| **RANGE** Western species; year-round resident. Found in a variety of habitats, from forested mountains with shrubby undergrowth to arid brush and chaparral; also common in backyard gardens and parks.

| **FOOD** Small insects and spiders gleaned from foliage.

| **NESTING** *Location:* From low in a bush to high in a tree. *Nest:* gourd-shaped, hanging nest woven from vegetation and spiderwebs; entrance near the top. *Eggs:* Usually 5–7; incubated by both parents for 12–13 days. *Fledging:* Leaves nest at about 18 days.

grayish face

coastal ♂

brown crown

Sightings

JAN	FEB	MAR	APR	MAY	JUN	JUL	AUG	SEP	OCT	NOV	DEC

Nuthatches
Family Sittidae

Short-tailed, acrobatic birds that climb up, down, and around tree trunks and branches. Suet feeders will likely attract any nuthatches living in your neighborhood.

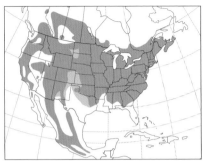

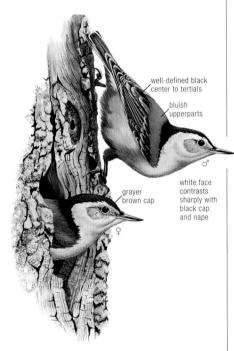

well-defined black center to tertials

bluish uppparts

♂

white face contrasts sharply with black cap and nape

grayer brown cap

♀

White-breasted Nuthatch
Sitta carolinensis, L 5¾" (15 cm)

When moving head-first down a tree trunk, the nuthatch probably gains a feeding advantage—the different perspective reveals insects hidden in bark crevices that other birds, like woodpeckers, might miss as they move upward. The nuthatch has especially long and strong hind claws that anchor it to a tree trunk.

IDENTIFICATION Common. Small, but larger than a chickadee, with a stocky, angular body, short tail, and wedge-tipped, dagger-like bill. It clings securely to tree bark with large, sharp-clawed feet that also serve to anchor a seed or nut that needs to be hammered open ("hatched") with its bill. Joins mixed-species foraging flocks in winter that often include chickadees and titmice.
■ **plumage** Black cap tops an all-white face and breast, with a variable amount of rust under the tail. **Female** has a crown that is grayish or, in the South, blackish like **male's**. Western birds (see photograph below) have longer bills.

Western White-breasted Nuthatches (two distinct groups) have longer bills and a different call than eastern birds.

■ **similar species** Red-breasted Nuthatch (page 153) has cinnamon underparts and a bold black line through the eye.

■ **voice** **Song** is a rapid series of nasal whistles. **Call** is a low-pitched, nasal *yank* in the East and a higher pitched *eehr* on the West Coast, with multiple high-pitched calls in the interior West.

RANGE Widespread species; year-round resident. Inhabits mature deciduous or mixed forests; also common in wooded suburbs, orchards, towns, and parks. Although nonmigratory, in some years numbers move south (irrupt) in fall and winter, but not as conspicuously or as often as Red-breasted Nuthatches.

FOOD Gleans insects from bark and foliage, sometimes pecking into bark crevices or chipping away bark to reach a beetle or bug; feeds nestlings mostly insects. Relies mainly on seeds in winter (acorns, beechnuts, and birdseed are important). Like chickadees and titmice, caches seeds in winter, usually removing their shells beforehand. Individual seeds are cached separately in a bark crevice, or sometimes on the ground. Nuthatches have excellent spatial memory, so most of the seeds are eventually retrieved and eaten.

The white outer tail feathers of the White-breasted Nuthatch are easiest to see on a bird in flight.

■ **feeding** Common feeder visitor. Likes suet, sunflower seeds, and shelled peanuts.

NESTING *Location:* In an old woodpecker hole or natural cavity. *Nest:* Bedding of bark strips, often lined with animal fur. Known to rub crushed insects around the entrance and on the inside of its nest cavity, possibly to repel predators. *Eggs:* Usually 5–9; incubated by female for 12–14 days. *Fledging:* Leaves nest at about 26 days.

■ **housing** Will use a nest box.

This eastern White-breasted Nuthatch has a shorter bill than the western subspecies (opposite).

Sightings

	JAN	FEB	MAR	APR	MAY	JUN	JUL	AUG	SEP	OCT	NOV	DEC

CACHING FOOD AND FINDING IT

Birds of many species are content to eat the food they find at the moment, but some species have evolved behavior that looks into the future. They *cache* food, storing it for retrieval later when food resources decline or become unavailable. Jays, crows, ravens, chickadees, titmice, and nuthatches regularly hoard seeds.

STASHING STRATEGIES

Western Scrub-Jays are known to store thousands of piñon nuts and seeds in a season—mostly in autumn—and then remember in late winter and spring where half are hidden. Scrub-Jays will steal one another's caches, so a bird looks around carefully to assure that another jay is not watching.

Chickadees and titmice do not use large caches. They stash each seed in a different place, a technique called *scatter-hoarding,* and apparently they can remember their cache sites a month later. Unlike jays and crows, which may store food miles away from the source, chickadees and titmice typically stash seeds close to where they found them.

FINDING HIDDEN CACHES

How do birds remember where their caches were hidden? Neuroscientists say that the hippocampus, a portion of the brain governing spatial memory, is larger in birds that cache seeds than in birds of comparable brain size that do not cache. Indeed, experiments show that cachers can recall "landmarks" such as rocks and shrubs at the site.

Holes excavated by the Acorn Woodpecker hold a single acorn that is hammered and wedged into place. A colony's granary tree may contain thousands of acorn holes that are reused for many years.

One of the most famous hoarders, the Acorn Woodpecker, stashes acorns in plain sight in holes drilled in trees—one acorn per hole. Thousands of holes are communal food larders for the woodpeckers' extended families.

Red-breasted Nuthatch

Sitta canadensis, L 4½" (11 cm)

The Red-breasted Nuthatch ("Little Yank") is the smaller cousin of the White-breasted Nuthatch ("Big Yank")—the nicknames refer to their calls and different sizes. In many locations, the Red-breasted is seen only in fall and winter.

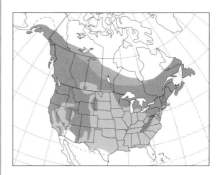

duller below than male

deep cinnamon underparts

prominent white supercilium

♀

♂

■ voice High-pitched, nasal **call** sounds like a toy tin horn: *yank yank* or *ehhnk ehhnk*.

RANGE Widespread species. Inhabits coniferous forests, typically spruce and fir; southern breeders live mostly in mountainous areas. In winter, many birds move south and into lowlands, but how far and how many vary greatly from year to year. In a good "irruption" year, they move deep into the South or into Western lowlands; other years, there are none.

FOOD Relies mostly on insects and spiders gleaned from tree bark in summer, and on seeds in winter (acorns, beechnuts, and birdseed are important).
■ feeding Common feeder visitor, but irregular. Eats suet, sunflower seeds, and shelled peanuts. Planting conifers in your yard will provide shelter and foraging locations for them.

IDENTIFICATION Common to uncommon. Attractively small and compact, about the size of a chickadee. Foraging behavior similar to the larger White-breasted Nuthatch, but with more restless, jerkier movements. Prefers conifers and often forages with mixed flocks of resident birds in winter.
■ plumage Striped head has a bold black line through the eye, white eyebrows, and a black cap; cinnamon underparts. **Female** and **immature birds** have a duller face pattern and paler underparts.
■ similar species White-breasted Nuthatch (pages 150–151) has a white face and underparts and is larger.

NESTING *Location:* Excavates its own hole in a tree; smears resin around the entrance to deter predators. *Nest:* Bedding of bark strips, often lined with animal fur. *Eggs:* Usually 5–6; incubated by female for 12–13 days. *Fledging:* Leaves nest at 18–21 days.
■ housing Rarely uses a nest box.

Sightings

	JAN	FEB	MAR	APR	MAY	JUN	JUL	AUG	SEP	OCT	NOV	DEC

Wrens
Family Troglodytidae

Found in most of North America, wrens are chunky with slender, slightly curved bills; tails are often uptilted. Loud and vigorous territorial defense belies the small size of most species.

bold white supercilium

rufous-brown upperparts

extensively rich buffy underparts

Carolina Wren
Thryothorus ludovicianus, L 5½" (14 cm)

The loud, rollicking song of the male Carolina Wren reverberates across backyards throughout the East. Pairs remain together throughout the year. State bird of South Carolina.

 IDENTIFICATION Common. Chunky wren with a sturdy, down-curved bill. Relatively tame and fearless in backyards, but sticks to cover and almost always stays low. Pairs may mate for life.
■ **plumage** Overall ruddy plumage: deep rusty brown above, cinnamon below. Bold white stripe above the eye and white throat.
■ **similar species** Slender Bewick's Wren (opposite), very rare in the East,

has pale (not cinnamon) underparts and a long, twitchy tail with white bars near the tip.
■ **voice** Vocal throughout the year. Male's **song** is a loud, rolling chant of *tea-kettle tea-kettle tea-kettle* with many variations and inflections. **Calls** include harsh notes and buzzy trills.

RANGE Eastern species; year-round resident. Inhabits brushy woods, clearings, and wooded backyards. Severe winters can devastate northern populations, but they often recover within a few years.

FOOD Gleans insects and spiders from the tree trunks, brushy tangles, woodpiles, and building crevices.
■ **feeding** The only wren that regularly visits bird feeders; suet feeders are visited most often, but also takes sunflower seeds.

NESTING *Location:* In a vine tangle or open tree cavity, rarely higher than 10 feet up. *Nest:* Bulky, domed cup of dried vegetation. *Eggs:* Usually 4–6; incubated by female for 12–14 days. *Fledging:* Leaves nest at 14–16 days.
■ **housing** More likely to nest in a sheltered building nook, open tool shed, or overturned flowerpot than in a nest box.

Sightings

JAN	FEB	MAR	APR	MAY	JUN	JUL	AUG	SEP	OCT	NOV	DEC

Bewick's Wren
Thryothorus bewickii, L 5¼" (13 cm)

Bewick's Wren is an enigma. The species is common in the West, but east of the Mississippi has declined so dramatically in the past 60 years that it has all but vanished there. The decline in the East is probably due to aggressive, nest-destroying House Wrens, whose numbers have increased with the disappearance of Bewick's Wrens.

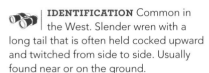

IDENTIFICATION Common in the West. Slender wren with a long tail that is often held cocked upward and twitched from side to side. Usually found near or on the ground.

■ **plumage** Upperparts vary: grayish brown in the Southwest, brown along the Pacific Coast, and reddish brown in the East; underparts are pale gray. Has a bold white stripe above the eye and white bars near the tip of the tail.

■ **similar species** Carolina Wren (opposite) does not occur in the West, has cinnamon underparts and no white in its tail, and is larger. House Wren (next page) lacks the white eye stripe and has no white in its shorter tail.

■ **voice** Quite vocal. **Song** is complex and varied, starting with short notes and buzzes and ending in a musical trill. **Calls** include a scratchy *jip* and scolding *bzzzzz*.

RANGE Mostly Western species, now rare in the East; mostly resident. Small numbers may persist in the Southeast, west of the Appalachians (where it is migratory). Western birds inhabit brushy woodland, coastal and desert scrub, and chaparral and are fairly common in many residential areas and parks.

FOOD Gleans insects and spiders from bark crevices, root tangles, and rocky crevices.

NESTING *Location:* near the ground in a rocky crevice, or sometimes an old woodpecker hole or tree cavity. *Nest:* Cup of dried vegetation. *Eggs:* Usually 5–7; incubated by female for about 14 days. *Fledging:* Leaves nest at 14–16 days.

■ **housing** Will use a nest box; may also use a sheltered building nook, open shed, and so forth.

white bars on long tail

western

grayish above

bold white supercilium

warm ruddy brown above

grayish white underparts

eastern

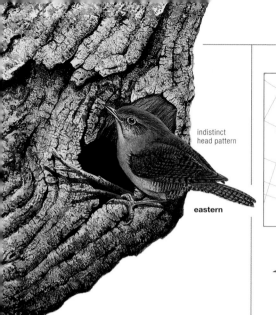

indistinct head pattern

eastern

tail of moderate length

juvenile

grayer above and paler below in West

western

House Wren

Troglodytes aedon, L 4¾" (12 cm)

The male House Wren's loud and bubbly song is a familiar summer sound in backyards across North America. The species was not always so common or widely distributed. The shrubby edges and open woods so perfect for House Wrens were scarce commodities in the primeval forests of pre-European North America, but today's fragmented woodlands and woodsy backyards mimic its traditional habitat, and the House Wren has flourished.

IDENTIFICATION Very common. Small wren with a moderately long tail. Fairly tame and approachable. Spends much of its time darting around in thickets and low in trees, occasionally descending to the ground. The male sings his territorial song from an exposed perch with such force that his whole body quivers from the effort.

■ **plumage** Plain, without strong patterns. Brown upperparts have fine black barring, most noticeable on the wings

and tail. The underparts are paler, with more fine barring on the back half. **Juvenile** has more buff below, often with indistinct scalloping on the breast, and is less barred than the adult.

■ **similar species** Carolina Wren (page 154) and Bewick's Wren (previous page) both have bold white stripes above the eye. Brown Creeper (page 158) has a bill that resembles the House Wren's, but has streaky upperparts and pure white underparts and climbs up vertical tree trunks.

■ **voice** Exuberant **song** is a cascade of bubbling whistled notes. **Calls** include a soft *chek* and a harsh scold.

RANGE Widespread species. Lives in open forests, thickets, woodland edges, and wooded towns

This ceramic birdhouse—a style that has been popular since colonial times—makes an attractive nest site for a family of House Wrens.

An old woodpecker hole—a valuable piece of forest real estate—is the perfect home for many cavity-nesting songbirds.

and suburbs. Moves to the southern tier of states and Mexico in winter. Spring **migration:** April–early May; fall migration: September–October.

FOOD Gleans insects and spiders from trees, saplings, shrubs, and the ground.

NESTING *Location:* In an old woodpecker hole, natural cavity, or enclosed crevice. *Nest:* Cup of dried vegetation. *Eggs:* Usually 5–8; incubated by female for about 14 days. *Fledging:* Leaves nest at 15–18 days. *Nest wars:* House Wrens are fierce competitors for nest holes and nest boxes—a limited commodity in most places. They are known to evict larger birds, puncture and remove eggs from nest sites they want, and sometimes kill nestlings and even adult birds. Common species that lose out include Tree Swallows, bluebirds, and chickadees. If you have House Wrens nesting in your backyard (they're otherwise delightful birds), put up multiple nest boxes to ease the pressure on other species.
■ housing Will use a nest box 4–5 feet up and many other human structures

with nooks and crannies—flowerpots, mailboxes, clothespin bags, discarded boxes, farm equipment. John James Audubon famously painted a pair nesting in an old hat.

Typical wren posture—the chunky body is held low and the tail uptilted.

Sightings

JAN	FEB	MAR	APR	MAY	JUN	JUL	AUG	SEP	OCT	NOV	DEC

Creepers
Family Certhiidae

A small family of forest birds with highly cryptic plumage. The Brown Creeper is the only member found in the New World.

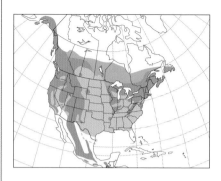

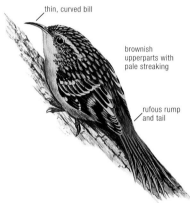

thin, curved bill

brownish upperparts with pale streaking

rufous rump and tail

Brown Creeper
Certhia americana, L 5¼" (13 cm)

This bird is hard to see. Perched vertically on a tree trunk, its back plumage almost perfectly matches the furrowed bark where it finds its food. Its thin, very high-pitched call is often the best clue that one is around.

IDENTIFICATION Fairly common. Smaller than a nuthatch, the creeper has a long, spiky-tipped tail, which it uses like a prop when climbing, and a thin, curved bill. It forages in a very predictable way: starting at the base of a large tree, it spirals up the trunk, poking into bark crevices, until it reaches the first large branches, at which point it flies to the base of a nearby tree and starts over. You can often watch the whole process a few times before losing sight of the bird.

■ **plumage** Brown, streaky upperparts; whitish below. In flight, the wing has a bold buff stripe.

■ **similar species** Nuthatches move up and down the trunk (rather than spiraling up like a creeper) and onto branches and are not streaked. Somewhat similar to House Wren (pages 156–157), but shape and behavior very different.

■ **voice** Thin and very high-pitched. **Song** is a variable *see see see titi see.* **Call** is a soft, sibilant *seee* or buzzier and doubled *tee-see* in the West.

RANGE Widespread. Inhabits woodlands with large trees, mainly conifers or mixed conifer-deciduous when breeding. Widespread and less choosy in winter, when it is as likely to be found in deciduous forest, suburbs, or parks. Spring **migration:** April; fall migration: October.

FOOD Gleans prey—insects and larvae, spiders and their eggs—from bark crevices.

NESTING *Location:* Behind a flap of loose tree bark. *Nest:* Cup of bark strips and twigs, adhered to the vertical bark flap with insect cocoons. *Eggs:* Usually 5–6; incubated by female for 13–17 days. *Fledging:* Leaves nest at 15–18 days.

Sightings

| JAN | FEB | MAR | APR | MAY | JUN | JUL | AUG | SEP | OCT | NOV | DEC |

Gnatcatchers
Family Sylviidae
Gnatcatchers—tiny, active birds with long tails—are part of a very large family that includes the Old World warblers.

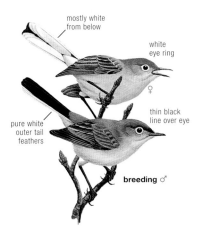

mostly white from below

white eye ring

♀

thin black line over eye

pure white outer tail feathers

breeding ♂

Blue-gray Gnatcatcher
Polioptila caerulea, L 4¼" (11 cm)

The insistent peevish call of the Blue-gray Gnatcatcher announces its early spring arrival in many parts of the country. New arrivals in the East are easy to spot in the budding branches, but later in the season, their treetop activities are often hidden from view. Western birds tend to stay lower down in oaks, piñons, and shrubs.

IDENTIFICATION Common. Small and slender, with a long tail. The gnatcatcher restlessly flits and hops from twig to twig. Even when perched, it keeps moving—its long tail swishing from side to side.
■ **plumage** Pale, silvery blue-gray upperparts; white eye ring; whitish underparts; black tail with white outer tail feathers (looks mostly white from below). **Breeding**

male has a thin, black eyebrow, absent in the **female** and winter male.
■ **similar species** The Bushtit (page 149), a Western bird, has a gray tail and travels in flocks (also see juvenile Verdin, page 148). The breeding male Black-tailed Gnatcatcher (not illustrated) of the desert Southwest has a full black cap.
■ **voice Song** is a series of thin, wheezy notes. **Call** is a querulous *speeeee*.

RANGE Widespread. Breeds mostly in moist deciduous forests in the East; in the West, breeding habitat includes oaks, piñons, and junipers. Winters in the southern tier of states, in coastal scrub, chaparral, and brushy areas as well as forests. Spring **migration:** March–early May; fall migration: mid-August–September.

FOOD Small insects and spiders. Usually gleans prey from foliage, but also in hovering flight or sallying after flushed prey.

NESTING *Location:* In a tree or shrub, anywhere from 3 to 80 feet up. *Nest:* Neat, high-walled cup of plant fibers, lichen, and bark flakes bound with spiderweb. *Eggs:* Usually 4–5; incubated by both parents for 11–15 days. *Fledging:* Leaves nest at 10–15 days.

Sightings

JAN	FEB	MAR	APR	MAY	JUN	JUL	AUG	SEP	OCT	NOV	DEC

Kinglets
Family Regulidae

A small family—just six species world-wide—of tiny, hyperactive birds that eat insects. Two species occur in North America.

slightly broken whitish eye ring

tiny bill

male's red crown usually concealed

♀

♂

pale olive underparts

Ruby-crowned Kinglet
Regulus calendula, L 4¼" (10 cm)

Backyard birders typically encounter the Ruby-crowned Kinglet in fall and winter. It breeds in mountainous areas and far to the north.

IDENTIFICATION Common. Tiny, somewhat plump songbird with a large head, short tail, and tiny bill. Very active, constantly flitting about and nervously flicking its wings.
■ **plumage** Plain, mostly olive green, with two white wing bars. Blank face is punctu-ated with a large black eye and white eye ring (broken above). **Male's** red crown is hidden except when the bird is agitated.
■ **similar species** Golden-crowned King-let (opposite) has black and white head stripes and a colorful crown. Hutton's Vireo (not illustrated), mainly from the West

Coast, is larger, has a thicker bill, and lacks the black panel next to the lower wing bar.
■ **voice** **Song** is a loud and complex series of high notes ending in warbled, three-note phrases. **Call** is a husky, scolding *je-dit*.

RANGE Widespread. Breeds in coniferous forests in Canada, New England, and the mountainous West. Win-ters at lower elevations in the southern and western U.S. and into Mexico. Winter habitat is diverse: woodlands of all types, thickets, chaparral, coastal scrub, sub-urban backyards, and city parks. Spring **migration:** March–early May; fall migra-tion: mid-September–October.

FOOD Gleans small insects and spiders from foliage and bark, often hovering in front of a leaf to pick off an insect or flying out after flushed prey. Eats small amounts of fruit in winter.
■ **feeding** Will feed on suet. Shrubs and vines with winter fruit attract kinglets to backyard gardens.

NESTING *Location:* In a conifer, from 4 to 100 feet up. *Nest:* Deep cup of plant fibers, lichen, moss, and pine needles, bound with spiderweb. *Eggs:* Usually 7–8; incubated by female for 12–14 days. *Fledging:* Leaves nest at about 16 days.

Sightings

	JAN	FEB	MAR	APR	MAY	JUN	JUL	AUG	SEP	OCT	NOV	DEC

Golden-crowned Kinglet
Regulus satrapa, L 4" (10 cm)

In winter, the tiny Golden-crowned Kinglet often joins small foraging flocks of insect-eating woodland birds such as Ruby-crowned Kinglets, Brown Creepers, Yellow-rumped Warblers, and chickadees. On cold winter nights, these hardy kinglets may seek shelter in a squirrel nest or tangle of tree roots.

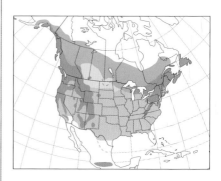

 IDENTIFICATION Fairly common. Tiny—smaller than the Ruby-crowned Kinglet—with a short tail and thin bill. Behavior is similar to Ruby-crowned: very active, constantly flitting about and nervously flicking its wings.
■ **plumage** Conspicuously striped head—white eyebrow bordered above and below with black. Mostly grayish olive above, paler below; darker wings with two white wing bars. Center of yellow crown is reddish orange on **male**, all yellow on **female**.
■ **similar species** Ruby-crowned Kinglet (previous page) is more olive above and yellow below and has a plain head and white eye ring.

■ **voice** **Song** is a series of accelerating *see* notes, ending in a lower pitched, jumbled warble. When flocking, a very high, sibilant jingling *tsii tsii tsii*. **Call** is a similar series of very high, thin notes: *see see see*.

RANGE Widespread. Breeds mainly in coniferous forests, a few in mixed or deciduous forests. In winter, many birds remain in breeding range, but most move south, where they are found in a wide variety of forested habitats, including wooded residential areas, towns, and parks. Spring **migration:** March–April; fall migration: October–November.

FOOD Gleans small insects and spiders from foliage and bark, often hovering in front of a leaf to pick off an insect or sallying out after flushed prey. Eats small amounts of fruit in winter.
■ **feeding** Suet is the best choice. Shrubs and vines with winter fruit attract kinglets to backyard gardens.

NESTING *Location:* In a conifer, from 6–50 feet up and suspended near the end of a branch. *Nest:* Deep cup of plant fibers, lichen, moss, and pine needles bound with spiderweb. *Eggs:* Usually 8–9; incubated by female for 12–14 days. *Fledging:* Leaves nest at about 16–19 days.

broad yellow stripe bordered by black stripe

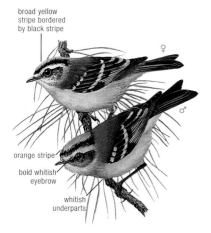

orange stripe

bold whitish eyebrow

whitish underparts

Sightings

JAN	FEB	MAR	APR	MAY	JUN	JUL	AUG	SEP	OCT	NOV	DEC

white belly and
undertail coverts

Thrushes
Family Turdidae

This large family with a worldwide distribution includes many outstanding
vocalists. Thrushes feed on insects and
fruits, and many species are migratory.

Eastern Bluebird
Sialia sialis, L 7" (18 cm)

*Known for their brilliant plumage, endearing
behavior, and attraction to nest boxes,
Eastern Bluebirds have millions of adoring
fans. State bird of Missouri and New York.*

IDENTIFICATION Common.
Bluebirds often allow close
approach and choose low perches where
they are easy to observe.
■ **plumage** Male has flashy blue upperparts; female's are more subdued. Rusty
color on breast and flanks wraps up behind
the ear coverts; belly is white. **Juvenile** is
heavily spotted, but has blue wings.
■ **similar species** Western Bluebird
(page 164) is very similar, but overlaps
little in range.
■ **voice** Simple musical **song** consists of a
rich warble: *chur chur-lee chur-lee*. **Call** is a
rising *chur-lee*.

RANGE Eastern species primarily;
year-round resident throughout
much of its range. Lives in open, rural

areas. **Migration** covers short distances,
and some bluebirds, even in northern
areas, don't migrate. Spring arrival in
southern Canada is as early as mid-March.

FOOD From spring to early fall,
bluebirds primarily eat insects. In
winter, they rely on small fruits.
■ **feeding** Offer live mealworms. Fruiting
trees and vines provide winter sustenance.

NESTING *Location:* In a natural
cavity or old woodpecker hole.
Nest: Cavity is filled with grass and other
plant material. *Eggs:* Usually 4–5; incubated by female for 11–19 days. *Fledging:* Leaves nest at about 19 days.
■ **housing** Will use a nest box.

rufous in both sexes
wraps around sides of
neck and includes throat

spotted

juvenile

ATTRACTING BLUEBIRDS

The juvenile Eastern Bluebird *(right)* is being fed mealworms by its mother, while the father *(left)* looks on. Offering live mealworms is a great way to get close-up looks at these beautiful birds.

Bluebirds are cavity-nesting thrushes that greatly benefit when houses (nest boxes) are provided to them. None of the three species of bluebirds lives in cities or heavily wooded suburbs—they require fields, pastures, and open woodlands more typical of rural areas.

■ **Housing** Bluebird houses need to be the correct size. You can purchase them ready-made or construct your own. The basic house measures 5 inches long by 5 inches wide by 10 inches high and has a 1½-inch entrance hole (1⁹/₁₆ inches for Western and Mountain Bluebirds) without an exterior perch. Plans are available online (see below). Mount your birdhouse on a predator-resistant metal pole about five feet above the ground. After the young have fledged, clean out the nest box. Where bluebirds are year-round residents, they may use the nest box for winter roosting. To find out more online, visit the North American Bluebird Society's website (www .nabluebirdsociety.org).

■ **The Competition** Competition for scarce natural cavities and birdhouses can be intense. Bluebirds often lose out to starlings, Tree Swallows, House Wrens, and House Sparrows. A bluebird house with the right size hole will exclude starlings, but if you see House Sparrows building a nest, remove their nesting material immediately.

■ **Mealworms** Live mealworms—a favorite food—can be purchased from many pet stores. Feed the birds in the morning and again toward evening.

Western Bluebird
Sialia mexicana, L 7" (18 cm)

Because they favor open parklike woods, Western Bluebirds have less contact with backyard birders than Eastern Bluebirds do. Both species are equally stunning and attracted to nest boxes.

IDENTIFICATION Common. Similar in structure to the Eastern Bluebird; has a plump body—bigger than a sparrow, smaller than a robin—and a large head.
■ **plumage** **Male's** upperparts are deep cobalt blue and can look very dark; breast and back are chestnut. **Female** has a grayish head and back, with a pale chestnut breast. **Juvenile** (not illustrated) is very similar to juvenile Eastern Bluebird.
■ **similar species** Eastern Bluebird (page 162) does not overlap much in range. Female Mountain Bluebird (not illustrated), a Western species, is grayer, has more uniform coloration, and lacks a rusty breast.
■ **voice** Simple **song** consists of a series of call notes—*few few fawee*—primarily heard at dawn. **Call** is a simple, mellow *few* or *peurr*.

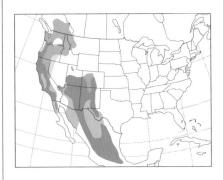

RANGE Western species; year-round resident throughout much of its range. Breeds in open woodlands, especially ponderosa pine, piñon, juniper, or oak; also found around orchards, farmland with scattered trees, and golf courses. **Migration** covers relatively short distances, often simply moving to a lower altitude.

FOOD In summer, insects are the primary food. Hunts from a perch, swooping down to the ground to capture an insect; sometimes gleans foliage or catches insects in midair. In winter, feeds mostly on small fruits and berries—mistletoe and juniper berries are favorites.
■ **feeding** Use live mealworms; rarely eats birdseed.

NESTING *Location:* In a natural tree cavity or old woodpecker hole. *Nest:* Cavity is filled with dry grass and other plant material. *Eggs:* Usually 4–5; incubated by female for 12–18 days. *Fledging:* Leaves nest at about 20 days. *Broods:* In many areas, 2 per year is normal.
■ **housing** Will use a nest box. The North American Bluebird Society (www.nabluebirdsociety.org) has good advice and nest box building plans.

gray sides to neck

♀

all-blue head

♂

gray undertail coverts

some dark rufous scapulars

JAN	FEB	MAR	APR	MAY	JUN	JUL	AUG	SEP	OCT	NOV	DEC

Hermit Thrush
Catharus guttatus, L 6¾" (17 cm)

The Hermit Thrush's song has inspired poets and writers. Frank Chapman, the inventor of the field guide, didn't curb his enthusiasm when in 1897 he wrote, "The Hermit's hymn echoes through the woods like the swelling tones of an organ in some vast cathedral." State bird of Vermont.

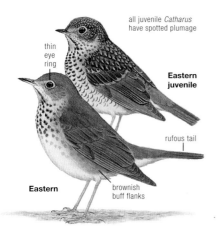

all juvenile *Catharus* have spotted plumage

thin eye ring

Eastern juvenile

rufous tail

Eastern

brownish buff flanks

IDENTIFICATION Common. Medium-size thrush—smaller than a robin—that has two habitual tics: it quickly raises its tail, then slowly lowers it, and it rapidly flicks its wings. Often seen hopping on the forest floor, keeping to the shadows, or visiting fruiting vines in migration or winter.

■ **plumage** Upperparts vary from rich brown to gray brown (in some Western birds), but reddish tail is always the brightest part. Eastern birds have brownish flanks; western birds have grayish flanks. White eye ring; buff breast with dark spots. **Juvenile** has spotted upperparts.

■ **similar species** The face and eye ring of Swainson's Thrush (next page) are more buff, and the color of its tail matches its back. In the East, the Wood Thrush (page 167) is larger, bright rufous above, with bold black spots underneath. See also the Fox Sparrow (page 191).

■ **voice** **Song** is a serene series of clear, flutelike notes, with successive songs on different pitches. **Calls** include *chup* or *chup-chup* and a wheezy, rising *zhwee*.

RANGE Widespread species. Breeds widely in northern and mountain hardwood and coniferous forests. Quite hardy and migrates relatively short distances. In winter, found in more open forest with brushy (berry-producing) tangles, including residential areas, towns, and parks. Spring **migration:** April–mid-May; fall migration: late September–early November.

FOOD Mostly insects and fruit. Searches for food on the forest floor and in low trees, sometimes hovering briefly to pick off an insect or berry. In winter, about half of its diet is small fruits.

NESTING *Location:* On the ground, hidden by overhanging vegetation, or sometimes in a low tree. *Nest:* Bulky cup of grass, other plant fibers, and a layer of mud. *Eggs:* Usually 4; incubated by female for 12–13 days. *Fledging:* Leaves nest at 12–13 days.

Sightings

JAN	FEB	MAR	APR	MAY	JUN	JUL	AUG	SEP	OCT	NOV	DEC

Swainson's Thrush
Catharus ustulatus, L 7" (18 cm)

Swainson's Thrush is a bird that backyard birders will most likely see during spring and fall migration. Berry-producing vines and shrubs often entice these retiring birds out into the open; the rest of the time, they stick to shady woodlands.

upperparts with a russet cast

olive gray upperparts

Pacific Coast

buffy flanks

Alaska

IDENTIFICATION Fairly common. Medium-size thrush. Unlike the Hermit Thrush, it does not flick its wings or cock its tail, but otherwise it has very similar behavior.

■ **plumage** Upperparts vary from russet brown (on the Pacific Coast) to olive brown (in most other areas), with a similar-colored tail. The lighter parts of the face are buff, as are the eye ring and lores, giving it spectacled look.

■ **similar species** Hermit Thrush (previous page) has a white eye ring and a reddish tail that contrasts with its back. Other "spotted thrushes" seen in the East during migration include Veery and Gray-cheeked Thrushes (not illustrated).

■ **voice Song** is an ascending spiral of flutelike whistles. **Calls** include a sharp *quirk* and a liquid *whit* (Pacific Coast).

RANGE Widespread species; summer resident. Breeds in northern and mountain forests; Pacific Coast birds also breed in streamside willows and shady canyons. Winters from Mexico to South America. Spring **migration:** mid-April–May; fall migration: September–mid-October.

FOOD Mostly insects and fruit. Searches for insects on the forest floor and in low trees. During fall migration, eats berries primarily.

NESTING *Location:* In a small tree, from 2 to 7 feet up. *Nest:* Compact cup of twigs, moss, and other plant material. *Eggs:* Usually 4; incubated by female for 10–14 days. *Fledging:* Leaves nest at about 14 days.

buffy eye ring and supraloral line

olive brown upperparts

widespread subspecies

brownish flanks

Sightings

JAN	FEB	MAR	APR	MAY	JUN	JUL	AUG	SEP	OCT	NOV	DEC

Wood Thrush

Hylocichla mustelina, L 7¾" (20 cm)

Considered by many to rival the Hermit Thrush in vocal ability, the Wood Thrush moved Longfellow to write, "And where the shadows deepest fell / The wood thrush rang his silver bell."

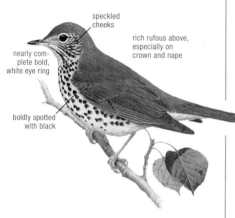

speckled cheeks

rich rufous above, especially on crown and nape

nearly complete bold, white eye ring

boldly spotted with black

■ **voice** **Song** is a dreamy, flutelike series of rising and falling notes—*eh-eh eee-o-lay*—followed by a complex trill. **Calls** include a staccato *pit pit pit pit.*

RANGE Eastern species; summer resident. Breeds in moist hardwood and mixed forests with dense undergrowth. Backyards bordering good habitat and even large urban parks are sometimes suitable, but unfortunately, Wood Thrush numbers have declined since the 1970s. Forest fragmentation—both here and in its winter home in southern Mexico and Central America—and brood parasitism by Brown-headed Cowbirds are thought to be major causes. Spring **migration:** April–May; fall migration: October.

IDENTIFICATION Common. Medium-large thrush—larger and more robust than Hermit and Swainson's Thrushes, and much easier to identify. It sticks to the ground and understory of its Eastern forest home and is particularly vocal in the early morning and at dusk.

■ **plumage** Very bright cinnamon-rufous upperparts—brightest on the crown—but equally impressive below, with bold black spots on a pure white background. The large, dark eye and white eye ring are prominent.

■ **similar species** Hermit and Swainson's Thrushes (page 165 and opposite) are smaller, less potbellied, less heavily spotted, and not as brightly colored, and they do not have a strong white eye ring. Larger Brown Thrasher (page 174) has a much longer tail and bill, and yellowish eyes.

FOOD Mostly insects and fruit. Searches for insects on the forest floor (typically with several hops and a pause, like a robin) and in low trees. Small fruits and berries are consumed year-round.

NESTING *Location:* In a sapling or shrub, about 10 feet up. *Nest:* Open cup of leaves and grass, with a layer of mud. *Eggs:* Usually 3–4; incubated by female for 11–14 days. *Fledging:* Leaves nest at 12–15 days.

Sightings

JAN	FEB	MAR	APR	MAY	JUN	JUL	AUG	SEP	OCT	NOV	DEC

Varied Thrush

Ixoreus naevius, L 9½" (24 cm)

An extremely attractive thrush of the dark forests of the Pacific Northwest, the Varied Thrush is seen more often in winter, when some birds move south out of their forest havens into more open areas, such as backyards, gardens, parks, and shady oak canyons.

juvenile

orange wing bars and markings on wing

orange superciliUM

♀

♂

black breast band

IDENTIFICATION Common. Large thrush—almost robin size, and sometimes associates with robin flocks in winter. Hops on the ground, tossing debris aside to look for insects. Male often perches high up (out of sight) during long bouts of singing.

■ **plumage** Intricate orange wing pattern and prominent orange stripe above the eye. **Male** has orange underparts crossed by a black breast band and steely blue upperparts. **Female** is less intensely colored with a faint gray breast band and brownish-gray upperparts. **Juvenile** has scalier-looking breast and white belly.

■ **similar species** American Robin (pages 170–171) lacks the bold orange stripe over the eye and has brick red (not orange) underparts, with no dark breast band.

■ **voice** Song is a series of long, trilled whistles; each eerie whistle is pitched differently and followed by a pause. **Call** is a soft, low *tschook*.

RANGE Pacific Coast and Alaska species. Breeds in moist coniferous and mixed forests with a closed canopy and also in alder and poplar groves farther north. In winter, many breeders move south and coastward (irregular to southern California, in small numbers), but some stay put. Winter habitat is more diverse and includes urban parks and backyards (sometimes even open lawns). Typical time frame for winter visitors is October–April.

FOOD Insects, fruits, berries, and nuts. Searches for insects on the forest floor (typically taking several hops and a pause, like a robin). Small fruits and berries are consumed year-round, but are the primary food in winter.

NESTING *Location:* In a conifer, 4–20 feet up. *Nest:* Open cup of twigs, moss, and grass, with a layer of mud. *Eggs:* Usually 3–4; incubated by female for about 12 days. *Fledging:* Leaves nest at 13–15 days.

Sightings

JAN	FEB	MAR	APR	MAY	JUN	JUL	AUG	SEP	OCT	NOV	DEC

HOW DO BIRDS STAY WARM?

Ducks, geese, and gulls stand on ice in freezing weather. Small birds visit feeders in a blizzard. Large and small alike, they can survive nights when temperatures dip far below zero. The reasons are a metabolic system and body design that combine to keep them warm—but there are limits.

A bird's overarching physiological requirement in cold weather is prevention of body heat loss, and birds' physiology and their behavior combine to minimize the loss.

PRESERVING BODY HEAT

Ducks, geese, and gulls would be especially vulnerable to frostbite on their feet and toes, which is prevented because their blood circulation slows and the blood is cooled as it passes through the feet. This reduces heat loss sufficiently to keep the feet from freezing.

You have probably noticed birds perching with their body feathers fluffed out on especially cold days. The air space between the warm skin and the feathers provides a warm-air buffer to keep cold air from reaching the skin.

An extraordinary mechanism in hummingbirds and swifts is called *torpor*. Overnight their metabolic rate is substantially lowered, and they slow their heartbeat and breathing greatly. Partially "shut down," the birds require much less body heat to survive.

BEHAVIORAL STRATEGIES

Behavior, too, is critical to birds' winter survival. They seek shelter in the dense foliage. Many species have learned to keep warm by using the shelter of buildings.

Of course, many birds that breed in the north migrate. Along with an absence of their insect food in the winter, their metabolism is not adapted to extremely cold weather, so they must leave.

This American Goldfinch isn't abnormally fat. Its breast feathers are fluffed out, trapping air warmed by body heat, which insulates the skin from winter's chill.

American Robin
Turdus migratorius, L 10" (25 cm)

This species' distinctive plumage and acceptance of human-dominated habitats make it one of our most familiar and beloved birds. In northern areas, the male's loud, caroling song is a welcome harbinger of spring. Exceptionally adaptable, robins nest from urban centers and backyards to remote wilderness areas above the Arctic Circle. State bird of Connecticut, Michigan, and Wisconsin.

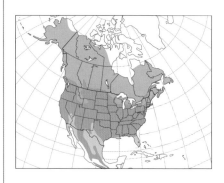

IDENTIFICATION Identification is easy and usually obvious. The robin has a pot-bellied look and an upright stance as it searches for food with a distinctive run-stop-run rhythm. A stopped bird cocks its head to one side to look (not listen) for the presence of an earthworm or grub. Robins also poke into leaf litter, flipping leaves out of the way in their search for insects. In winter and migration, they often occur in large flocks.

■ **plumage** Brick red underparts are its most familiar attribute; also note its gray upperparts, yellow bill, white chin, and white eye arcs. Eastern birds have small white tail spots, visible in flight. **Male** has a darker head and deeper red underparts than **female. Juvenile** has a spotted breast.

■ **similar species** Compare to male Eastern Towhee (page 183). Juvenile might be confused with other spotted thrushes, such as the Hermit Thrush (page 165), but has gray upperparts and head.

■ **voice** Loud caroling **song** has a cheerful, bubbling quality. It is composed of phrases

juvenile

heavily spotted

♀

usually paler than male

white spot

bold white broken eye ring

yellow bill

♂

brick red underparts

Small berries are swallowed whole by American Robins, but larger fruits are pecked at.

broken with short pauses: *cheerily-cheer up-cheerio*. Its song can be confused with that of other birds that sing in phrases broken with pauses, such as tanagers and grosbeaks. **Calls** include a low mellow *pup* and a doubled or trebled *chok* or *tut*.

RANGE Widespread species. Robins are common and pervasive in North America, as both breeding and wintering birds. Most birds are migratory to some extent, but some southern breeders remain in the same area year-round. Spring **migration:** February–April; fall migration: October–November.

FOOD Insects, earthworms, and berries. From spring to fall, backyard robins forage conspicuously on lawns for earthworms. In many locations, winter flocks have no fixed address, but wander in search of fruit—after the trees or vines are stripped of food, the flock moves on.

■ **feeding** Comes to a feeder that offers live mealworms. To promote earthworms (and robins) around your home, use organic fertilizers and avoid insecticides.

Fruiting trees, shrubs, and vines will encourage flocks to linger in winter—holly, sumac, crabapple, and pyracantha are good choices.

NESTING *Location:* Sheltered site in a tree, shrub, or man-made structure, from 5–15 feet up. *Nest:* Untidy, bulky, open cup of plant material, lined with mud and finished off with fine grass. *Eggs:* Usually 4; incubated by female for 12–14 days. *Fledging:* Leaves nest at 14–16 days. *Broods:* In most areas, 2 per season; sometimes 3.

■ **housing** Robins are not shy about nesting around homes, which may help to protect their nest from predators such as raccoons. If you have a porch with a suitable recess or even a protected window-sill, you might find robins nesting there. A nesting platform added to a sheltered location will attract them.

These hungry nestling American Robins will be ready to leave their crowded nest in about a week.

Sightings

	JAN	FEB	MAR	APR	MAY	JUN	JUL	AUG	SEP	OCT	NOV	DEC

Mockingbirds & Thrashers
Family Mimidae

Long-tailed songbirds noted for the rich variety and volume of their songs. Most species forage on or near the ground and have a solitary lifestyle.

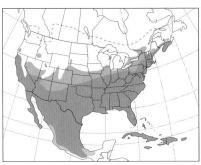

dark eye

yellow eye

spotted

white outer tail feathers

juvenile

Northern Mockingbird
Mimus polyglottos, L 10" (25 cm)

The male Northern Mockingbird is a masterful singer who weaves the songs of many other species into his own large repertoire. State bird of Arkansas, Florida, Mississippi, Tennessee, and Texas.

IDENTIFICATION Common. Slender, long-tailed bird that is often conspicuous around backyards. Its habitual wing flashing exposes large white wing patches and may serve as a territorial defense, to startle predators, or to flush insects—no one is certain.
■ **plumage** Gray above, white below. Has dark wings with a large white patch, white outer tail feathers, and yellowish eyes. **Juvenile** has faintly spotted breast and dark eyes.

■ **similar species** Loggerhead Shrike (not illustrated) is an uncommon predatory songbird with a similar overall pattern, but has a stubby, hooked bill, and a black face mask.
■ **voice** **Song** is a mix of original and imitative phrases, each repeated several times. Unmated males often sing at night. **Calls** include a loud, sharp *check*.

RANGE Widespread species; year-round resident. Favors thickets and brushy areas with open ground nearby—a good description of many backyards.

FOOD Eats a full menu of insects in spring and summer. Winter food is primarily berries—fruiting shrubs are vigorously defended from other birds.
■ **feeding** Will visit a suet feeder. Plant fruiting trees, shrubs, and vines for winter sustenance.

NESTING *Location:* In a dense shrub or tree, usually 3–10 feet up. *Nest:* Bulky open cup of twigs, grass, and other plant material. *Eggs:* Usually 3–4; incubated by female for 12–13 days. *Fledging:* Leaves nest at 12–16 days.

extensive white wing patch

Sightings

	JAN	FEB	MAR	APR	MAY	JUN	JUL	AUG	SEP	OCT	NOV	DEC

Gray Catbird
Dumetella carolinensis, L 8½" (22 cm)

The thicket-loving Gray Catbird has a surprisingly wide distribution, reaching almost to the Pacific Ocean in the northern tier of states and southern Canada. The only mainland states that it avoids breeding in are Nevada and California.

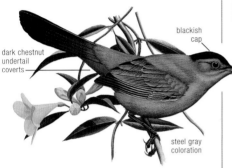

dark chestnut
undertail
coverts

blackish
cap

steel gray
coloration

IDENTIFICATION Common. Slender, long-tailed, dark gray bird, smaller than a mockingbird, that inhabits backyard shrubbery. Its behavior is somewhat furtive and skulking, with short, low flights that rarely take it far. However, around most backyards, a nesting pair of catbirds gets used to the hubbub, and you're almost as likely to see one perching openly on a lawn chair or visiting a birdbath.

■ plumage All gray except for a blackish skullcap, a long black tail, and inconspicuous chestnut undertail coverts. **Juvenile** has pale undertail coverts with a hint of rust color.

■ similar species None.

■ voice **Song** is a rapidly delivered mix of melodious, nasal, and squeaky notes, interspersed with catlike *mew* notes; also mimics other birds' calls and songs. Most frequent **call** is a nasal, down-slurred *mew*.

RANGE Widespread species. Favors thickets, brushy forest undergrowth, tangled vines, and suburban backyards with dense shrub plantings. Winters along the East Coast, and south into the Caribbean and Central America. Spring **migration:** April–May; fall migration: September–early November.

FOOD Mainly insects in spring and summer; more small fruits and berries on migration and during the winter.

NESTING *Location:* In a dense shrub or tree, usually 3–10 feet up. *Nest:* Bulky open cup of twigs, weed stems, vines, and other plant material. *Eggs:* Usually 4; incubated by female for 12–14 days. *Fledging:* Leaves nest at 11–15 days.

Even with a partial view, the gray plumage and blackish cap of the Gray Catbird are unmistakable.

JAN	FEB	MAR	APR	MAY	JUN	JUL	AUG	SEP	OCT	NOV	DEC

Brown Thrasher
Toxostoma rufum, L 11½" (29 cm)

The only thrasher in the eastern half of North America (eight species of thrasher occur in the West). The East has more uniform habitat and climate than the West, and the Brown Thrasher is widespread throughout the region. State bird of Georgia.

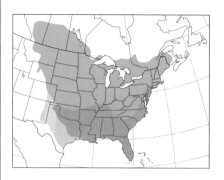

IDENTIFICATION Common to uncommon. Long-tailed, yellow-eyed, mostly rufous bird—larger than a mockingbird—that lurks in thickets and feeds mostly on the ground, sweeping aside leaf litter and soil in pursuit of hidden insects. In winter, when it eats mainly berries, it spends less time on the ground. Most flights are short, jerky affairs that hug the ground; however, a singing male usually selects a high perch to proclaim his breeding territory.

rufous upperparts

long rufous tail

streaked underparts

illustrated), a southern Texas specialty, is grayer above and has a longer bill.
■ **voice** **Song** is a series of varied melodious phrases, each phrase often repeated two or three times. **Calls** include a loud, smacking *spuck* and a low *churr*.

RANGE Eastern and Midwestern species; scarce in the western part of its range. Favors thickets, brushy forest edges, briar tangles, shelterbelts, and suburban backyards with dense shrub plantings. Winters along the East Coast and throughout much of the South. Spring **migration:** late March–early May; fall migration: late August–early November.

FOOD Mainly insects in spring and summer; more small fruits and nuts (particularly acorns) on migration and during the winter.
■ **feeding** Comes to suet and seed feeders, particularly in winter.

■ **plumage** Rich rufous upperparts and tail; two whitish wing bars. Underparts are extensively streaked.
■ **similar species** Wood Thrush (page 167) is short tailed with distinct spots (not streaks) on its underparts. In the South, a wintering Brown Thrasher often occupies the same habitat as the Hermit Thrush (page 165), which has less rufous upperparts, spotted underparts, and a shorter tail and bill. Long-billed Thrasher (not

NESTING *Location:* In a dense shrub or tree, usually 3–6 feet up; sometimes on the ground. *Nest:* Bulky open cup of twigs, weed stems, and other plant material. *Eggs:* Usually 4–5; incubated by both parents for 11–14 days. *Fledging:* Leaves nest at 9–12 days.

Sightings

JAN	FEB	MAR	APR	MAY	JUN	JUL	AUG	SEP	OCT	NOV	DEC

Curve-billed Thrasher
Toxostoma curvirostre, L 11″ (28 cm)

The Curve-billed Thrasher—the common thrasher from the Sonoran Desert of Arizona east to the brushlands of Texas— can be very conspicuous when calling loudly from atop a saguaro or prickly pear cactus (or street sign).

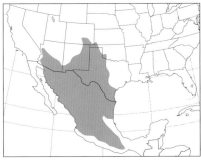

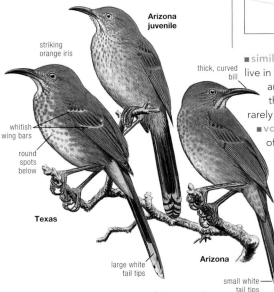

Arizona juvenile

striking orange iris

thick, curved bill

whitish wing bars

round spots below

Texas

large white tail tips

Arizona

small white tail tips

■ **similar species** Other similar thrashers live in the Southwest—Bendire's, Crissal, and Le Conte's (not illustrated)—but they are uncommon species, very rarely seen in backyards.

■ **voice** Long, melodic **song** consists of low trills and warbles. **Call** is a loud *whit-wheet* (in Arizona and New Mexico) or *whit-whit* (in Texas).

RANGE Southwestern species; year-round resident. Favors arid brush and cactus-rich desert. Often inhabits suburban desert communities, especially where cholla cactus grows or, in Texas, around prickly pear thickets.

IDENTIFICATION Common. A sturdy thrasher with strong legs and feet tough enough to perch on spiny cacti. Sometimes lurks in dense vegetation, but feeds on open ground, often walking or running from place to place. Most flights are short and jerky and keep near the ground. Has striking orange eyes and a heavy, downcurved bill.

■ **plumage** Overall dingy, brownish gray with spotted or mottled underparts and a white-tipped tail. **Juvenile** has a shorter bill and paler eyes. Southern Arizona subspecies has underparts with blurry mottling, less white in the tail, and no wing bars.

FOOD A wide variety of insect prey is uncovered or excavated from the ground. Diet is supplemented with seeds, wild berries, and cactus fruit.

■ **feeding** Comes to suet, mealworm, and seed feeders.

NESTING *Location:* In a dense shrub or tree, usually 3–6 feet up; sometimes on the ground. *Nest:* Bulky open cup of twigs, weed stems, and other plant material. *Eggs:* Usually 4–5; incubated by both parents for 11–14 days. *Fledging:* Leaves nest at 9–12 days.

Sightings

JAN	FEB	MAR	APR	MAY	JUN	JUL	AUG	SEP	OCT	NOV	DEC

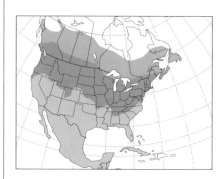

Waxwings
Family Bombycillidae

Waxwings have sleek crests, silky plumage, and yellow-tipped tails. Of three species in the world, two occur in North America.

streaked underparts

juvenile

crest

yellow tail tip

yellowish belly

Cedar Waxwing
Bombycilla cedrorum, L 7¼" (18 cm)

The curious name—waxwing—derives from the bright red, waxy secretions produced at the tips of the secondary wing feathers. Their function, if any, is unknown.

 IDENTIFICATION Common. A bluebird-size, extremely social bird with an arboreal lifestyle that revolves around fruiting trees. Amiable flocks feed high in fruiting trees and might go unnoticed but for their constant, high-pitched calling. When breeding, pairs may nest close together and do not defend a territory.

■ **plumage** Very sleek. Brown crest; black "bandit's mask"; toasty brown and yellow underparts; white undertail coverts; plain wings except for the red waxy tips. **Juvenile** is streaked below.

■ **similar species** Bohemian Waxwing (not illustrated) breeds in the far north, but occurs sporadically with Cedar Waxwings in the northern U.S. in fall and winter. Look for rufous (not white) undertail coverts and white wing markings.

■ **voice** No song (not territorial). **Call** is a soft, high-pitched, trilled whistle: *zeeee.*

RANGE Widespread species. Breeds and winters in open forests, riparian corridors, orchards, and wooded (and berried) residential areas. **Migration** timing is difficult to assess; birds return to northernmost breeding areas in May–June and depart by late fall or early winter.

FOOD Searches for berry-producing trees and shrubs. Supplements its summer diet with insects.

NESTING Starts to breed as late as July–August in some areas. *Location:* In a tree, usually 6–20 feet up. *Nest:* Loose open cup of twigs, weed stems, and other plant material. *Eggs:* Usually 3–5; incubated probably by female for 12–14 days. *Fledging:* Leaves nest at 14–18 days.

Sightings

JAN	FEB	MAR	APR	MAY	JUN	JUL	AUG	SEP	OCT	NOV	DEC

Wood-Warblers
Family Parulidae

More than 50 species of wood-warblers (warblers) breed in North America. These colorful sprites are beloved by birders. Many backyards host migrating warblers in spring and fall.

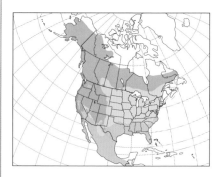

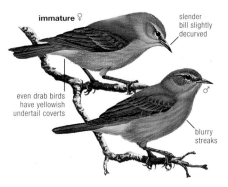

immature ♀

slender bill slightly decurved

even drab birds have yellowish undertail coverts

♂

blurry streaks

Orange-crowned Warbler
Oreothlypis celata, L 5" (13 cm)

This widespread warbler is much more common in the West than in the East. The Orange-crowned is a hardy bird that winters farther north than most warblers.

IDENTIFICATION Common to uncommon. Plain warbler that often probes into dead leaf clusters.
■ **plumage** Very plain; olive green and yellowish overall; orange crown rarely visible. Note dark line through the eye, blurry streaks on the chest, and yellow undertail coverts. Western birds are more yellow; northern breeders (which winter in the Southeast) are duller.
■ **similar species** Pine Warbler (page 180) has wing bars and white undertail coverts. Very similar to Tennessee Warbler (not illustrated).
■ **voice** **Song** is a high-pitched staccato trill. **Call** is a sharp, metallic *chip*.

RANGE Widespread species. Breeds in brushy coastal canyons and mountain thickets and across the northern edge of the boreal forest. In the South or along the Pacific coast, look for this species in winter in backyard gardens. Spring **migration:** March–April in the West, mid-April–May in the East; fall migration: mid-August–October in the West, late September–October in the East.

FOOD Insects in summer; also small berries and nectar.
■ **feeding** Comes to suet and peanut butter feeders in winter and also to hummingbird feeders.

NESTING *Location:* On or near the ground. *Nest:* Open cup of twigs and other plant material. *Eggs:* Usually 4–5; incubated by female for 11–13 days. *Fledging:* Leaves nest at 10–13 days.

Pacific ♂

split eye ring

brighter overall and more of a lemon yellow below

Sightings

JAN FEB MAR APR MAY JUN JUL AUG SEP OCT NOV DEC

GALLERY OF WARBLERS

In his first field guide, Roger Tory Peterson described warblers as "the sprightly butterflies of the bird world." Here is a sampling of colorful spring males. More than 50 species breed in North America; they often pass through backyards on migration during spring (mainly May) and fall (mainly September).

WIDESPREAD WARBLERS

YELLOW WARBLER	WILSON'S WARBLER
COMMON YELLOWTHROAT	YELLOW-BREASTED CHAT

WESTERN WARBLERS

BLACK-THROATED GRAY WARBLER	TOWNSEND'S WARBLER
HERMIT WARBLER	RED-FACED WARBLER

EASTERN WARBLERS

GOLDEN-WINGED WARBLER	NORTHERN PARULA
BLACK-THROATED GREEN WARBLER	BLACKBURNIAN WARBLER
CERULEAN WARBLER	MAGNOLIA WARBLER
PROTHONOTARY WARBLER	BLACK-AND-WHITE WARBLER
KENTUCKY WARBLER	AMERICAN REDSTART

RARE WARBLERS

KIRTLAND'S WARBLER	RUFOUS-CAPPED WARBLER

Pine Warbler
Dendroica pinus, L 5½" (14 cm)

Unlike many bird names, this one rings true: Pine Warblers do indeed have a close connection to pine forests—they breed almost nowhere else. These hardy warblers winter almost entirely in the United States, in the Southeast and eastern Texas.

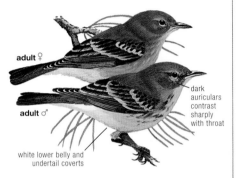

adult ♀

adult ♂

dark auriculars contrast sharply with throat

white lower belly and undertail coverts

IDENTIFICATION Common. The Pine Warbler is long tailed and somewhat heavy billed for a warbler, and its feeding actions are slower and more deliberate than most warblers. Quite gregarious in winter, they often mix in with small flocks of Eastern Bluebirds, Yellow-rumped Warblers, and Chipping Sparrows.

■ **plumage** Unstreaked, olive upperparts; two wing bars; white undertail coverts. There is a sharp contrast between the dark ear coverts and throat. **Male** is yellow below with streaks on the sides and a white belly. **Female** is duller. **Immature female** is exceptionally drab.

■ **similar species** Orange-crowned Warbler (page 177) lacks wing bars and has yellow undertail coverts. Pine Warblers (except immature female) are very similar to fall Bay-breasted and Blackpoll Warblers (not illustrated).

■ **voice Song** is a twittering, musical trill that varies in speed. **Call** is a flat, sweet *chip*.

RANGE Eastern species. Breeds in southern pine forests and denser mature pine or mixed forests in the north. Spring **migration:** April; fall migration: late September–mid-October.

FOOD Eats insects all year; winter diet is supplemented with small berries and seeds.

■ **feeding** Comes to suet feeders in winter and even takes sunflower seeds.

NESTING *Location:* Concealed in a pine, usually 30–50 feet up. *Nest:* Deep, open cup of twigs, pine needles, and other plant material. *Eggs:* Usually 4; incubated by both parents for about 10 days. *Fledging:* Leaves nest at about 10 days.

brownish above

immature ♀

pale wraps around auriculars

whitish below

immature ♂

long tail projection past undertail coverts

Sightings

	JAN	FEB	MAR	APR	MAY	JUN	JUL	AUG	SEP	OCT	NOV	DEC

Yellow-rumped Warbler

Dendroica coronata, L 5½" (14 cm)

There are two regional groups with distinctly different head patterns that were once considered to be separate species— "Audubon's Warbler" in the West and the widespread "Myrtle Warbler."

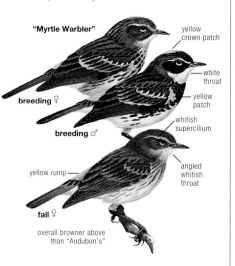

"Myrtle Warbler"

yellow crown patch

white throat

yellow patch

breeding ♀

breeding ♂

whitish supercilium

yellow rump

angled whitish throat

fall ♀

overall browner above than "Audubon's"

■ **voice** **Song** is a soft warble, trailing off at the end. **Call** of "Myrtle" is a flat *check*, a sharper *chip* is given by "Audubon's."

 RANGE Widespread species. Breeds in coniferous and mixed woodlands. Winters farther north than any other warbler. Spring **migration:** March–early May; fall migration: late September–October.

FOOD Eats insects all year; winter diet is often berries.

NESTING *Location:* Most often in a conifer, usually 4–50 feet up. *Nest:* Open cup of twigs, pine needles, and other plant material. *Eggs:* Usually 4–5; incubated by female for 12–13 days. *Fledging:* Leaves nest at 10–12 days.

IDENTIFICATION Common to abundant; often in winter flocks. It is often the first and last warbler you'll see during the year.
■ **plumage** A yellow rump patch and a patch of yellow on the sides are features of all ages, sexes, and regional groups. Northern and Eastern birds ("**Myrtle**") have a thin whitish eyebrow and a white throat that extends to a point behind the ear region; **breeding male** has a mottled black chest and bold white wing bars. Western birds ("**Audubon's**") have a more rounded, *yellow* throat (sometimes whitish in immature females); **breeding male** has a black chest and large white wing patch.
■ **similar species** Magnolia and Cape May Warblers (not illustrated) are smaller "eastern warblers" with yellowish rumps.

"Audubon's Warbler"

most have pale yellow in rounded throat patch

fall ♀

yellow rump

yellow throat

extensive white

breeding ♂

JAN	FEB	MAR	APR	MAY	JUN	JUL	AUG	SEP	OCT	NOV	DEC

Towhees & Sparrows
Family Emberizidae

Large family of seed-eating birds that contains many species that frequent backyard feeders. They all have conical bills for cracking open seeds, and most are seen on or near the ground.

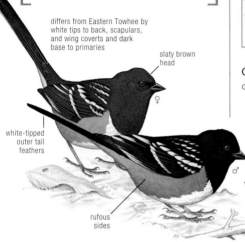

differs from Eastern Towhee by white tips to back, scapulars, and wing coverts and dark base to primaries

slaty brown head

♀

white-tipped outer tail feathers

♂

rufous sides

Spotted Towhee
Pipilo maculates, L 7½" (19 cm)

The Spotted and Eastern Towhees were once considered a single species, the "Rufous-sided Towhee."

IDENTIFICATION Common. A large, chesty sparrow with a long tail that recalls a thrasher. Often stays out of sight in thickets or under shrubbery.
■ **plumage** The long tail has white-tipped outer tail feathers. **Male** has a black hood, ruby red eyes, and black upperparts neatly spotted with white. **Female** is slate brown where the male is black.
■ **similar species** Eastern Towhee (opposite) lacks the white spots on upperparts.
■ **voice Song** starts with short whistled notes and ends with a simple, loud, buzzy trill (coastal birds give just the trill).

Call is a scratchy, up-slurred *reee-eh?* or a descending, raspy mewing in the Rockies.

RANGE Widespread species; casual in the East. Breeds in chaparral, brushy mountain slopes, and riparian thickets. Resident in many locations. Spring **migration:** March–early May; fall migration: mid-September–October.

FOOD Eats insects all year, if available; winter diet includes berries, nuts, and seeds.
■ **feeding** Visits a platform feeder or takes seeds on the ground.

NESTING *Location:* Usually on the ground. *Nest:* Cup of dried leaves and grasses. *Eggs:* Usually 3–4; incubated by female for 12–13 days. *Fledging:* Leaves nest at 8–10 days.

juvenile

streaked

JAN	FEB	MAR	APR	MAY	JUN	JUL	AUG	SEP	OCT	NOV	DEC

Eastern Towhee
Pipilo erythrophthalmus, L 7½" (19 cm)

Both the Eastern Towhee's song (drink-your-tea) and call (chewink or towhee) are easy to remember. That's very helpful, because this attractive sparrow has a talent for hiding in the underbrush.

milk chocolate
upperparts and head

♀

white base to
primaries in all
plumages

white-tipped
outer tail
feathers

black head
and back

♂

rufous
sides

RANGE Widespread species. Is partial to forest edges with dense tangles, overgrown fields, and thickets. Year-round resident in some Southern areas. Spring **migration:** March–early May; fall migration: late September–October.

FOOD Eats insects all year, if available; winter diet includes berries, nuts, and seeds.
■ **feeding** Common at platform feeders or takes seeds scattered on the ground.

NESTING *Location:* Usually on ground. *Nest:* Cup of dried leaves and grasses. *Eggs:* Usually 3–4; incubated by female for 12–13 days. *Fledging:* Leaves nest at 8–10 days.

IDENTIFICATION Common to uncommon. Like the related Spotted Towhee, a large and chesty bird with a long tail that recalls a thrasher. Its noisy foraging under the shrubbery will often alert you to its presence.
■ **plumage** Very dapper and neatly patterned. A white mark on the wings and white-tipped outer tail feathers are easy to see when a bird flushes. **Male** has a black hood, ruby red eyes, black upperparts, and rufous sides. **Female** is chocolate brown where the male is black. In Florida, adults have pale yellowish eyes.
■ **similar species** Spotted Towhee (opposite) has white spots on the upperparts. The two species overlap along rivers in the Great Plains and interbreed.
■ **voice** Full **song** is a loud, ringing *drink-your-tea!* or shortened *drink-tea.* **Calls** include an up-slurred *chewink* or *towhee* and, in Florida, a clearer, even-pitched *swee.*

Florida ♂

yellowish
white iris

juvenile

streaked

Sightings

JAN	FEB	MAR	APR	MAY	JUN	JUL	AUG	SEP	OCT	NOV	DEC

Canyon Towhee

Melozone fusca, L 8" (20 cm)

The Canyon Towhee and its Pacific coast relative the California Towhee (next page) were considered the same species, the "Brown Towhee," until 1989. Both are sedentary birds, and their ranges don't overlap.

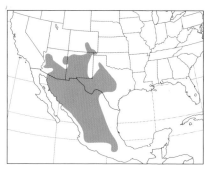

pale rufous crown

buffy throat

whitish belly with inconspicuous breast spot

IDENTIFICATION Common. Large, long-tailed sparrow that sticks to the ground and low bushes. Fairly tame and approachable as it scratches and pecks for food, hopping from place to place. Sometimes becomes very tame around homes, even entering open doors. Usually seen alone or in a pair, occasionally with a small flock of other sparrows.

This hopper feeder is large enough for a Canyon Towhee to perch on with ease.

■ plumage Plain brownish gray overall; rufous crown sometimes raised into a short crest; and a buff throat encircled by a "necklace" of dark streaks with a "stickpin" breast spot. **Juvenile** is faintly streaked below.

■ similar species Abert's Towhee (not illustrated) is a secretive, desert towhee with warm brown plumage, black face, and pale bill that is also seen in backyards.

■ voice **Song** opens with a call note, followed by sweet, slurred notes. **Call** is a shrill *chee-yep* or *chedep.*

RANGE Southwest species; year-round resident. Lives in a variety of arid habitats: desert scrub, dry foothills, canyon slopes, arroyos, and desert-community backyards.

FOOD Mostly seeds. Supplements diet with insects.

■ feeding Eats black-oil sunflower seeds, milo, or millet at a platform feeder or takes seeds scattered on the ground.

NESTING Nesting behavior not well known. *Location:* In a small tree or shrub, usually 3–12 feet up. *Nest:* Bulky cup of twigs and grasses. *Eggs:* Usually 3–4; incubated by female for 12–13 days. *Fledging:* Leaves nest at 8–10 days.

Sightings

	JAN	FEB	MAR	APR	MAY	JUN	JUL	AUG	SEP	OCT	NOV	DEC

California Towhee
Melozone crissalis, L 9" (23 cm)

From southern California to southern Oregon, this simple brown bird enlivens many backyard feeders. A mated pair remains together throughout the year and is often seen foraging side by side or staying in touch by calling back and forth to each other.

IDENTIFICATION Common. Large, long-tailed sparrow that sticks to the ground and low bushes. Fairly tame and approachable as it scratches in the leaf litter or open ground looking for food. Hops from place to place or makes short, jerky flights on short, broad wings.
■ **plumage** Very plain; medium-brown overall with a darker tail. Face and breast are suffused with orange-buff and bordered below by short, faint streaks; has a thin, orange-buff eye ring. **Juvenile** is faintly streaked below.
■ **similar species** Larger, darker brown California Thrasher (not illustrated) has a long downcurved bill and a very long tail, but occurs in similar habitat.
■ **voice Song,** heard mostly in late afternoon, is a series of *chink* notes strung into a loose accelerating series. **Call** is a sharp *chink*, like some Fox Sparrows.

RANGE West Coast species; year-round resident. Lives in a variety of brushy habitats from coastal lowlands up to about 4,000 feet in the mountains: chaparral, coastal sage, streamside thickets, open woodlands, and shrubby suburban and urban backyards. One of the most sedentary species, rarely moving far from where it nests.

FOOD Mostly seeds. Supplements diet with insects, especially when feeding young. Also feeds on small berries and green shoots.
■ **feeding** Very common feeder bird, where it is often seen in the company of White-crowned and Golden-crowned Sparrows. Prefers black-oil sunflower seeds, cracked corn, and millet at a platform feeder or seeds scattered on the ground. Vulnerable to free-roaming cats.

NESTING *Location:* In a small tree or shrub, sometimes on a sheltered building ledge, usually 4–12 feet up. *Nest:* Loosely constructed cup of twigs and grasses. *Eggs:* Usually 3–4; incubated by female for about 14 days. *Fledging:* Leaves nest at about 8 days, when still unable to fly well.

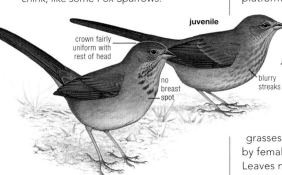

juvenile

crown fairly uniform with rest of head

no breast spot

blurry streaks

Sightings

JAN	FEB	MAR	APR	MAY	JUN	JUL	AUG	SEP	OCT	NOV	DEC

HOW LONG DO BIRDS LIVE?

The scientific record is very incomplete, but longevity records in birds can be tracked in two different ways: from zoo records of captive birds, and from banding records of wild birds that are recaptured at a later date.

■The Champions In 1892, the Moscow Zoo acquired a male adult Andean Condor, which died in 1964 at the age of 72—a record that still stands. Other families with birds whose life spans have surpassed 50 years in captivity include pelicans, hawks and eagles, cranes, owls, and parrots. Although not strictly reliable, parrot owners often claim life spans in excess of 60 years for their pets; an *Amazona* parrot named Jimmy reportedly survived to the age of 104 in Liverpool, England.

■Wild Birds The rigors of life in the wild—predation, disease, starvation, harsh weather, migration, and more—end most (if not all) birds' lives before they die of old age. Many birds perish in their first year of life, largely due to inexperience. The median life span of the typical songbird is probably one to three years; on average, larger birds live longer.

The following list gives the ages of the oldest wild birds documented by banding records for 16 of the species found in this book. These are maximum documented ages—the *average* wild bird has a much shorter life span.

MAXIMUM DOCUMENTED LIFE SPAN IN THE WILD			
SPECIES	YEARS-MONTHS*	SPECIES	YEARS-MONTHS*
Canada Goose	33-03	European Starling	15-03
Mourning Dove	31-04	American Robin	13-11
Red-tailed Hawk	29-09	Downy Woodpecker	11-11
Great Horned Owl	28-00	Eastern Bluebird	10-06
Common Grackle	23-01	American Goldfinch	10-05
Blue Jay	17-06	Barn Swallow	8-01
American Crow	16-04	Carolina Wren	7-08
Northern Cardinal	15-09	Brown Creeper	4-05

*Data from the U.S. Geological Survey's Patuxent Wildlife Research Center website
(www.pwrc.usgs.gov/bbl/homepage/longvlst.cfm), as of September 2010

American Tree Sparrow
Spizella arborea, L 6¼" (16 cm)

Far to the north, in muskeg and brushy tundra, this hardy sparrow raises its family during the Arctic summer. In the fall, flocks migrate south to spend the winter months in weedy fields, at forest edges, and at backyard feeders, particularly after a heavy snow.

breeding

largest
Spizella

spot

 RANGE Widespread species. Breeds in Alaska and northern Canada. In winter, common in the northern tier of states, but scarce near the southern and western edge of its winter range. Spring **migration:** March–April; fall migration: mid-October–late November.

 FOOD Seeds in winter; mostly insects in summer.
■ **feeding** Common winter feeder bird in North (mostly in rural areas). Black-oil sunflower seeds and millet are preferred.

IDENTIFICATION Fairly common. Has a bicolored bill—dark above, bright yellow below. During winter, small flocks forage on the ground with juncos and other sparrows, or strip seeds from dried weed stalks. Despite its name, it is not particularly associated with trees, although flushed birds often alight there.
■ **plumage** Distinct rusty cap and eye line; rusty-striped back; two white wing bars. Underparts are mostly gray, with rufous sides of the breast and buff flanks. Note the central breast spot ("stickpin").
■ **similar species** Field Sparrow (page 190) is smaller, lacks the breast spot, and has a paler face and pink bill. Chipping Sparrow (next page) is also smaller, lacks the breast spot, and is duller below. Also, compare Song Sparrow (pages 192–193).
■ **voice** **Song** begins with several clear notes, followed by a variable, rapid warble; it is heard in late winter, before migration. **Call** is a cheerful, musical *teedle-eet*.

NESTING *Location:* On the ground or low in a dwarf willow. *Nest:* Cup of grasses and moss. *Eggs:* Usually 3–5; incubated by female for 12–13 days. *Fledging:* Leaves nest at about 9–10 days; able to fly 5–6 days later.

In winter, the American Tree Sparrow's central breast spot can be hard to see.

Sightings

JAN	FEB	MAR	APR	MAY	JUN	JUL	AUG	SEP	OCT	NOV	DEC

Chipping Sparrow
Spizella passerina, L 5½" (14 cm)

The Chipping Sparrow ("Chippy") breeds in every mainland U.S. state and Canadian province or territory, except remote Nunavut. Its love of open areas with scattered trees—a good description of many backyards—has made it a well-known and popular bird. The male's loud trilling song is heard all day long in spring and early summer, although some people mistake it for an insect.

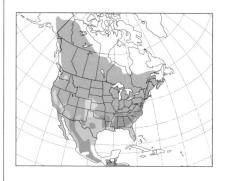

IDENTIFICATION Common. Slender and well-proportioned sparrow, with a fairly long tail. In fall and winter, small flocks gather on lawns and at bird feeders, often loosely associated with other birds, such

white supercilium

dark eye line in all plumages

breeding

as bluebirds, wintering warblers, and other sparrows. If flushed, the whole group flies up to a nearby tree, but soon returns to the ground. The bill is black in summer, dull pinkish in winter.
■ **plumage** Dark eye line extends from the bill to behind the eye. **Breeding adult** has a chestnut cap, gray face, and white eyebrow; **winter adult** has streaked crown with some rufous, buff face and eyebrow. **First-winter** bird has little or no rufous in crown and a buff (not grayish) breast.

Juvenile (seen into October) has prominently streaked underparts.
■ **similar species** Field Sparrow (page 190) has a pale head and white eye ring, with no dark line through the eye. American Tree Sparrow (previous page) is larger and more richly colored below and has a breast spot and a sharply two-toned bill.
■ **voice** **Song** is a long, rapid trill of dry *chip* notes; all the notes are on one pitch, giving it a mechanical or insectlike quality. **Call** is a high, sharp *tsik* or *seep*.

RANGE Widespread species. Breeds across the continent in wooded suburbs and towns, city parks, golf courses, orchards, and farmland. Wilder breeding locations include open woodlands (especially pine woods), forest edges, and clearings—from lowlands to high in the mountains. Highly migratory, it winters in the southern tier of states and as far north as the Mid-Atlantic. Spring **migration:** mid-March–mid-May; fall migration: late August–early November.

FOOD Eats mostly insects in summer and feeds insects to nestlings. Insects are sometimes taken in midair after a short chase, but most are gleaned from the ground or vegetation. The rest of the year, forages

winter
adult

contrasty
gray rump
often hidden

streaked
crown

juvenile

streaky
juvenile
seen into
October

1st winter

buffy
breast

primarily on the ground for seeds of wild grasses and weeds.

■ **feeding** Common feeder bird, often seen in small flocks. It prefers to take seed scattered on the ground or on a platform feeder. Black-oil sunflower seeds, millet, and cracked corn are good choices.

NESTING *Location:* In a tree, often a conifer, shrub, or vine tangle, usually 3–20 feet up. *Nest:* Rather flimsy cup of grasses and root-lets. *Eggs:* Usually 4; incubated by female for 10–15 days. *Fledging:* Leaves nest at about 9–12 days. *Broods:* 2 per year.

In fall, Chipping Sparrows replace (molt) all their feathers.

In spring, Chipping Sparrows undergo a second molt that replaces only the head feathers.

Sightings

	JAN	FEB	MAR	APR	MAY	JUN	JUL	AUG	SEP	OCT	NOV	DEC

Field Sparrow

Spizella pusilla, L 5¾" (15 cm)

This pale, wide-eyed sparrow breeds in brushy clearings and overgrown pastures. Its plaintive, whistled song is a delightful accompaniment to spring and summer days in many rural areas of the East.

IDENTIFICATION Common. Medium-size sparrow with a long tail. Easy to overlook in winter, when they are much quieter and infrequent at bird feeders. The stout bill is completely pink, as are the legs.

■ **plumage** Overall pale; gray and rufous tones combine for a "toasty" appearance (drabber in western part of range). Blank gray face with a bright white eye ring, a rusty patch behind the eye, and a rusty crown. Grayish underparts, suffused with tan on the breast and sides. **Juvenile** has a streaked breast.

■ **similar species** Chipping Sparrow (previous pages) has a dark eye line, no eye ring, and a darker bill. American Tree Sparrow (page 187) is larger and has a breast spot, and its bill is sharply two toned.

■ **voice** **Song** begins with several sweet whistles, then accelerates into a trill (tempo increasing "like a Ping-Pong ball dropped on a tabletop"). **Call** is a clear *chip*.

RANGE Widespread species, declining in many areas. Breeds in overgrown pastures, brushy woodlands with clearings, power-line cuts—usually not close to human habitation. Winters in similar habitat and in large, less brushy fields of tall grasses or sedges. Some birds are resident; northern breeders move south. Spring **migration**: mid-March–early May; fall migration: mid-October–early November.

FOOD In summer, insects and small seeds. Primarily seeds in winter.

■ **feeding** Not particularly attracted to feeders. Visitors prefer millet and cracked corn scattered on the ground.

NESTING *Location:* On the ground or low in a small shrub or sapling. *Nest:* Cup woven of grass. *Eggs:* Usually 3–5; incubated by female for 10–12 days. *Fledging:* Leaves nest at about 7–8 days; able to fly 5–6 days later.

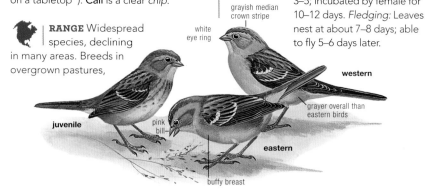

grayish median crown stripe

white eye ring

western

grayer overall than eastern birds

juvenile

pink bill

eastern

buffy breast

Sightings

JAN	FEB	MAR	APR	MAY	JUN	JUL	AUG	SEP	OCT	NOV	DEC

Fox Sparrow
Passerella iliaca, L 7" (18 cm)

Fox Sparrows have plumage that varies from region to region, and the different groups may someday be split into different species.

rufous streaking on gray back

rufous in cheek

rufous tail

rufous streaking below

"Red"

IDENTIFICATION Common but shy. In the East, only the **"Red Fox Sparrow"** occurs. In the Rockies and Great Basin, only the **"Slate-colored"** occurs, and only in summer when it breeds there. **"Sooty"** breeds in the Pacific Northwest; **"Thick-billed"** breeds in the mountains of California and Oregon. In winter, all three western types can occur together in the Pacific region.

■ **plumage** All are large and have under-parts heavily marked with triangular spots that merge into a larger spot on the breast.

■ **similar species** Song Sparrow (pages 192–193) is much smaller and has a bold face pattern and streaked back.

■ **voice** **Song** combines sweetly slurred whistles and short trills; trills are harsher in western birds. **Call** of most birds is a smacking *tschup*, like a Brown Thrasher.

RANGE Widespread species. Different types breed in different habitats. In winter, found in undergrowth, also in suburban yards. Spring **migration:** early March–late April; fall migration: late September–late November.

FOOD In summer, mostly insects; otherwise, primarily seeds.
■ **feeding** Seeds on the ground.

NESTING *Location:* On the ground. *Nest:* Open cup of grass. *Eggs:* Usually 2–4; incubated by female for 12–14 days. *Fledging:* Leaves nest at about 9–11 days.

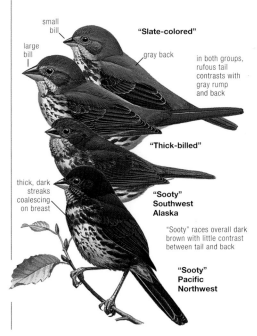

small bill

"Slate-colored"

large bill

gray back

in both groups, rufous tail contrasts with gray rump and back

"Thick-billed"

thick, dark streaks coalescing on breast

"Sooty" Southwest Alaska

"Sooty" races overall dark brown with little contrast between tail and back

"Sooty" Pacific Northwest

Sightings

JAN	FEB	MAR	APR	MAY	JUN	JUL	AUG	SEP	OCT	NOV	DEC

Song Sparrow
Melospiza melodia, L 6¼" (16 cm)

If you see a brown, streaky sparrow in your backyard, consider the Song Sparrow first—it's the most widespread and abundant American sparrow. In spring and summer, the male selects an exposed, eye-level perch and proclaims his territory with a loud and musical song.

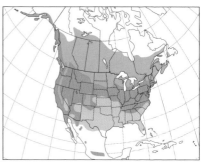

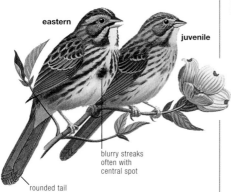

eastern

juvenile

blurry streaks
often with
central spot

rounded tail

IDENTIFICATION Very common. Medium-size sparrow with a fairly long, rounded tail. Backyard pairs are often quite tame and conspicuous as they move around the shrubby borders and undergrowth. Undulating flight has a jerky quality and the tail is constantly pumped up and down. In areas where they are resident, the male defends his territory year-round. Individual territories are often small, and it is not uncommon for multiple pairs to be present in large backyards with good habitat. In winter, migrant Song Sparrows from farther north may join the resident birds that come to your feeder, but never occur in big flocks. Song Sparrows vary regionally in color and size—more than 30 subspecies occur in the U.S. and Canada, from blackish streaked in coastal California; paler and smaller in the desert Southwest; darker and redder in the Pacific Northwest; and larger and grayer in Alaska—but they still look and sound undeniably like Song Sparrows.

■ **plumage** Striped face exhibits a dark crown, pale eyebrow, dark line through the eye, and two dark streaks ("whiskers," or more precisely, moustachial and malar stripes) below the eye. The underparts are variably streaked on the sides and breast,

Each male Song Sparrow has a repertoire of 8 to 10 songs; he usually repeats the same song 5 to 15 times before switching to a new one.

The short, rounded wings of the Song Sparrow make flying through brushy thickets easier.

and the streaking often converges into a central breast spot.

■**similar species** Fox Sparrow (page 191) is larger and lacks a boldly striped face. Other common, backyard sparrows lack heavily streaked underparts. Lincoln's Sparrow (not illustrated) is smaller and has a buff breast with fine streaking.

■**voice** **Song** is a series of notes with a noticeable trill in the middle or as a final flourish. **Call** is a distinctive *chemp*.

RANGE Widespread species. Breeds across the continent in brushy areas, often near fresh or salt water. Also common around suburban homes, parks, rural hedgerows, farmland, and other altered habitats if there is sufficient shrubbery or brush for nesting and foraging. Northern breeders migrate south, where they winter in similar habitat. Spring **migration:** March–April; fall migration: October–November.

FOOD Eats mostly insects in spring and summer; feeds insects to nestlings. The rest of the year, forages for seeds and birdseed at feeders and sometimes eats small berries. Often forages by scratching into leaf litter in dense cover; also picks insects from foliage.

■**feeding** Common feeder bird, but comes most readily to a feeder placed close to good cover. It prefers seeds scattered on the ground or on a platform feeder. Black-oil sunflower seeds, millet, and cracked corn are good choices.

NESTING *Location:* On the ground or low in a shrub or vine tangle. *Nest:* Open cup of grasses, leaves, and rootlets. *Eggs:* Usually 3–5; incubated by female for 12–14 days. *Fledging:* Leaves nest at about 10–12 days; able to fly 5–6 days later.

California races are very dark

northwestern races are dark and ruddy

dark malar stripe

southwestern desert races are small and pale

Sightings

| JAN | FEB | MAR | APR | MAY | JUN | JUL | AUG | SEP | OCT | NOV | DEC |

Lark Sparrow
Calamospiza melanocorys, L 7" (18 cm)

The Lark Sparrow is a bird of open spaces. In the mid-1800s, when there was more cleared land in the East, Lark Sparrows colonized the new habitat. Today, most of those open fields are gone, reverted to forest or gobbled up by urban and suburban sprawl, and the Lark Sparrow is retreating to its core range in the Great Plains and the West.

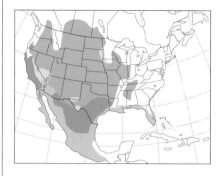

IDENTIFICATION Fairly common. This medium large sparrow has such a distinctive head pattern that, unlike many sparrows, its identification is easy. Lark Sparrows are often seen conspicuously perched along roadsides, on fences, utility lines, and shrubs, or feeding on open ground. In winter and migration, gathers in large flocks.

■ **similar species** None.

■ **voice** **Song** begins with two loud, clear notes, followed by a long jumble of clear notes, trills, and buzzes. **Call** is a soft, sharp *tsip*, often given in a rapid series and frequently delivered in flight.

RANGE Central and Western species. Breeds and winters in open areas where grassy areas intermix with trees and shrubs, such as pastures, prairies, hedgerows, roadsides, sagebrush, and desert scrub. Year-round resident in some areas, but the majority vacate their breeding range, moving south into Mexico. Spring **migration:** March–May; fall migration: August–mid-October.

distinctive head pattern; dark breast spot

whitish at base of primaries

juvenile

extensive white in tail

subdued head pattern; streaked below

FOOD Weed and grass seeds are the primary food; insects make up about 25 percent of the diet.

■ **feeding** Occasional feeder visitor; prefers millet and cracked corn scattered on the ground.

NESTING *Location:* Usually on the ground. *Nest:* Cup woven of grass. *Eggs:* Usually 4–5; incubated by female for 11–12 days. *Fledging:* Leaves nest at about 9–12 days.

■ **plumage** Harlequin face pattern is unique; also note the dark central breast spot. In flight, the long black tail shows bold white corners (similar to an Eastern or Spotted Towhee). **Juvenile** has a subdued face pattern and light streaking on the breast.

Sightings

JAN	FEB	MAR	APR	MAY	JUN	JUL	AUG	SEP	OCT	NOV	DEC

Harris's Sparrow

Zonotrichia querula, L 7½" (19 cm)

The heartland of North America is where you'll find the Harris's Sparrow—wintering on the Great Plains and breeding in northern Canada.

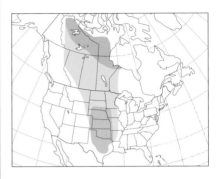

black crown and bib

large pink bill

breeding

brushy areas on the southern Great Plains. Spring **migration:** late March–late May; fall migration: October–early November.

 FOOD Insects, seeds, and berries. Winter diet primarily seeds and some berries.
■ **feeding** Visits feeders in winter.

NESTING *Location:* Breeds at the northern edge of the boreal forest in northern Canada—where there are no conventional backyards! Its nest went undiscovered until 1931.

IDENTIFICATION Fairly common. Large, bigger than a White-crowned Sparrow. Small winter flocks feed on the ground and often mix with more numerous smaller sparrows. Has pink bill and legs.
■ **plumage** **Breeding adult** has a mostly black head and gray cheeks. **Winter adult** has an all-black or partially black throat. **Immature** bird has less black on the head and a black whisker mark.
■ **similar species** Adult male House Sparrow (page 236) has a black bib, but is smaller and lacks the pink bill.
■ **voice** **Song** comprises two or three long, pure-toned whistles on the same pitch; rarely heard away from breeding grounds. **Call** is a loud *wink*.

RANGE Great Plains and northern Canada species. Winters in

winter adults

dark postocular spot in all plumages

immature

dark chest patch

brownish flank streaking

Sightings

	JAN	FEB	MAR	APR	MAY	JUN	JUL	AUG	SEP	OCT	NOV	DEC

White-crowned Sparrow
Zonotrichia leucophrys, L 7" (18 cm)

In many areas this attractive "crowned" sparrow is best known as a winter visitor to backyards—especially along the West Coast, where it is abundant.

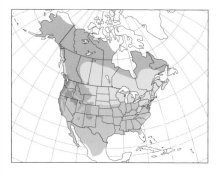

white supraloral

black-and-white head stripes

"Gambel's" adult

rufous-brown lateral crown stripes on all immatures

"Nuttall's" adult

"Eastern" immature

RANGE Widespread species. Breeds in Canadian tundra, in the Western mountains, and along the West Coast north of Santa Barbara. Most birds are highly migratory, but some along the West Coast are resident. Spring **migration:** mid-March–mid-May; fall migration: September–mid-November.

FOOD In summer, eats mostly insects; primarily seeds the rest of the year; sometimes berries or buds.
■ **feeding** Scattered seed on the ground.

NESTING *Location:* Usually on the ground or low in a bush. *Nest:* Open cup of grass and weed stems. *Eggs:* Usually 4–5; incubated by female for about 12 days. *Fledging:* Leaves nest at about 8–10 days.

IDENTIFICATION Common. Medium large, flocking sparrow. There are five subspecies with subtle geographic variation. Bill color varies from pinkish to orange to yellow.
■ **plumage** **Adult** has bold black and white crown stripes. **Immature** bird has brown and light tan crown stripes. **Juvenile** (seen only in nesting areas) has streaked underparts.
■ **similar species** White-throated Sparrow (opposite) has a contrasting white throat and a yellow spot in front of the eye. Immature Golden-crowned Sparrow (page 198) on the West Coast has grayish bill and an indistinct crown pattern.
■ **voice** **Song**—heard all winter—is made up of mournful whistles, followed by jumbled notes and ending in a buzz or trill. **Calls** include a loud *pink* and a sharp *tseep*.

"Gambel's" juvenile

dark superloral

reddish pink bill

"Eastern" adult

Sightings

	JAN	FEB	MAR	APR	MAY	JUN	JUL	AUG	SEP	OCT	NOV	DEC

White-throated Sparrow
Zonotrichia albicollis, L 6¾" (17 cm)

The two color morphs of this species behave differently—which is almost unheard of in the bird world. Tan-striped birds are nonaggressive and attentive parents; white-striped birds are socially dominant and poor parents. Mixed-morph pairs that strike the right balance of aggression and nurturing are most successful.

yellow supraloral spot; dark bill

tan-striped morph

white-striped morph

juvenile

white throat; richly colored back

IDENTIFICATION Common. Medium-large woodland sparrow that feeds on the ground along forested edges, darting for cover if disturbed. It may reemerge in response to *pishing* and can occur in large flocks in winter.
■ **plumage** Conspicuous and strongly outlined white throat; also, a yellow spot in front of the eye. **White-striped morph** has clean black and white head stripes. **Tan-striped morph** has tan and dark brown head stripes, with duller, dingy-looking plumage on the face, throat, and underparts. **Juvenile** birds have heads like the tan-striped morph and a streaked breast.
■ **similar species** White-crowned Sparrow (opposite) lacks the contrasting white throat and the yellow spot in front of the eye.
■ **voice Song**—heard all winter—is a thin, mournful whistle, generally two single notes followed by three triple notes (*pure sweet Canada Canada Canada*). **Calls** include a sharp *pink* and a drawn-out, lisping *tseep*.

RANGE Widespread species. Very common to abundant in the East in winter; uncommon to rare along the West Coast. Winters in brushy woodland thickets, forest edges, wooded suburban neighborhoods, and urban parks. Breeds in coniferous and mixed forests, often in dense brush near water. Spring **migration:** late March–mid-May; fall migration: mid-September–early November.

FOOD In summer, eats mostly insects; primarily seeds the rest of the year, or sometimes berries or tree buds.
■ **feeding** Scattered seeds on the ground or at a platform feeder. White-striped adults are dominant.

NESTING *Location:* Usually on the ground, concealed by shrubbery. *Nest:* Open cup of grass and weed stems. *Eggs:* Usually 4–5; incubated by female for 11–14 days. *Fledging:* Leaves nest at about 8–9 days; able to fly well about a week later.

Sightings

JAN	FEB	MAR	APR	MAY	JUN	JUL	AUG	SEP	OCT	NOV	DEC

Golden-crowned Sparrow

Zonotrichia atricapilla, L 7" (18 cm)

A West Coast specialty that breeds in western Canada and Alaska but winters from Vancouver to San Diego in brushy thickets and in shrubby backyards.

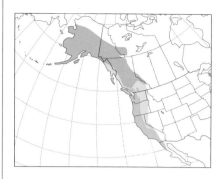

 IDENTIFICATION Fairly common. Medium-large woodland sparrow. In winter, it is often found with flocks of White-crowned Sparrows, though it favors denser cover. Although close in size, the Golden-crowned is obviously larger and heavier set than the White-crowned.

■ **plumage** **Breeding adult** has an extensive black cap with a bright yellow forecrown and gray face. **Winter adult** has dusky brown cap with dingy yellow forecrown and browner face. **Immature's** face is very plain brown, with just a tinge of dull yellow on the forecrown (can be hard to see).

■ **similar species** Immature White-crowned Sparrow (page 196) is similar, but paler overall, with a light tan eyebrow, central crown stripe, and paler bill.

■ **voice** **Song**—a series of three or more plaintive, whistled notes (*oh dear me*)—is heard year-round. **Calls** include a soft *tseep* and a flat *tsick*.

 RANGE West Coast species. Winters in dense brush, forest thickets, chaparral, backyard gardens, and urban parks. Breeds in mountain thickets at the tree line and also in alder and willow patches in coastal Alaska. Entire population is migratory. Spring **migration:** late March–mid-May; fall migration: late September–early November.

FOOD Not a seed specialist; eats a varied diet of seeds, buds, berries, and insects throughout the year.
■ **feeding** Scattered seeds on the ground or at a platform feeder.

NESTING *Location:* Usually on the ground, concealed by shrubbery. *Nest:* Bulky cup of grass and weed stems. *Eggs:* Usually 3–5; incubated by female for 11–12 days. *Fledging:* Leaves nest at 9–11 days; probably able to fly well about a week later.

dull yellow forehead; head pattern otherwise muted

immature

yellow crown with broad black eyebrow

breeding

winter adult's crown pattern much more muted

mostly dark bill

winter adult

Sightings

JAN	FEB	MAR	APR	MAY	JUN	JUL	AUG	SEP	OCT	NOV	DEC

RARE BIRDS

"Rare" is a relative word that changes meaning depending on how big an area you are considering—there's "backyard rare," all the way up to globally rare.

■ **Rare in Your Yard** The thrill of a sighting new or unexpected species can happen right in your backyard. Of course, what's rare in your yard may be common somewhere nearby with a different habitat, such as a marsh, pine forest, or grassland. Many birders keep a yard list of all the species they have seen there—in many parts of the country, reaching 100 or more species over a period of years is a reasonable goal.

■ **Rare in Your Region** Every region has scarce species that require extra effort or visits to special habitats to see. That might mean multiple boat trips off the West Coast to see a Flesh-footed Shearwater or a trek up a New England mountain to search for Bicknell's Thrush. Some regional rarities are irregular visitors to the region from elsewhere, such as a Rufous Hummingbird in the East or a Rose-breasted Grosbeak in the West.

■ **Rare in North America** More than 900 species of birds have been recorded in North America, but almost 200 are North American rarities—vagrants from beyond our shores that are not seen on our continent every year.

■ **Rare in the World** Of the almost 10,000 species of living birds, BirdLife International estimates that 1,200 species are threatened with extinction and 190 species are critically endangered. Critically endangered North American species include California Condor, Eskimo Curlew, Ivory-billed Woodpecker, and Bachman's Warbler, the last three likely extinct.

Choosy and rare, Kirtland's Warbler breeds in jack pines 5–20 feet tall, mostly in Michigan, and winters primarily in the Bahamas.

Dark-eyed Junco

Junco hyemalis, L 6¼" (16 cm)

Little flocks of these dapper sparrows—known to many as "snowbirds"—show up at backyard feeders across the continent as winter weather is about to set in. Juncos can also be summer breeding birds, for instance, throughout New England, across the mountainous West, and along much of the Pacific Coast. Their plumage varies geographically more than any other American sparrow—the juncos in the East look quite different from those out West.

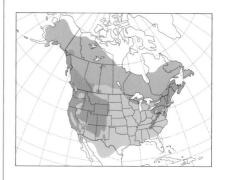

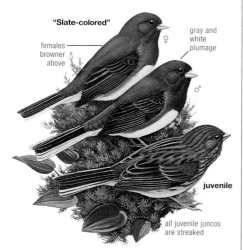

"Slate-colored"

females browner above

gray and white plumage ♀

♂

juvenile

all juvenile juncos are streaked

IDENTIFICATION Very common. There are two useful field marks that almost all juncos share: a pale pink bill, and flashing white outer tail feathers. The three most common subtypes are the "Slate-colored Junco" in Alaska and east of the Rockies; "Oregon Junco" in the northern Rockies and farther west; and "Gray-headed Junco" in the southern Rockies. Two other types with small western ranges are illustrated but not described: the "White-winged" (breeds in mountains of Wyoming, South Dakota, and Montana) and "Pink-sided" (breeds mainly in central Montana

and northern Wyoming). The "Red-backed" (not illustrated) breeds from mountains of central Arizona to western Texas.

■ **plumage** "Slate-colored" male is uniformly dark gray above and on breast, and white below; female is paler and brownish gray above. "Oregon" male has a slate black hood and rufous-brown back and sides; female has a gray hood. "Gray-headed" has a gray hood, gray underparts, and a neat rufous back. All **juveniles** are brown and streaky, but have white outer tail feathers.

■ **similar species** Distinctive, but complicated by regional varieties—in the Rocky Mountain states, different varieties mix together in winter. "Slate-colored" is uncommon to rare in the West.

■ **voice** Song is most often a simple trill, on one pitch; it is also heard in winter. **Calls** include a sharp *dit* and rapid twittering, often heard in flight.

dark lores

pale gray head and underparts

pale bill

rufous back

"Gray-headed"

Although rare, birds with aberrant plumages, like this mostly white junco, are occasionally seen.

"Slate-colored" ♂

all subspecies have white outer tail feathers

RANGE Widespread species. Breeds across the continent in a wide variety of forested habitats with open areas for foraging. Most populations are migratory, particularly the "Slate-colored." Small flocks of 10–30 birds stay together through the winter, concentrated around open areas with nearby trees, where they often mix with other sparrows and finches. Spring **migration:** March–April; fall migration: October–November.

FOOD Eats mostly insects in spring and summer, and feeds insects to nestlings. The rest of the year, forages for seeds and eats small berries. ■ **feeding** One of the most common species at winter bird feeders. It prefers seeds scattered on the ground or on a platform feeder. Hulled sunflower seeds, millet, and cracked corn are good bets.

NESTING *Location:* Usually on the ground, sheltered by rocks or vegetation. *Nest:* Open cup of fine twigs, leaves, and rootlets. *Eggs:* Usually 3–5; incubated by female for 12–13 days. *Fledging:* Leaves nest at 9–13 days.

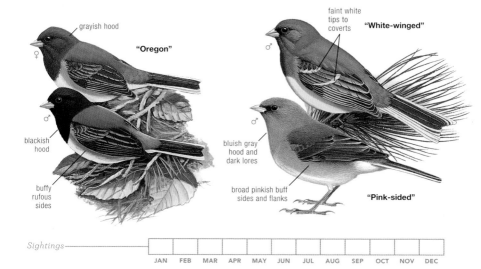

grayish hood

"Oregon"

blackish hood

buffy rufous sides

faint white tips to coverts

"White-winged"

bluish gray hood and dark lores

broad pinkish buff sides and flanks

"Pink-sided"

Sightings

JAN	FEB	MAR	APR	MAY	JUN	JUL	AUG	SEP	OCT	NOV	DEC

Cardinals, Tanagers, & Grosbeaks
Family Cardinalidae

This family of medium-size songbirds now includes all of the tanagers that breed in North America. Bright colors—reds, yellows, and blues—and bold patterns enliven the male plumage of many species, and most have heavy bills to deal with a diet of insects, seeds, and fruit.

long crest

black surrounds red bill

♂

dark bill

♀

overall buffy brown and dull red

juvenile ♂

Northern Cardinal
Cardinalis cardinalis, L 8¾" (22 cm)

The bright red male Northern Cardinal ("redbird"), with its conspicuous crest, is one of the most recognizable and popular birds in North America. Its stylish plumage has gotten it "elected" to state bird by seven states (more than any other) and enshrined as the name of numerous athletic teams. State bird of Illinois, Indiana, Kentucky, North Carolina, Ohio, Virginia, and West Virginia.

IDENTIFICATION Very common. Fairly large songbird with a pointed crest, triangular red bill, and long tail. Although sometimes secretive, the male cardinal sings from an exposed perch. The general public often mistakenly identifies any bright red bird as a cardinal, especially Westerners who grew up in the East. But with the exception of desert-dwelling cardinals in southern Arizona and New Mexico, there are *no* cardinals west of the Great Plains.

■ **plumage** **Male** is completely red, except for a small black mask and black chin. **Female** is tawny brown, tinged with red on the crest, wings, and tail. **Juvenile** resembles female, but has a blackish bill.

■ **similar species** Other prominently red birds include male Scarlet Tanager (page 204), Summer Tanager (page 205), male House Finch (page 226), and male Purple Finch (page 227), none of which has a crest. In the Southwest, Pyrruloxia (not illustrated) has a crest and some red plumage, but is grayer and has a rounded, yellow bill.

■ **voice** Loud, liquid whistling **song** with many variations, including *cheer cheer cheer* and *purty purty purty*; both sexes sing almost year-round. Common **call** is a sharp *chip*.

In spring the male Northern Cardinal is fiercely territorial. His own reflection in a window or car mirror may cause him to spend hours trying to repel the imaginary intruder.

RANGE Eastern and Midwestern species; year-round resident. Found in a variety of habitats, including woodland edges, thickets, vine tangles, backyard gardens, towns, and urban parks. Abundant in the Southeast. Locally common around desert washes, mesquite groves, and riparian woodlands in the Southwest. Cardinals generally expanded their range to the north in the 20th century.

A baby Northern Cardinal may leave its nest before being able to fly adequately.

FOOD Varied diet consists mostly of insects in spring and summer, but also includes fruit, berries, leaf buds, flowers, and the seeds of weeds and grasses; feeds insects to nestlings. In winter, forages mainly for seeds and small berries.

■ **feeding** Very common at all types of feeders, but prefers seeds scattered on the ground, especially sunflower seeds, safflower seeds, and cracked corn. Fruiting trees and shrubs offer both food and nesting locations. A frequent victim of free-roaming cats.

NESTING *Location:* Hidden in a dense shrub or low tree, usually 3–10 feet up. *Nest:* Open cup of twigs, grasses, and bark strips. *Eggs:* Usually 3–4; incubated by female for 12–13 days. *Fledging:* Leaves nest at 9–11 days; male may care for the recently fledged young while female begins the next nesting attempt. *Broods:* 2–3 per year.

Sightings

	JAN	FEB	MAR	APR	MAY	JUN	JUL	AUG	SEP	OCT	NOV	DEC

Scarlet Tanager
Piranga olivacea, L 7" (18 cm)

The luminous red plumage of the male Scarlet Tanager seems better suited to a tropical jungle than the Eastern hardwood forests where it breeds. It does winter in the tropics, but by that time of year, the male has molted into a somber greenish plumage.

wings contrast darker to olive green back

small bill

1st spring ♂

♀

brownish

1st fall ♂

black shoulder contrasts with greenish wings

IDENTIFICATION Common. Medium-size, compact songbird with a short tail and fairly heavy, pale bill. Forages slowly in the leafy treetops where, despite the male's brilliance, it can be hard to see. Your best looks will often be in spring before the leaves have fully emerged.
■ plumage Breeding male is vivid red and black, becoming a splotchy red and green in late summer when in molt. **Fall adult male** is bright olive green above and greenish yellow below with black wings. **Female** is like the fall male, but has greenish brown wings. **Immature male** is like female, but has partially black wings.
■ similar species Female Summer Tanager (next page) is larger and has mustard to orangish yellow (not greenish) plumage, a larger bill, and paler wings and tail.
■ voice Robin-like **song**, but much

harsher, with loud, burry phrases. **Call** is a hoarse *chip-burr*.

RANGE Eastern species; summer resident. Breeds in mature deciduous forest with a high leafy canopy, often in oaks. Winters in South America. Spring **migration:** mid-April–late May; fall migration: September–mid-October.

FOOD Mostly insects, gleaned from leaves; sometimes hovers while gleaning. Small fruits and berries are important in late summer and during fall migration.

NESTING *Location:* In a tree, usually 20–50 feet up. *Nest:* Loosely woven cup of twigs, weed stems, and other plant material. *Eggs:* Usually 4; incubated by female for 13–14 days. *Fledging:* Leaves nest at 9–15 days.

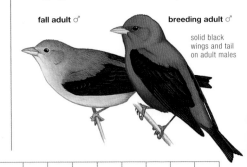

fall adult ♂

breeding adult ♂

solid black wings and tail on adult males

Summer Tanager
Piranga rubra, L 7¾" (20 cm)

Bees and wasps may seem a hazardous food source, but the Summer Tanager specializes in them. The wasp or bee is usually caught in midair.

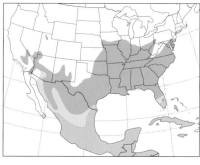

red head and patches elsewhere; greenish wings

1st spring ♂

overall rosy red

adult ♂

RANGE Widespread species; summer resident. Breeds in open deciduous woods, pine-and-oak woodlands, bottomland forests, and in the Southwest, riparian forests. Winters from central Mexico to South America. Spring **migration:** early April–early May; fall migration: late August–October.

FOOD Mostly insects in spring and summer. Small fruits and berries are part of its diet in late summer and during fall migration.

NESTING *Location:* In a tree, usually 10–35 feet up. *Nest:* Loosely woven cup. *Eggs:* Usually 4; incubated by female for 11–12 days. *Fledging:* Leaves nest at about 10 days.

IDENTIFICATION Common to uncommon. Medium-size songbird—bigger than Scarlet Tanager—with a large, pale bill. Forages sluggishly in the leafy treetops and often sits motionless, when only its loud call reveals its presence.
■ **plumage** **Adult male** entirely rosy red. **Female** mustard yellow below, darker above; some females have blurry patches of red. **First-spring male** usually has red head and scattered patches of red plumage.
■ **similar species** Female Scarlet Tanager (opposite) is smaller and has greenish plumage, a smaller bill, and wings darker than upperparts. Also compare Northern Cardinal (pages 202–203).
■ **voice** Robin-like **song** of slurred, whistled notes with short pauses. **Call** is a staccato *ki-ti-tuck.*

large bill

some females with patchy dull red

red morph ♀

overall ochre plumage

Sightings

	JAN	FEB	MAR	APR	MAY	JUN	JUL	AUG	SEP	OCT	NOV	DEC

Western Tanager
Piranga ludoviciana, L 7¼" (18 cm)

The striking black-and-yellow male Western Tanager, with its bright red head, is one of the most colorful summer species of Western pine forests. Normally a treetop species, migrating birds are often seen foraging lower down in suburban gardens and urban parks.

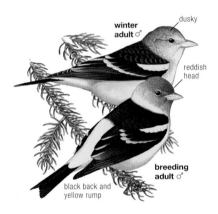

winter adult ♂

dusky

reddish head

black back and yellow rump

breeding adult ♂

■ **IDENTIFICATION** Common. Medium-size, compact songbird with a short tail and fairly heavy, pale bill. Although brightly plumaged, it can be quite inconspicuous when foraging high in the canopy.

■ **plumage** Breeding male has a red or orangish red head, but is otherwise bright yellow with black back, wings, and tail and two wing bars (front yellow, rear white). **Fall adult male** loses red on head (some are red-tinged on forehead and chin); back plumage has pale edges. **Female** is olive green to olive gray above and dull yellow below, with two whitish wing

gray back and white wing bars

larger bill than Scarlet ♀

bars. Some females look quite gray and drab, with limited yellow below.
■ **similar species** Female Bullock's (page 224) and Hooded Orioles (page 222) have longer, pointy bills and much longer tails.
■ **voice** Robin-like **song**, but much harsher, with loud, burry phrases. **Calls** include a rising *pit-er-ick.*

RANGE Western species; summer resident. Breeds in open conifer and pine-and-oak woodlands, often at high elevations. Winters sparingly in coastal southern California—mostly in residential gardens and around flowering eucalyptus—but primarily in Mexico and Central America. Spring **migration:** mid-April–early June; fall migration: mid-July–early October.

FOOD Mostly insects. Small fruits and berries are important in late summer and during fall migration.
■ **feeding** Will occasionally visit feeders for fruit.

NESTING *Location:* In a conifer, 8–60 feet up. *Nest:* Flimsy cup of twigs and weed stems. *Eggs:* Usually 4; incubated by female for 13–14 days. *Fledging:* Leaves nest at 10–11 days.

Sightings

JAN	FEB	MAR	APR	MAY	JUN	JUL	AUG	SEP	OCT	NOV	DEC

Indigo Bunting
Passerina cyanea, L 5½" (14 cm)

Seen singing from an overhead wire against a bright sky, the male Indigo Bunting looks black—only when he is lower down can his electric blue coloration be appreciated.

♀
faint blurry streaks

fall

winter adult ♂

RANGE Eastern and Midwestern species; summer resident. Breeds in brushy thickets, overgrown fields, roadsides, and shelterbelts. Spring **migration:** mid-April–early June; fall migration: mid-September–mid-October.

FOOD Mixed diet of insects, seeds, buds, and berries.
■ feeding Will occasionally visit feeders.

NESTING *Location:* In a dense shrub or sapling, 1–3 feet up. *Nest:* Neat woven cup of dried vegetation. *Eggs:* Usually 3–4; incubated by female for 12–13 days. *Fledging:* Leaves nest at 9–12 days.

IDENTIFICATION Common. Small, compact songbird with a short, triangular, pale bill. Most foraging takes place in high weeds and brushy thickets. When flushed, swishes tail from side to side.
■ plumage Breeding male is entirely blue. Winter adult male and first-spring male are patchy brown and blue. Female and immature are all brown with two faint wing bars and diffuse streaking on the underparts.
■ similar species Blue Grosbeak (not illustrated) is larger and has a heavier bill and broad cinnamon wing bars. Also see Eastern Bluebird (page 162).
■ voice Cheerful **song** is a series of sweet, variously pitched phrases, usually paired: *sweet-sweet chew-chew sweet-sweet.* **Call** is a sharp *spit*; flight call is a husky *bzzzt*.

patchy blue

1st ♂ spring

deep blue

breeding adult ♂

Sightings

	JAN	FEB	MAR	APR	MAY	JUN	JUL	AUG	SEP	OCT	NOV	DEC

Rose-breasted Grosbeak

Pheucticus ludovicianus, L 8" (20 cm)

The flashy, male Rose-breasted Grosbeak sings his slow warbling song hidden in the treetops. His song is sweetly melodic, but the call note given by both sexes—eek! like the sound of a sneaker on a gym floor—is unique and easier to learn.

 IDENTIFICATION Fairly common. Medium-large, robust songbird with a huge, pale, triangular bill. Usually forages in the leafy treetops, but sometimes visits bird feeders.

breeding adult ♂

rose red

■ **plumage** Breeding male is black and white, except for a rosy pink bib and underwings. **Winter adult male** (seen during fall migration) has brown-edged feathering on head and back. **Female** is brown above, with streaked underparts, a strong white eyebrow, and two wing bars. **First-fall male** resembles the female but is more buff, often with a few red feathers on the breast.

■ **similar species** Female Purple Finch (page 227) is much smaller and has a smaller, darker bill and no white in the wings. Compare to female and immature Black-headed Grosbeak (opposite); their ranges have some overlap.

■ **voice** Warbling **song** is a series of singsong, robin-like phrases. **Call** is a sharp squeak *eek!*

 RANGE Eastern and Midwestern species; summer resident. Breeds in deciduous and mixed woodlands and woodland edges, pastures, orchards, and suburban and rural backyards. Winters in Central America and Cuba. Spring **migration:** mid-April–early June; fall migration: late August–mid-October.

FOOD Mixed diet of insects, seeds, buds, and fruit. Feeds nestlings mostly insects. During fall migration, feeds almost entirely on fruit.

■ **feeding** Visits feeders, especially in spring. Prefers sunflower seeds.

NESTING *Location:* In a shrub or small tree, 4–20 feet up. *Nest:* Loose cup of twigs and dried vegetation. *Eggs:* Usually 4; incubated by both parents for 11–14 days *Fledging:* Leaves nest at 9–12 days.

winter adult ♂

breeding adult ♂

♀

streaked below

Sightings

JAN	FEB	MAR	APR	MAY	JUN	JUL	AUG	SEP	OCT	NOV	DEC

Black-headed Grosbeak
Pheucticus melanocephalus, L 8¼" (21 cm)

Even though male Rose-breasted and Black-headed Grosbeaks look completely different, the two species are closely related. They have almost identical songs and occasionally interbreed on the Great Plains. The females of the two species are very similar.

darker upper mandible than Rose-breasted

buffy breast; streaking largely limited to sides and flanks ♀

burnt orange

breeding adult ♂

IDENTIFICATION Common. Medium-large, robust songbird with a huge triangular bill that is dark above and pale below. In late summer and fall, forages in fruiting bushes and trees.

■ **plumage** Breeding male has a black head, black-and-white wings, and cinnamon orange underparts. **Female** is brown above, with light streaking on tawny underparts, and has a strong white eyebrow and two wing bars. **First-fall male** is rich buff below, with little or no streaking.

■ **similar species** Female Purple Finch (page 227) is smaller overall and has a smaller, darker bill and no white in the wings. Female and immature

Rose-breasted Grosbeaks (previous page) tend to have heavier streaking on whiter underparts and a paler (not two-toned) bill; first-fall male usually has some pink feathers on the breast.

■ **voice** Warbling **song** is a series of sing-song, robin-like phrases. **Call** is a sharp *pik!* (not as squeaky as Rose-breasted's).

RANGE Western and Great Plains species; summer resident. Breeds in a variety of open woodlands (oak, conifer, piñon-juniper, riparian) from lowlands to mountains, as well as in woodsy suburban and rural backyards. Winters mainly in Mexico. Spring **migration:** early April–mid-May; fall migration: mid-July–September.

FOOD Mixed diet of insects, seeds, buds, and fruit. Feeds nestlings mostly insects. During fall migration, feeds almost entirely on fruit.

■ **feeding** Visits feeders; prefers sunflower seeds.

NESTING *Location:* In a thicket or tree 6–12 feet up, often near a stream. *Nest:* Loose cup of twigs, grasses, and other dried vegetation. *Eggs:* Usually 3–4; incubated by both parents for 12–14 days. *Fledging:* Leaves nest at about 12 days.

Sightings

JAN	FEB	MAR	APR	MAY	JUN	JUL	AUG	SEP	OCT	NOV	DEC

Starlings
Family Sturnidae

Widespread Old World family of chunky, often glossy songbirds that also includes the mynas.

yellow bill

triangular wings

glossy plumage

breeding ♂

European Starling
Sturnus vulgaris, L 8½" (22 cm)

First introduced in New York's Central Park in 1890—in a misguided plan to introduce all the birds mentioned in Shakespeare's works into the United States—it spread across the continent by the late 1940s.

 IDENTIFICATION Abundant. Stocky and short-tailed songbird with a sharply pointed bill, often seen strutting about lawns and parking lots. Starlings form very large flocks in winter, often with blackbirds.

■ **plumage** **Breeding** bird is glossy black, with a yellow bill (blue-based in male; pink-based in female). **Fresh fall** bird is densely speckled with white and buff, with a black bill; by late winter, the speckles are worn off, revealing the glossy black feathering. **Juvenile** is uniformly grayish brown.

■ **similar species** Other blackish birds include the Brewer's Blackbird (page 212), Red-winged Blackbird

plumage heavily spotted with white

fresh fall

slender dark bill

short tail

(page 213), and Brown-headed (page 218) and Bronzed Cowbirds (page 219). Blackbirds have longer tails and shorter, never yellow bills.

■ **voice** Extremely varied. Elaborate, lengthy **song** with rattles, buzzes, clicks, and squealing notes. Often mimics other species. **Calls** include whistled *wheeeeoooo* and buzzy *dzeeer,* among others.

juvenile

overall grayish brown

dull, blurred streaks

RANGE Widespread, non-native species. Very common around human structures but also occupies more natural settings. Avoids dense forest and unbroken desert.

FOOD Mixed, opportunistic diet of insects, berries, and seeds.

NESTING *Location:* In a tree cavity, sheltered building crevice, or nest box. Aggressively evicts many native species from scarce nest holes. *Nest:* Untidy cup of twigs, grasses, and other dried vegetation. *Eggs:* Usually 5–7; incubated by both parents for 12–15 days. *Fledging:* Leaves nest at 20–22 days.

Sightings

JAN	FEB	MAR	APR	MAY	JUN	JUL	AUG	SEP	OCT	NOV	DEC

HOW DO BIRDS CHANGE COLOR?

Most birds that are year-round residents in North America look the same all year, although their plumage may be slightly duller or brighter in different seasons. But there are two very common and familiar exceptions to this rule: the European Starling (opposite) and the American Goldfinch (pages 230–231). Their colors and patterns change dramatically when they molt, and the changes come about in two different ways.

WORN FEATHERS

In early fall, the starling has spotted coloration. Its fresh black feathers have pale tips that contrast brightly against the dark background color of the plumage. By the time spring arrives, the bird's entire appearance has changed. It is all dark, even subtly iridescent, and the spots are gone. It has not grown new dark feathers, though. Rather, the pale tips have *worn off* during the winter, exposing the glossy black plumage.

NEW FEATHERS

The goldfinch's appearance, on the other hand, changes because it *molts* a new set of body feathers in both the fall and spring. The brilliant yellow body and black forehead are lost in autumn and replaced with drab grayish and brownish—with yellow confined to the male's shoulder.

In the early spring, the male's bright yellow feathers gradually grow in. The black crown patch returns, too.

This spring plumage is the "breeding" plumage, a product of improved seasonal diet and greater hormonal activity. Chemicals ingested by the goldfinch in its food are transformed physiologically into the bright yellow pigment. A male's brilliance signals to the female that he is fit to breed. After the breeding season is over, the twice-annual molt cycle resumes, and the dull hues return.

This male American Goldfinch, seen in April, is molting into breeding plumage. The remaining brown body feathers will soon be replaced with bright yellow ones and the cap will become solidly black.

Blackbirds, Grackles, & Orioles
Family Icteridae
Large New World family of medium-to-large songbirds with sharply pointed bills. Plumage varies from all black to brilliant yellows and oranges.

males have yellow eyes

dark eye

♂

glossy

♀

grayish brown

wings uniformly dark

immature ♂

Brewer's Blackbird
Euphagus cyanocephalus, L 9" (23 cm)

Historically, Brewer's Blackbird was more of a Western species, but over the past hundred years, it has pioneered new breeding territory to the northeast.

IDENTIFICATION Very common. A slim blackbird that forages on the ground, walking with an alert, upright stance or probing the soil with its tail elevated. Occurs in a large winter flock with other species, such as cowbirds and Red-winged Blackbirds. Eyes are bright yellow in male, dark in female.

■ **plumage** **Male** is black, with strong purple iridescence on the head and greenish iridescence on the body. **Female** is a dull, brownish gray. **Immature male** sometimes has buff feather tips.

■ **similar species** Common Grackle (page 216) is larger and has a much longer tail; smaller Brown-headed Cowbird (page 218) has smaller, thicker bill and shorter tail; and female Red-winged Blackbird (opposite) is streaked. Similar Rusty Blackbird (not illustrated), in the East in fresh plumage, has a strong face pattern and feathers tipped broadly with rust.

■ **voice** **Song** is a wheezy, unmusical *quee-ee* or *k-seee*. Typical **call** is a harsh *check*.

RANGE Mostly Western species. Inhabits a wide variety of open habitats, from city sidewalks and suburban lawns to open woodlands and mountain meadows. In winter, large flocks congregate around agricultural operations. **Migration** is poorly understood, and wintering groups are somewhat nomadic.

FOOD Insects, seeds, and berries; more insects in summer, more seeds and grains in winter.
■ **feeding** Will visit feeders.

NESTING *Location:* Usually in a tree, from 20 to 40 feet up. *Nest:* Bulky cup of twigs, grasses, and other dried vegetation. *Eggs:* Usually 4–6; incubated by female for 12–14 days. *Fledging:* Leaves nest at 13–14 days.

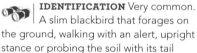

Sightings

	JAN	FEB	MAR	APR	MAY	JUN	JUL	AUG	SEP	OCT	NOV	DEC

Red-winged Blackbird

Agelaius phoeniceus, L 8¾" (22 cm)

In northern areas, the male Red-winged Blackbird's song—konk-la-ree—signals the end of winter, even if the marsh he's staking claim to is just starting to thaw.

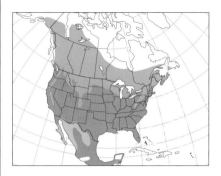

IDENTIFICATION Common to abundant. A stocky, short-tailed blackbird that forages on the ground, sometimes in immense winter flocks. The male's red shoulders are striking when he's singing and displaying, but largely hidden otherwise.

■ **plumage** Male is glossy black, with red shoulder patches broadly tipped in golden yellow. **Female** is dark brown above, heavily streaked below, and often orangish on face and throat. **First-year male**'s body is heavily scalloped with warm brown.

■ **similar species** Male Tricolored Blackbird (not illustrated) of California has a white border to the red shoulder patch; female has a blackish belly. Juvenile Brown-headed Cowbird (page 218) is smaller, with a thicker bill.

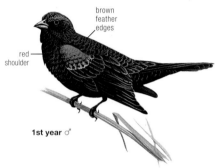

brown feather edges

red shoulder

1st year ♂

■ **voice** **Song** is a liquid, gurgling *konk-la-ree*, ending in a trill. **Call** is a flat *chack*.

RANGE Widespread species. In winter, large flocks (often including grackles, cowbirds, and starlings) sometimes roost in suburban neighborhoods. Spring **migration:** early February–early April; fall migration: September–November.

FOOD Insects, seeds, and berries, mostly grain in winter.
■ **feeding** Will visit feeders.

NESTING Semicolonial. *Location:* Usually woven into marsh vegetation, from 3 to 15 feet up. *Nest:* Open cup of grass and reeds. *Eggs:* Usually 3–4; incubated by female for 11–13 days. *Fledging:* Leaves nest at 11–14 days.

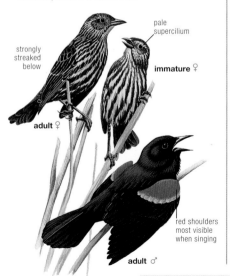

pale supercilium

strongly streaked below

immature ♀

adult ♀

red shoulders most visible when singing

adult ♂

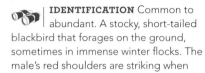

Sightings

JAN	FEB	MAR	APR	MAY	JUN	JUL	AUG	SEP	OCT	NOV	DEC

Great-tailed Grackle

Quiscalus mexicanus, L male 18" (46 cm);
female 15" (38 cm)

*Twenty years ago, the Great-tailed
Grackle was rare over most of California,
but now it's common in the southern
half of the state. The species continues
to spread north and west, thanks to
urbanization and irrigation.*

juvenile

long
bill

flat crown
and pale eye

♀

purple
gloss

♂

shorter
tail

very long, keel-
shaped tail

Grackle (not illustrated) overlaps
with Great-tailed on the
Texas-Louisiana coast;
Boat-taileds there have
dark eyes.

■ **voice Song** is a loud series of
whistles, trills, fast ratchet-like
clacks, and other weird sounds.
Most common **call** is a low-pitched
chuck.

RANGE Widespread spe-
cies. Inhabits farmlands,
prairies, wetlands; also common
in developed areas. **Migration** is not well
understood; northern breeders usually
move south for winter.

IDENTIFICATION Common to
abundant. A large grackle with a
very long, keel-shaped tail and piercing
yellow eyes. Flocks often gather in town
centers and city parks well after dark, pro-
claiming their presence with a cacophony
of sound.
■ **plumage Male** is glossy black. **Female**
is smaller and shorter tailed than male;
dark brown above and cinnamon buff
below. **Juvenile** has dark eyes and shows
diffuse streaking below.
■ **similar species** Common Grackle
(pages 216–217) is much smaller, with a
shorter tail and shorter, thicker bill; gloss on
head contrasts with body. Similar Boat-tailed

FOOD Omnivorous. Diet includes
insects, small animals, bird eggs,
plant matter, and human refuse.
■ **feeding** Will visit feeders, whether or
not you want them. Considered a crop
pest in some areas and a nuisance bird by
many urbanites.

NESTING Colonial. *Location:*
In dense shrubs, a low tree, or
marsh vegetation (especially in West),
usually 2–20 feet up. *Nest:* Bulky, woven
cup of grass and reeds. *Eggs:* Usually
3–4; incubated by female for 13–14 days.
Fledging: Leaves nest at 12–15 days.

Sightings

JAN	FEB	MAR	APR	MAY	JUN	JUL	AUG	SEP	OCT	NOV	DEC

WHY DO SOME BIRDS FLOCK TOGETHER?

Flocks of birds are a common sight. Many flocks are small feeding aggregations of the same species or mixed species, but large flocks in the hundreds are not uncommon, and spectacular flocks of hundreds of thousands can occur in winter and during migration.

■Feeding Flocks Although competition for food can be intense within a feeding flock, the benefits must outweigh the disadvantages. Having more individuals searching for food increases the chances of locating a rich food source that all can share. In open areas, large blackbird flocks often feed in an organized way, birds in the rear leapfrogging to the front and thereby alternating time at that prime feeding location.

■Safety in Numbers Probably the greatest benefit of flocking is the increased number of watchful eyes and ears, on the lookout for any danger. In large blackbird flocks, adults allow younger birds to flock with them, but the dominant adults are usually found near the safer center of the flock. The young birds at the vulnerable edges benefit from the adults' greater experience at finding food, but also help to protect the center of the flock. If a predator, such as a hawk, is sighted, members of a flock often choose to harass it rather than flee. Many predators hunt by stealth and can be repelled by mobbing groups of smaller birds. When a hunting falcon or hawk deliberately pursues a flock, birds such as sandpipers, pigeons, and starlings fly together in tight groups that change direction in unison, thereby confusing a predator that relies on pursuing an individual bird.

In fall and winter, large roaming flocks of blackbirds are a common sight in rural areas, where they forage in fields during the day and gather at dusk to roost in groves of trees.

Common Grackle
Quiscalus quiscula, L 12½" (32 cm)

Up close, the Common Grackle is a stunning species whose plumage shimmers with iridescent blue, purple, and bronze tones, set off by striking yellow eyes and a long, flared tail. However, it causes extensive crop damage, gathers in huge, noisome, winter flocks, and is therefore often officially "controlled" (killed) in large numbers.

IDENTIFICATION Abundant. A medium-size grackle with a long, graduated tail, yellow eyes, and a heavy bill. The male holds his tail in a deeply keeled shape—the central tail feathers lowered and the outer ones raised and flared—during the breeding season and engages in other ritualized display postures related to courtship (see photographs). This grackle is a familiar sight in many Eastern backyards, striding across the lawn looking for an insect meal or singing its loud creaking song from the treetops, often in groups and sometimes

This is the "head-down" display given by the male to the female both before and after copulation.

The "bill-up" display is a threat given in response to the approach of another male.

well after dark. There are two basic plumage types with different glossy coloration in the male: the "Purple Grackle" is found in the Southeast and north along the coast to southern New England; the "Bronzed Grackle" occupies the rest of the range (mainly north and west of the Appalachians). From a distance, both types look plain black.

■ **plumage** Male "Bronzed Grackle" has a bronze-tinted body and wings that contrast with its blue head. **Male "Purple Grackle"** has a purplish body and head, with a green-glossed back (in Florida) or a more variegated, purple-green back (farther north). **Female** of both types is smaller, browner (less glossy), and shorter tailed than male. **Juvenile** is plain brown with dark eyes and faintly streaked breast.

■**similar species** Brewer's Blackbird (page 212) has a shorter, unflared tail and smaller bill. Great-tailed Grackle (page 214) is much larger, with a longer bill, more striking tail, and uniform, purple gloss—not with different gloss colors on head and body as seen in "Bronzed Grackles." Boat-tailed Grackle (not illustrated), of the Atlantic and Gulf coasts, is larger (almost Great-tailed size) and has a longer, more keel-shaped tail and longer bill.

■**voice Song** is a short, creaky *readle-eak*. **Call** is a loud, deep *chuck*.

RANGE Eastern and Midwestern species. Inhabits fields with scattered trees, open woodlands, farmlands, and marshes; also common in developed areas, suburban yards, towns, and cities. Range is slowly expanding northward and westward. In the East, although still common, numbers have significantly decreased in the past 30 years. Northern "Bronzed Grackle" breeders move south for the winter. In winter, birds gather in large flocks that often seek out conifer stands for a night roost. Spring **migration:** mid-February–April; fall migration: late September–early November.

FOOD Omnivorous and opportunistic. Diet is mostly insects and some grain when breeding; otherwise, mainly grain (waste corn is a favorite),

The "song spread" display is a ritualized posture often seen early in the breeding season.

seeds (especially acorns), and some fruit and scavenged garbage. Usually forages in flocks when not breeding.

■**feeding** Will visit feeders, whether or not you want them.

NESTING Semicolonial; typically nests in small colonies of 10–50 pairs, sometimes more. *Location:* Often in a conifer, usually 3–20 feet up. *Nest:* Bulky cup of twigs and grass. *Eggs:* Usually 3–4; incubated by female for 12–15 days. *Fledging:* Leaves nest at 12–15 days.

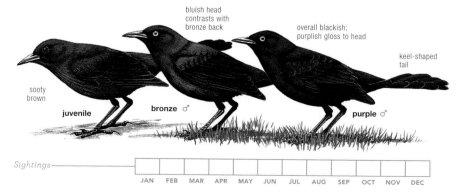

bluish head contrasts with bronze back

overall blackish; purplish gloss to head

keel-shaped tail

sooty brown

juvenile

bronze ♂

purple ♂

Sightings

JAN	FEB	MAR	APR	MAY	JUN	JUL	AUG	SEP	OCT	NOV	DEC

Brown-headed Cowbird

Molothrus ater, L 7½" (19 cm)

This pariah of the bird world is a brood parasite—it lays its eggs in other birds' nests to be raised by the hosts. Once a more restricted species, our fragmented agricultural and suburban landscapes have allowed it to spread across the continent. Its impact on many nesting songbirds can be substantial—a single female may lay 40 eggs per season.

juvenile

juvenile streaked
below, scaly above

♀

♂

brown
head

IDENTIFICATION Common to abundant. This small, compact blackbird—about the size of a large sparrow—has a stout, sharp-tipped bill and a short tail. It usually feeds on the ground, typically walking around with its tail cocked up. In spring, the male conspicuously displays to and chases females; after mating, the female lurks at the forest's edge looking for nests to host her eggs.
■ **plumage** Male is black with a greenish gloss and dark brown hood. **Female** is grayish brown above, paler below. **Juvenile** is paler than female, with pale scalloping on upperparts and lightly streaked below; molting males have patches of black plumage.
■ **similar species** Larger Bronzed Cowbird (opposite) has red eyes (adults) and a much heavier bill. Female House Finch (page 226) and female Red-winged

Blackbird (page 213) are similar to juvenile.
■ **voice** Male's **song** is a squeaky gurgling. **Calls** include a harsh rattle and squeaky whistles.

RANGE Widespread species. Inhabits open grassland with scattered trees, including woodland edges, fields, pastures, and residential areas; avoids unbroken forest. In winter, joins large flocks of starlings and other blackbirds. Northern breeders move south for winter. Spring **migration:** mid-March–mid-April; fall migration: August–October.

FOOD Seeds, grain, and some insects.
■ **feeding** Will visit feeders. If cowbirds visit your feeders in spring and summer, consider taking them down rather than aiding this species.

NESTING No nest and no parental care. Brood parasite of many different species—including warblers, vireos, flycatchers, and sparrows—which raise the cowbird's young. Usually 1 egg is laid in a nest and incubation takes 11–12 days. The young cowbird develops very rapidly, leaving the nest at about 10 days and fed by the host parent for an additional 2 weeks.

Sightings

| JAN | FEB | MAR | APR | MAY | JUN | JUL | AUG | SEP | OCT | NOV | DEC |

Bronzed Cowbird
Molothrus aeneus, L 8¾" (22 cm)

*Like its close relative, the better known
Brown-headed Cowbird, the Bronzed
Cowbird is a brood parasite, laying its
eggs in other birds' nests.*

southwestern ♀

grayish
overall

dark overall,
less glossy
than male

Texas ♀

 IDENTIFICATION Common.
Medium-size but heavyset blackbird, about the size of a Red-winged
Blackbird. Has a thick-based bill, a thick
neck ruff (male only), and red eyes. In
spring, the male's bizarre courtship display includes strutting and bowing with
his neck ruff expanded, interspersed with
hovering flights above the female's head.
■ **plumage** Male is black with a bronzy
gloss, becoming strongly blue-glossed on
wings and tail. **Female** is brownish black
(in Texas) or grayish (farther west); plumage is not glossy. **Juvenile** is dark brown
(in Texas) to grayish and lightly streaked
(farther west) and has dark eyes.
■ **similar species** Smaller Brown-headed
Cowbird (opposite) has dark eyes and a
shorter, smaller bill. Female Brewer's
Blackbird (page 212) is darker brown
and has dark eyes and a thinner, more
pointed bill.
■ **voice** Male's **song** is a series of odd,
squeaky gurgles. **Call** is a rasping *chuck*.

RANGE South Texas and southwestern species. Inhabits open

woodlands and suburban lawns. In winter, joins large flocks of other blackbirds
around feedlots. **Migration** is not well
known: there are spring movements in
Texas in March, with southbound movements in September. Some winter in
southern Louisiana and, increasingly,
in Florida.

FOOD Seeds, grain, and
some insects.
■ **feeding** Will visit feeders.

NESTING No nest and no parental care. Brood parasite of many
different species—including jays, cardinals, sparrows, and orioles—which raise
the cowbird's young. Usually 1 egg is laid
in a nest and incubation takes 10–13 days.

dark
eye
dark
brown

red eye

**southwestern
juvenile**

thick
bill

glossy
plumage

southwestern ♂

Eastern Meadowlark
Sturnella magna, L 9½" (24 cm)

In spring, the male Eastern Meadowlark defends his few acres of meadow by singing from a conspicuous fence post or roadside bush. What to our ears is a sweetly melodic song is serious business for the meadowlark. Any trespassing males are vigorously pursued until beyond his territorial borders; intruders that resist may be physically attacked.

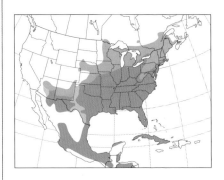

 IDENTIFICATION Common, but decreasing in the East due to habitat loss. A robin-size, chunky songbird with a short tail and long, pointed bill. White tail feathers are seen when a bird takes flight. Foraging is done on the ground, and flocks of meadowlarks often gather together in fall and winter.
■ **plumage** Black V-shaped breast band on bright yellow underparts; upperparts are cryptically patterned. Head has bold stripes. **"Lilian's Meadowlark,"** a Southwestern desert-grasslands subspecies, is much paler above and has more white in the tail. **Juvenile** has streaks on the breast.
■ **similar species** Yellow of throat on Eastern does not extend up onto the face as in Western Meadowlark (opposite).
■ **voice Song** is a clear, whistled *see-you see-yeereoo;* sings in winter. Distinctive **call** is a high, buzzy *drzzt,* given as a rapid chatter in flight.

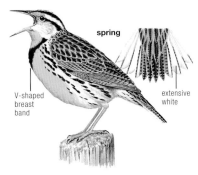

spring

V-shaped breast band

extensive white

RANGE Eastern and Southwestern species. Inhabits native grasslands, old pastures, roadsides, and other open areas. Northern breeders move south for winter. Spring **migration:** March–April; fall migration: mostly in October.

FOOD Insects, especially grasshoppers and crickets, in summer; mostly weed seeds and grain in fall and winter.

NESTING *Location:* On the ground, in dense grass. *Nest:* Cup of grass with a domed roof woven into surrounding grass and a large side entrance. *Eggs:* Usually 3–5; incubated by female for 13–15 days. *Fledging:* Leaves nest at 11–12 days, when able to run, but not fly.

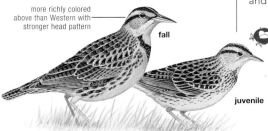

more richly colored above than Western with stronger head pattern

fall

juvenile

Sightings

	JAN	FEB	MAR	APR	MAY	JUN	JUL	AUG	SEP	OCT	NOV	DEC

Western Meadowlark
Sturnella neglecta, L 9½" (24 cm)

An emblematic bird of the wide-open Western landscape. In the Great Plains and upper Midwest, its range overlaps that of the Eastern Meadowlark. Even though the two species look very similar, they sing different songs and rarely interbreed. State bird of Kansas, Montana, Nebraska, North Dakota, Oregon, and Wyoming.

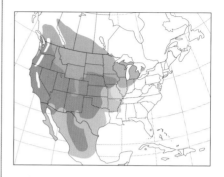

IDENTIFICATION Common. A robin-size, chunky songbird with a short tail and long, pointed bill. Behavior and structure very similar to Eastern Meadowlark.
■ **plumage** Black V-shaped breast band on bright yellow underparts; upperparts are cryptically patterned. Head with bold stripes; yellow of throat extends higher up onto the face than in Eastern Meadowlark. **Juvenile** has streaks on the breast.
■ **similar species** Eastern Meadowlark (opposite) has a diagnostically different song and call. Eastern (except "Lilian's") also has darker upperparts, less yellow in the face, paler cheeks, and more white in the tail (especially "Lilian's Meadowlark"); Western looks shorter legged, favors more sparsely vegetated fields, and flies with less rapid wing beats.
■ **voice** Long, melodious **song** starts off with several clear whistles and ends with complex gurgling and bubbling notes. **Call** is a blackbird-like *chuck*.

RANGE Western and Midwestern species. Inhabits dry rangelands, native grasslands, roadsides, large pastures, desert grasslands, and, in winter, other open areas such as croplands, feedlots, large lawns, and golf courses. Northern breeders move south for winter. Spring **migration:** March–April; fall migration: September–October.

FOOD Insects, especially grasshoppers and crickets, in summer; mostly weed seeds and grain in fall and winter.

NESTING *Location:* On the ground, in tall grass. *Nest:* Cup of grass with a domed roof woven into surrounding grass and a tunnel side entrance. *Eggs:* Usually 3–5; incubated by female for 13–15 days. *Fledging:* Leaves nest at 10–12 days, when able to run but not fly.

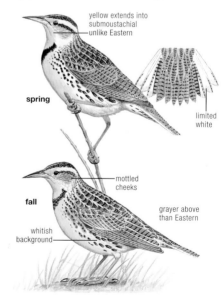

yellow extends into submoustachial unlike Eastern

spring

limited white

mottled cheeks

fall

grayer above than Eastern

whitish background

Sightings

	JAN	FEB	MAR	APR	MAY	JUN	JUL	AUG	SEP	OCT	NOV	DEC

Hooded Oriole
Icterus cucullatus, L 8″ (20 cm)

This striking oriole has benefited from the extensive planting of fan palms—a favorite nest location—in residential and urban areas of California and the Southwest.

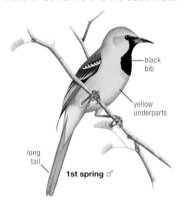

black bib

yellow underparts

long tail

1st spring ♂

migration: mid-March–April; fall migration: early August–mid-September.

FOOD Insects, spiders, fruits, and nectar from flowering trees.
■ **feeding** Often visits hummingbird feeders and takes offerings of cut fruit.

NESTING *Location:* In a shade tree, palm, or shrub, 10–45 feet up. *Nest:* Suspended cup deftly woven of grasses and plant fibers, entered from the top. *Eggs:* Usually 4; incubated by female for about 13 days. *Fledging:* Leaves nest at about 14 days.

IDENTIFICATION Common. A slender, long-tailed oriole with a relatively thin, noticeably downcurved bill with a bluish base.
■ **plumage** **Adult male** is deep yellow (orange in Texas) with a black face and throat. **Female** is olive above, yellowish below (orange tinted in Texas). **First-spring male** has a black face and throat.
■ **similar species** Stockier female Bullock's Oriole (page 224) has a grayish-white belly and straighter bill. Orchard Oriole (opposite) is smaller with a shorter bill.
■ **voice** **Song** is a rapid series of jumbled whistles and short chatters. **Calls** include a rising, whistled *wheet* (loud and strident in males) and rapid chattering.

RANGE Primarily Western species; summer resident. Commonly nests in ornamental fan palms and shade trees around suburban yards. Winters in Mexico and Belize. Spring

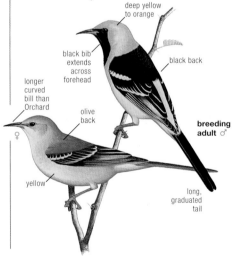

deep yellow to orange

black bib extends across forehead

black back

longer curved bill than Orchard

olive back

♀

yellow

breeding adult ♂

long, graduated tail

Sightings

JAN	FEB	MAR	APR	MAY	JUN	JUL	AUG	SEP	OCT	NOV	DEC

Orchard Oriole

Icterus spurius, L 7¼" (18 cm)

*The Orchard Oriole is North America's
smallest oriole. Seen flitting through
the shrubbery or gleaning insects in the
treetops, an olive-and-yellow female can
be reminiscent of a warbler.*

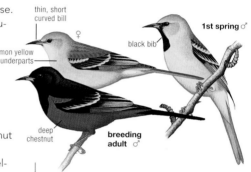

thin, short
curved bill

♀

lemon yellow
underparts

black bib

1st spring ♂

deep
chestnut

breeding
adult ♂

IDENTIFICATION Fairly common. A small oriole—much
smaller than a Baltimore Oriole—with
a relatively short tail and a thin, pick-
like, downcurved bill with a bluish base.
Actively forages in shrubs and deciduous trees, gleaning insects and
sometimes probing flowers for
nectar; often flicks its tail side-
ways. Is loosely territorial; in ideal
habitat, several pairs may nest in the
same tree.

■ **plumage** **Adult male** has a black
hood and upperparts, with rich chestnut
underparts (can look all dark in poor
light). **Female** is olive green above, yellow below with two crisp white wing bars.
First-spring male has a neat black bib and
lores, but otherwise resembles female;
sings like an adult male.

■ **similar species** Larger, stockier female
Baltimore Oriole (page 225) has orangish
underparts and a longer, heavier bill. All
vireos and warblers are smaller and have
shorter tails. Hooded Oriole (opposite) is
larger with a longer bill.

■ **voice** **Song** is a short series of musical
whistles with raspy notes, down-slurred
at the end. **Calls** include a blackbird-like
chuck and rapid chattering.

RANGE Eastern and Midwestern species; summer resident.
Favors forest edges and shade trees in
suburbs, farms, and shelterbelts. Winters
from Mexico to northern South America.
Spring **migration:** late March–mid-May;

fall migration: mid-July–early September.
Adult males are gone by early August.

FOOD Insects, spiders, fruits,
and nectar. All ages shift to a
fruit-based diet by the end of July, prior
to migration. Usually forages lower than
Baltimore Orioles and Bullock's Orioles.
■ **feeding** Occasionally visits hummingbird feeders and takes offerings of cut fruit.

NESTING *Location:* On the outer
branches of a tree, 10–50 feet up;
sometimes in loose colonies. *Nest:* Hanging cup about 4 inches long, attached to
a forked branch and woven of grasses
and long plant fibers; entered from the
top. *Eggs:* Usually 4–6; incubated by
female for 12–14 days. *Fledging:* Leaves
nest at 11–14 days.

Sightings

JAN	FEB	MAR	APR	MAY	JUN	JUL	AUG	SEP	OCT	NOV	DEC

Bullock's Oriole
Icterus bullockii, L 8¼" (21 cm)

The striking adult male Bullock's Oriole looks obviously different from its Eastern counterpart, the Baltimore Oriole, but from 1973 to 1995, the two species were considered the same species, called the "Northern Oriole." Their ranges overlap in a narrow corridor on the Great Plains, where they interbreed.

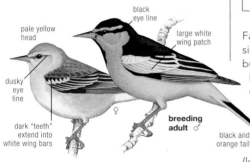

black eye line

pale yellow head

large white wing patch

dusky eye line

dark "teeth" extend into white wing bars

♀

breeding adult ♂

black and orange tail

Fall immature Baltimore Oriole (opposite) can look very similar to Bullock's, but is orangish (never lemon yellow) and lacks the dusky eye line, and its white upper wing bar is smooth and broad (not serrated).

■ **voice** Song is a mix of whistles and harsher notes. **Calls** include a harsh *cheh* and dry chattering (lower and slower than Hooded's).

IDENTIFICATION Common. The widespread "orange oriole" of the West. Stocky, with a relatively short tail and straight, pointed bill. Actively forages from low in shrubs to high in leafy treetops.
■ **plumage** Adult male is orange with a black eye line, crown, and chin stripe; black wings with a large white patch. **Female** and **immature** birds have a gray back, grayish white belly, and dull lemon yellow head, breast, and tail. Both show some trace of a dark eye line; upper wing bar has serrated ("toothed") pattern. **First-spring male** has a black chin and eye line; more orange than female.
■ **similar species** Female Hooded Oriole (page 222) is more slender, has a thinner, downcurved bill and longer tail, and is olive above and completely yellowish below.

black lores and chin

1st ♂ spring

RANGE Western species; mostly summer resident. Breeds in open woodland and where shade trees grow. Winters primarily in Mexico, with a few in coastal southern California. Spring **migration:** mid-March–early May; fall migration: mid-July–mid-September.

FOOD Insects, spiders, fruits, and nectar.
■ **feeding** Visits hummingbird feeders and takes offerings of cut fruit or jelly.

NESTING *Location:* In a tree or shrub, usually 10–20 feet up. *Nest:* Hanging pouch about 4–5 inches long, suspended from a forked branch and woven of long plant fibers; entered from the top. *Eggs:* Usually 4–5; incubated by female for 11–14 days. *Fledging:* Leaves nest at about 14 days.

Sightings

JAN	FEB	MAR	APR	MAY	JUN	JUL	AUG	SEP	OCT	NOV	DEC

Baltimore Oriole
Icterus galbula, L 8¼" (21 cm)

This "meteor of birds," as Emily Dickinson described the stunning male Baltimore Oriole, breeds throughout much of the East. State bird of Maryland.

no eye line

fall immature

smooth wing bar

IDENTIFICATION Common. The "orange oriole" of the East. Stocky, with a relatively short tail and straight, pointed bill. Actively forages high in the canopy.
■ plumage Adult male is bright orange with a black hood and back; orange shoulder bar. **Adult female** is pale orange below and has two white wing bars and a dull orange tail; some have an almost solidly dark hood and back (like male), but most have dusky orange to olive faces and backs. Most **immature females** are dull and have gray on their belly.
■ similar species Female Orchard Oriole (page 223) is much smaller and more slender, greenish above and completely yellow below. See Bullock's Oriole (opposite) for differences between fall immature birds.
■ voice Song is a sweet, flutelike series of notes. **Calls** include a rich *hew-li* and a series of rattles.

RANGE Eastern species; mostly summer resident. Breeds in deciduous woodlands and where shade trees grow, including residential areas. Winters primarily in Central and South America, with small numbers in the Southeast. Spring **migration:** early April–late May; fall migration: late August–early October.

FOOD Insects, berries, and nectar.
■ feeding Visits hummingbird feeders and takes offerings of cut fruit and jelly.

NESTING *Location:* In a tall tree, near the end of a drooping branch, usually 20–30 feet up. *Nest:* Hanging pouch about 4–6 inches long, suspended from a forked branch and woven of long plant fibers; entered from the top. *Eggs:* Usually 4–5; incubated by female for 12–14 days. *Fledging:* Leaves nest at 12–14 days.

spring adult ♀

black hood

maximum black

black and orange tail

1st ♀
spring

Sightings

JAN	FEB	MAR	APR	MAY	JUN	JUL	AUG	SEP	OCT	NOV	DEC

Finches
Family Fringillidae

Large, worldwide family of seed-eating birds. Many North American species nest in the North. In fall, flocks of "winter finches" may roam far to the south, but how far and how many birds vary from year to year.

orangish variant ♂

curved culmen

muted brown back

very indistinct face pattern ♀

House Finch
Carpodacus mexicanus, L 6" (15 cm)

Originally a bird of the West, House Finches spread throughout the East after caged birds were released on Long Island in 1940—about 50 years later, eastern birds met western birds on the Great Plains.

IDENTIFICATION Very common. A sparrow-size finch with a stubby bill, slightly curved on top. Some males are yellow or orange, a dietary deficiency.
■ **plumage** Male has red forehead, eyebrow, throat, breast, and rump, with long, brownish streaks on underparts. **Female** and **juvenile** are grayish brown, with a plain face and heavy streaking below.
■ **similar species** Purple Finch (opposite) has a shorter, notched tail and larger (not arched) bill; male Purple has less streaking below; female Purple has a strongly patterned face.

■ **voice** **Song** is a lively warble of three-note phrases, usually ending in a nasal *wheer*. **Call** is a whistled *wheat*.

RANGE Widespread species; year-round resident. Mainly found around people, also in native habitats.

FOOD Seeds, buds, and fruit. Buds of trees are important in spring; fruits in fall and winter.
■ **feeding** Very common feeder visitor.

NESTING *Location:* Often on a building, usually 5–7 feet up. *Nest:* Open cup of grass. *Eggs:* Usually 4–5; incubated by female for 13–14 days. *Fledging:* Leaves nest at 12–15 days.
■ **housing** Will use a nest box or nesting platform, or sometimes a hanging planter.

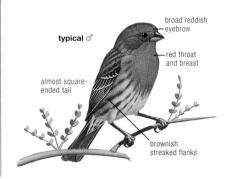

broad reddish eyebrow

typical ♂

red throat and breast

almost square-ended tail

brownish streaked flanks

Sightings

JAN	FEB	MAR	APR	MAY	JUN	JUL	AUG	SEP	OCT	NOV	DEC

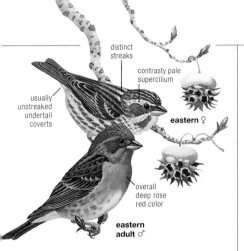

distinct streaks

contrasty pale supercilium

usually unstreaked undertail coverts

eastern ♀

overall deep rose red color

eastern adult ♂

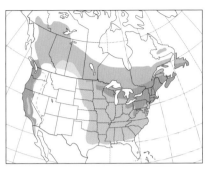

Purple Finch
Carpodacus purpureus, L 6" (15 cm)

The male Purple Finch is raspberry red, not purple. In winter, it ranges irregularly south throughout much of the eastern United States and moves to lower elevations in the West. State bird of New Hampshire.

 IDENTIFICATION Fairly common. About the size of a House Finch, but chunkier, with a larger head. Forages in trees and shrubs.
■ **plumage** Adult male is raspberry red on head, breast, and rump; its back and wings are tinged pinkish. **Female** and **juvenile** are brown and white, with a strongly patterned head and boldly streaked underparts. Western birds are buffier and diffusely streaked below.
■ **similar species** See House Finch (opposite) for differences. Cassin's Finch (next page), of the West, has a longer, straighter bill, longer wings, and streaked undertail coverts. Male Cassin's is brightest red on crown; female Cassin's has finer, sharper streaking below.
■ **voice** Song is a rich, continuous warble (shorter in the West). **Calls** include a musical *chur-lee* and a sharp *pit*.

 RANGE Widespread species. Favors moist coniferous forests

(East) or oak-and-conifer woodlands and riparian areas (West). Spring **migration:** February–May; fall migration: September–December.

 FOOD Seeds, buds, fruit; some insects.
■ **feeding** Feeder visitor, preferring black-oil sunflower seeds. Also feeds in berry-producing trees.

NESTING *Location:* In a tree, usually 15–20 feet up. *Nest:* Compact cup of twigs. *Eggs:* Usually 3–5; incubated mostly by female for 12–13 days. *Fledging:* Leaves nest at 13–16 days.

Pacific coast ♀

less obvious streaks than eastern

overall brownish tint

notched tail

Pacific coast adult ♂

Sightings

| JAN | FEB | MAR | APR | MAY | JUN | JUL | AUG | SEP | OCT | NOV | DEC |

Cassin's Finch
Carpodacus cassinii, L 6¼" (16 cm)

If you live in the Rockies, Cascades, or Sierra Nevada and have yellow pines, firs, or quaking aspens as your backyard scenery, then Cassin's Finches are probably your avian neighbors.

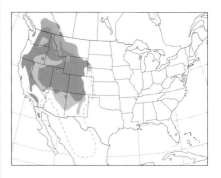

 IDENTIFICATION Fairly common. Slightly larger than either Purple or House Finch, with trimmer, more angular features, a longer and more sharply pointed bill, and longer wings.
■ **plumage** Streaked undertail coverts, wings, and back with whitish edges and streaks ("frosty"). **Adult male** has a red cap, brown moustachial stripe, and pink wash on breast and rump. **Female** and **juvenile** are brown and white, with a lightly patterned head and underparts with fine, crisp streaking.
■ **similar species** House Finch (page 226) has a shorter bill with a curved culmen and shorter wings. Male House Finch has a well-defined red bib and eyebrow; female House has heavily streaked underparts and is browner overall. Purple Finch (previous page) has a shorter, slightly more curved bill, shorter wings, and unstreaked undertail coverts. Male Purple Finch is more extensively washed with red (male Cassin's is brightest red on crown); female Purple has a more patterned face and coarser, blurry streaking below,
■ **voice** Song is a rich, continuous warble, more complex than that of a Western Purple Finch or House Finch. **Calls** include a dry *kee-up* or *tee-dee-yip*, given in flight.

RANGE Western species. Breeds in open coniferous forest in Western mountain ranges. Movements are unpredictable, but in some years, birds are seen in nearby lowlands, especially in spring. Like other "winter finch" species, winter numbers vary from year to year.

FOOD Seeds, buds, and berries, plus some insects. Craves salt, and visits areas with mineral-rich soil.
■ **feeding** Feeder visitor, mostly in winter. Prefers black-oil sunflower seeds.

NESTING Semicolonial; defends only a 15- to 75-foot territory around its nest. *Location:* Often in a large conifer, usually 30–40 feet up. *Nest:* Loose cup of twigs, weeds, and other dried vegetation. *Eggs:* Usually 4–5; incubated by female for 12–14 days. *Fledging:* Leaves nest at about 14 days.

adult ♀

distinct streaks

thick malar streak

crimson red crown

long bill with straight culmen

pale pink

adult ♂

streaked undertail coverts

fine streaks

Sightings

	JAN	FEB	MAR	APR	MAY	JUN	JUL	AUG	SEP	OCT	NOV	DEC

Lesser Goldfinch
Carduelis psaltria, L 4½" (11 cm)

This small, social finch is rarely found alone. Groups are often seen along brushy roadsides, particularly where thistles grow in abundance.

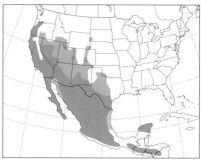

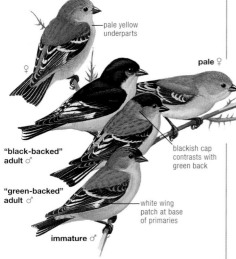

pale yellow underparts

pale ♀

"black-backed" adult ♂

blackish cap contrasts with green back

"green-backed" adult ♂

white wing patch at base of primaries

immature ♂

white undertail coverts, and lacks green tones to upperparts; it has a broad wing bar.

■ **voice** **Song** is a rambling, complex jumble of musical phrases and call notes, often including imitations of other species' calls. **Calls** include high, slurred whistles of *tee-yee?* or *tee-yur*.

RANGE Western species; primarily year-round resident. Most common in California and central Texas. Lives in a variety of habitats at different elevations, often in well-planted (or weedy) residential areas. In northern breeding areas, it arrives in April–May and departs in September–October.

FOOD Mostly seeds, tree buds, berries, and some insects. Favors seeds of thistle, purple coneflower, and other composite plants.

■ **feeding** Feeder visitor. Prefers black "thistle" (nyjer) and sunflower hearts.

NESTING Loosely colonial. *Location:* In a tree or shrub, usually 5–30 feet up. *Nest:* Compact cup of fine grass. *Eggs:* Usually 4–5; incubated by female for about 12 days. *Fledging:* Leaves nest at about 11 days.

IDENTIFICATION Common. Very small—smaller than an American Goldfinch—with a short, notched tail. Feeds quietly in weedy fields. Most easily detected when a flock takes flight and birds are calling. The male's white wing patch is prominent in flight.

■ **plumage** Two subspecies differ in adult male plumage: the **"black-backed"** (from Colorado to Texas) has solidly black upperparts; the **"green-backed"** (Southwest and West Coast) has a black cap but an olive back. **Adult female** is dull olive above and pale yellow below; dullest females are grayer above, paler below. **Immature male** has a blackish forehead.

■ **similar species** Female American Goldfinch (pages 230–231) is larger, has

American Goldfinch

Carduelis tristis, L 5" (13 cm)

Abundant, widespread, and beautiful, the American Goldfinch is a premier backyard bird. In early spring, you can easily observe the slow, patchy progression of feather replacement (molt) in the brownish winter male. It takes a period of weeks (late March–early April) until his transformation into a brilliant yellow-and-black bird is complete. State bird of Iowa, New Jersey, and Washington.

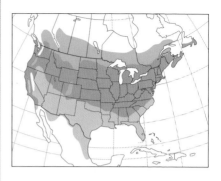

breeding ♀

black wings and tail; bright yellow body; white under tail

breeding ♂

black forehead and forecrown

IDENTIFICATION Common. Small, stocky finch with a short, notched tail. Most backyard birds congregate around feeders, but they are also very attracted to ornamental plantings of composite flowers, such as purple coneflower, black-eyed Susan, and sunflower. Bounds up and down in flight, often giving its distinctive "potato-chip" flight call (*per-chik-o-ree*) as it moves from place to place. Bill is pinkish in summer, dark in winter.

■ **plumage** All adult birds have white uppertail and undertail coverts; white wing bars are thin (worn down) in summer, bold (fresh) in winter. **Breeding male** is bright

yellow with a black cap. **Winter adult male** is tan above, pale gray below, with a yellow face and throat. **Breeding female** is olive brown above, yellow below. **Winter female** is drab gray overall, with just a hint of yellow. **Juvenile** (until November) has buff wing markings and rump.

■ **similar species** Female Lesser Goldfinch (previous page) has yellow undertail coverts, which separates it in all plumages from American Goldfinch; it is also smaller and has a yellow belly, greenish upperparts, and a white patch at base of primaries.

■ **voice** Song is a lively series of trills, twitters, and *suwee* notes. Call is a rising *suwee*; its flight call, *per-chik-o-ree* (sounds like "po-ta-to chip").

The American Goldfinch molts its body feathers twice a year—the bright yellow male of summer molts into a coat of brown feathers in fall.

The American Goldfinch is a strict vegetarian, rarely consuming any insects. Its favorite foods are tiny seeds, often pulled directly from a flower head.

RANGE Widespread species. Inhabits overgrown fields, pastures, and roadsides with shrubs and trees for nesting; often found near watercourses and in well-planted (or weedy) residential areas. Northern breeders migrate south in fall. Spring migration: April–May; fall migration: October–December.

FOOD Mostly seeds; very few insects. Favors seeds of thistles, wild sunflowers, other composite flowers, and many different weeds and grasses. Feeds nestlings a regurgitated mash of seeds with some insects.
■ feeding Very common feeder visitor. Prefers nyjer and hulled sunflower seeds.

NESTING Very late nester in the East (July–August), perhaps timed to coincide with peak of late-summer seed abundance. *Location:* In a vertical fork of a tree or shrub, usually 5–20 feet up. *Nest:* Compact cup of fine grass and plant fibers, often bound with spiderweb and lined with plant down. *Eggs:* Usually 4–6; incubated by female for 12–14 days. *Fledging:* Leaves nest at about 11–17 days.

yellow shoulder; brownish back

prominent wing bars

winter adult ♂

whitish undertail coverts

winter ♀

juvenile

notched tail

Evening Grosbeak
Coccothraustes vespertinus, L 8" (20 cm)

During some winters in the East, flocks of these big noisy finches irrupt southward. Rarely, they'll travel as far as the Mid-Atlantic and Midwest. In recent decades, big irruptions have become rare.

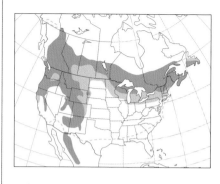

 IDENTIFICATION Fairly common. A big, starling-size finch with a huge, pale bill, large head, barrel-chested body, and short tail. Its flight is undulating. Winter flocks produce a loud chorus of shrill notes as they move around. They frequent bird feeders, or forage in seed-bearing trees and on the ground below.

white primary patch

■**plumage Adult male** has a dark-brown-and-yellow body, yellow forehead and eyebrow, and single white wing patch. **Adult female** is grayish tan with a dark whisker below the bill, two white wing patches, and a white-tipped tail. **Juvenile male** resembles adult male, but is yellower overall.

■**similar species** None.

■**voice Song** is undeveloped, rarely heard. **Calls** include a loud, ringing *clee-ip* and shrill *peer.*

RANGE Widespread species. Breeds in coniferous and mixed forests. An unpredictable migrant: winter irruptions vary from year to year and place to place; many birds spend the winter where they breed or move to lower elevations.

FOOD Seeds and insects (in summer), with some berries. Tree seeds, especially those of box elder, ash, locust, and maple, are a major component of its diet.

■**feeding** Platform or hopper feeders are best. Prefers sunflower seeds.

NESTING *Location:* In a tree, often a conifer, usually 20–60 feet up. *Nest:* Loose cup of twigs, grass, and pine needles. *Eggs:* Usually 3–4; incubated by female for 12–14 days. *Fledging:* Leaves nest at about 14 days.

yellow forehead and eyebrow

white patch on inner wing

large bill

breeding ♂

juvenile ♂

female with gray on head and back; buffy below

short tail with white tail spots

breeding ♀

Pine Siskin

Spinus pinus, L 5" (13 cm)

The most common of the irruptive "winter finches," at first glance the Pine Siskin looks more like a small, streaky sparrow. Some winters, large numbers of this sociable bird move far to the south and are common at backyard thistle feeders, where they join the ranks of American Goldfinches.

thin, sharply pointed bill

pale wing bars

juvenile

streaked underparts

prominent yellow wing stripe and yellow patches at base of tail

IDENTIFICATION Common. A small, goldfinch-size finch with a thin, sharply pointed bill and short, notched tail. In addition to frequenting feeders, winter flocks forage in seed-bearing trees and weedy patches, easily hanging upside down to extract seeds.
■ **plumage** Sexes are similar, but female has less yellow on wings and tail. **Adult** is darker above, whitish below, and prominently streaked everywhere, with two whitish wing bars. A yellow wing stripe and the base of the tail are mostly hidden on perched bird, but conspicuous in flight. Rare **"green morph,"** probably male, is extensively yellow on wings, face, and underparts and greenish on back. **Juvenile** has an overall yellow tint, lost by late summer.
■ **similar species** Streaky female House Finch (page 226) is larger, has a thicker bill and longer tail, and lacks yellow in the wings and tail.

■ **voice** **Song** is lengthy jumble of sweet and buzzy notes; similar to that of American Goldfinch, but huskier. Most common **call** is a very buzzy, rising *zreeeeee*; also gives a harsh, descending *chee* in flight.

RANGE Widespread species. Breeds in coniferous and mixed forests of the North and mountainous West. An unpredictable migrant: winter irruptions vary from year to year and place to place, likely due to fluctuating food supply; in nonirruptive years, birds spend the winter mainly within their breeding range.

FOOD Seeds and tree buds; some insects.
■ **feeding** Common feeder visitor, preferring nyjer and hulled sunflower seeds. Although smaller, it is usually dominant over Purple Finches and American Goldfinches.

NESTING Often in loose colonies. *Location:* In a tree, usually 10–40 feet up. *Nest:* Shallow cup of twigs, grass, and bark strips. *Eggs:* Usually 3–4; incubated by female for about 13 days. *Fledging:* Leaves nest at 14–15 days.

Sightings

JAN	FEB	MAR	APR	MAY	JUN	JUL	AUG	SEP	OCT	NOV	DEC

WINTER FINCH IRRUPTIONS

Years may pass with the array of species at your winter feeders staying essentially the same. Then, suddenly, in one late fall or early winter, an unexpected invasion occurs. It is a "winter finch irruption," and it brings exciting new birds to your yard.

An irruption occurs when the conifer cone crop in northern forests, particularly on spruces, is poor and offers little or no winter food for seed-eating birds. They must travel south in the autumn to survive. This arises periodically in different tree species, different regions, and different years. Therefore, it is difficult or impossible to predict which autumn might produce an invasion, where it might occur, or which species might be involved.

MAJOR IRRUPTIONS

Among the species in this book, Purple Finches, Pine Siskins, and Common Redpolls are especially known for irruptions. American Goldfinches from the north may also come south in large numbers. Cassin's Finches sometimes make large-scale down-elevation movements, as well. A larger finch, the Evening Grosbeak, formerly irrupted south into the northern states. However, the population of this species has

been declining at the edge of its geographic range, and feeder watchers in the East have not seen a major invasion by these beautiful birds for decades.

Finches are not the only birds that irrupt. Mountain Chickadees sometimes move down to lower elevations in winter and may travel far away from the mountains. Black-capped Chickadees and Red-breasted Nuthatches are also known for major irruptions, often in the same winter.

Goldfinches at winter feeders are sometimes joined by Pine Siskins like these. The siskins migrate southward only in years when trees are seedless in the northern forest.

Common Redpoll
Acanthis flammea, L 5¼" (13 cm)

These attractive finches breed in the far North. They move south in fall, but some years they irrupt farther south. Birds west of the Rockies irrupt less frequently.

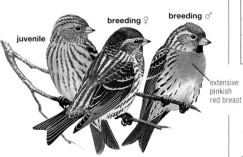

juvenile

breeding ♀

breeding ♂

extensive pinkish red breast

IDENTIFICATION Fairly common. A small "winter finch" with a blocky head, compact body, and deeply notched tail. The short bill is triangular shaped and mostly yellow. In irruption years, flocks frequent trees with winter seeds, such as birches and alders, or roam through weedy fields; some birds show up at feeders, where they are highly prized visitors.

■ **plumage** Both sexes have a red forehead ("poll") and black chin. **Winter male** has a rosy breast and sides (more intense in summer) and buff flanks with brown streaking. **Winter female** has whitish underparts with buff flanks and more streaking than male (darker in summer).

■ **similar species** Scarce Hoary Redpoll (not illustrated) breeds and winters even farther north. When seen, it is almost always with Common Redpolls. Differences from Common include: pale rump, unstreaked undertail coverts, smaller bill, faint flank streaks, and paler ("hoary") overall appearance.

■ **voice Song** combines trills and twittering. **Calls** include a rising *swee-ee-eet* when perched; flight call is a dry, scratchy *chit* or series of *chit* notes.

RANGE Northern species. Breeds in the boreal forest and Arctic tundra scrub. A winter visitor across northern North America (late October– April); unpredictable farther south.

FOOD Winter flocks feed on the ground or in seed-bearing trees.
■ **feeding** Feeder visitor. Prefers nyjer and hulled sunflower seeds.

NESTING *Location:* In a low shrub. *Nest:* Untidy cup of fine twigs, grass, and moss. *Eggs:* Usually 4–6; incubated by female for 10–11 days. *Fledging:* Leaves nest at 11–14 days.

winter ♀

buffy flanks with streaks

streaked undertail coverts

winter ♂

pink

Sightings

JAN	FEB	MAR	APR	MAY	JUN	JUL	AUG	SEP	OCT	NOV	DEC

Old World Sparrows
Family Passeridae

Two Old World sparrows were introduced to North America: the ubiquitous House Sparrow; and the Eurasian Tree Sparrow, found only in a small area of the Midwest around St. Louis.

bill paler

head pattern more subdued

chestnut nape

blackish bill and bib

fall ♂

white wing bar

breeding ♂

House Sparrow
Passer domesticus, L 6¼" (16 cm)

House Sparrows (also called "English Sparrows") were introduced in New York City in 1851. By the early 1900s, the species had spread to California.

 IDENTIFICATION Abundant. Compared to our native sparrows, the House Sparrow looks big-headed with a heavy bill, stout build, and short tail. It hops on the ground, perches in bushes, and is usually found in flocks, except when breeding.

■ **plumage** Male has a black bib, gray crown, and black bill. In fall, new plumage is edged with gray, and the bill is yellowish at its base. By spring, the gray edges wear away, revealing the black bib and chestnut colors. Nondescript **female** is best identified by the combination of buff eye stripe, streaked back, and dingy, unstreaked underparts.

■ **similar species** Compare to immature White-crowned Sparrow (page 196) and female House Finch (page 226).

■ **voice** Most common **call** is an honest-to-goodness *chirp.* Flocks chatter, sounding like a room full of talkative people.

 RANGE Widespread non-native species; year-round resident. Abundant in human-altered habitats, especially urban parks, vacant lots, backyards, and farmyards.

FOOD Eats weed seeds and grain; also insects while breeding.
■ **feeding** Visits feeders, often in unwanted numbers. Winter flocks "go to bed early" and are "late risers."

NESTING *Location:* In a cavity, building crevice, or nest box. *Nest:* Untidy construction of grasses, twigs, and bits of trash. *Eggs:* usually 4–6; incubated by both parents for 10–13 days. *Fledging:* Able to fly at about 14 days.

buffy eyebrow

♀

pale bill

plain underparts; dark streaked back

Sightings

	JAN	FEB	MAR	APR	MAY	JUN	JUL	AUG	SEP	OCT	NOV	DEC

INTRODUCED BIRDS

"Introduced" birds are nonnative species that have been deliberately or unintentionally relocated by humans and have gone on to establish permanent, self-sustaining populations. Some of these species have been so successful that they are now a dominant feature of the continent's birdlife; almost all are detrimental to our native species. The major groups are detailed below.

■The Big Three The Rock Pigeon, European Starling, and House Sparrow are three of the most common birds in North America. These three species originated in Europe, and all were introduced more than 100 years ago. Starlings and House Sparrows are aggressive species that nest in cavities, often displacing native species such as chickadees, titmice, bluebirds, and House Wrens. A fourth species, the Eurasian Collared-Dove, is currently exploding across North America and becoming a common backyard bird in many areas.

■Game birds and Waterfowl Over the years, attempts have been made to introduce many different species for sport hunting. The Ring-necked Pheasant has been the most successful and is found in open country across the continent. The invasive Mute Swan from Eurasia, imported for its decorative beauty, is destroying many East Coast and Great Lakes wetland habitats by overgrazing the fragile vegetation there.

■Parrots and Parakeets Most species found in the wild are descendants of escaped cage birds native to the neotropics. Large parrot populations occur in southern parts of California, Texas, and Florida. More

The Monk Parakeet is native to South America, but small numbers of these hardy birds have taken up residence in cities as far north as Chicago and New York.

than 15 species have been reported as breeding in the wild. The Monk Parakeet is the most northerly species, found in small numbers in cities of the Northeast, Midwest, and Texas, as well as being widespread in southern Florida.

[APPENDIX]

Glossary

ABA American Birding Association, publisher of *Birding.*

accidental A frequency category denoting an unusual or exceptional occurrence. In the ABA Checklist Area, it indicates a species that has been recorded five or fewer times overall, or fewer than three times in the past 30 years.

alternate plumage Plumage worn by an adult bird during the breeding season, produced by a partial molt before breeding. *Breeding plumage* and *nuptial plumage* are synonyms.

AOU American Ornithologists' Union, publisher of the *Check-list of North American Birds,* now in its seventh edition.

apical spot A spot at the tip of a feather.

auriculars A group of lacy feathers covering the ear (aural) openings, often bordered with contrasting stripes or lines. *Ear coverts* and *cheek* are synonyms.

axillaries A cluster of feathers in the bird's "armpit" that are recognizably longer than the underwing coverts.

bare parts Those areas of a bird's body completely without feathers.

basic plumage For most birds, the plumage worn for the longest time each year and produced by a complete molt. *Nonbreeding plumage* and *winter plumage* are synonyms.

bend of the wing The joint between the outer wing and the inner wing, where a bird's wing angles back noticeably. *Wrist* and *carpal* are synonyms.

binomial nomenclature The scientific name for an organism, consisting of two words—the first being the name of the genus, the second the specific species name.

biological species concept (BSC) Defines a species as a genetically cohesive group of populations that is reproductively isolated from other such groups. Compare *phylogenetic species concept.*

breeding plumage See *alternate plumage,* a synonym.

call notes Bird sounds that are generally shorter than songs and seem to convey a specific message, such as begging calls, alarm calls, and contact calls (or chip notes). These are generally innate rather than learned.

carpal bar A bar on the inner wing formed by contrasting secondary coverts.

casual A frequency category denoting a pattern of occurrence less than annual. In the ABA Checklist Area, it indicates there are six or more records, including at least three records in the past 30 years.

cere A band of skin covering the bill's base.

cline A gradual change in certain characteristics of individuals of the same species, evident in a geographic progression from one population to the next.

common name A name other than the scientific name by which an organism is called. These include the standard English names adopted by the AOU.

coverts The small feathers that partially overlay the flight feathers of the wing and tail at their bases. See also *greater coverts, lesser coverts,* and *median coverts.*

culmen Ridge of the upper mandible from base to tip.

dimorphic Two forms of the same species or population that differ in some aspect of plumage, size, or shape. Sexually dimorphic species show fixed differences between the sexes. Compare *polymorphic.*

ear coverts See *auriculars,* a synonym.

endemic Restricted to a given geographic area.

eye crescent A partial eye ring visible either above or below—or both above and below—the eye.

eye line A colored line that passes across the eye.

eye ring A circle of colored feathers fully encircling the eye. Compare *eye crescent* and *orbital ring*.

family The level of taxonomic classification above genus and below order, into which evolutionarily related genera are placed.

flight feathers The major feathers of the wing (primaries, secondaries) and the tail feathers (rectrices).

flight notes Calls usually given by a bird in flight, whether during nocturnal migration or from perch to perch.

gape The juncture of the maxilla and the mandible.

genus (plural, genera) The level of taxonomic classification above species and below family.

gonys The ridge formed where the two segments of the lower mandible join.

greater coverts A single row of feathers that partially overlays the flight feathers of the wing.

humerals A third set of flight feathers on the uppermost wing bone (humerus) that overlaps the secondaries as the wing folds. These are well developed in long-winged birds.

Humphrey-Parkes system A system for naming plumages and molts that does not use terms related to seasons. See *basic plumage* and *alternate plumage*.

hybrid The offspring of breeding (hybridizing) between individuals of different species. First-generation hybrids are known as *F1 hybrids*.

immature Not fully adult, either in some specific area of development, such as plumage, or as a whole.

iris The colored area of the eye surrounding the pupil.

juvenal plumage Feather coat worn by juvenile birds after they have molted their natal down. It consists of the first true contour feathers.

lateral crown stripe A stripe of darker feathers along the sides of the crown and above the supercilium.

lesser coverts Multiple rows of overlapping feathers of the wing that partially overlay the median coverts.

leucism An abnormal paleness occurring in a bird's plumage due to a dilution of pigmentation.

lores A small area located between the eye and the base of the bill.

malar stripe A distinctively colored stripe located below the submoustachial stripe and adjacent to the throat.

mandible The lower half of the bill. Compare *maxilla*.

mantle An alternate term often used to describe the back, scapulars, and upperwing coverts of gulls as a whole.

maxilla The upper part of the bill, also called the *upper mandible*. Compare *mandible*.

median coverts A single row of feathers lying between the lesser and greater coverts of the wing.

median crown stripe A contrasting line of feathers down the center of the crown.

mirror The subterminal white spots near the primary tips of many gull species.

molt The orderly replacement of old feathers with new feathers.

monotypic A taxonomic category that contains only a single taxon; for example, a monotypic species has no subspecies.

morph Usually describes a fixed color variation within a population or entire species.

moustachial stripe A dark facial stripe that extends from the gape and follows the lower border of the auriculars.

nail The hard, hooked tip of the upper mandible.

nominate subspecies The first type of the species to be described for a polytypic species. The subspecies name is the same as the second word of the species name.

nonbreeding plumage See *basic plumage,* a synonym.

orbital ring Ring of bare skin immediately surrounding the eye. Compare *eye ring.*

passerine Relating to all birds in the order Passeriformes, known as perching birds, which includes the songbirds.

patagium The leading edge of the inner wing. If this area is conspicuously dark, it forms a *patagial bar.*

pelagic Of the ocean.

phylogenetic species concept (PSC) Defines a species as "the smallest diagnosable cluster of individual organisms within which there is a parental pattern of ancestry and descent." Compare *biological species concept.*

plumage The collective term for all the feathers that cover a bird's body. Also known as *pterylosis.*

polymorphic Relating to species or populations that show fixed variations, such as color morphs.

polytypic A taxonomic category containing two or more representatives of the category immediately below it. For example, a polytypic species contains two or more subspecies.

postocular stripe A stripe extending back from the eye.

prealternate molt An annual partial molt in the late winter and early spring that results in alternate plumage. Not all species have a prealternate molt.

prebasic molt An annual complete molt, usually in late summer or early fall, that results in basic plumage.

primaries The long flight feathers of the outer wing.

primary coverts Small feathers arranged in rows that overlay the base of the primaries.

primary projection The length of the primaries projecting beyond the longest tertial feather on the folded wing.

rare A frequency category denoting abundance scarcer than uncommon but more numerous than casual. Refers to species that occur annually, but in low numbers.

rectrices (singular, rectrix) The long flight feathers of the tail. *Tail feathers* is a synonym.

remiges (singular, remix) The flight feathers—primaries and secondaries—of the wing.

rump The area between the back and the uppertail coverts.

scapulars A group of feathers that overlays the area where the wing attaches to the body.

scientific name The two-part species designation devised by Linnaeus. See *binomial nomenclature.*

secondaries The flight feathers of the inner wing.

song Patterned vocalizations usually given by males to attract mates or defend a territory.

species The level of taxonomic classification below genus and above subspecies. See *biological species concept* and *phylogenetic species concept* for differing definitions of species.

spectacles A pale eye ring that connects with the supraloral area, contrasting with the rest of the face.

subadult A bird that has not attained full adult plumage.

submoustachial stripe A stripe (usually pale) located below the moustachial stripe and above the malar stripe.

subspecies The level of taxonomic classification below species, containing individuals from a particular geographic region where the large majority of individuals are morphologically distinct from other individuals of the same species from a different area. *Race* is a synonym.

supercilium Pale feathers forming a stripe on the side of the head above the eye. *Eyebrow* is a synonym.

supraloral The part of the supercilium between the eye and the bill, located just above the lores.

tarsus (plural, tarsi) The section of leg directly above a bird's foot (the upper section of the avian foot).

taxonomy The classification of organisms, assigning names and relationships.

tertials Prominent feathers, usually three in number, that overlay the secondaries on the folded wing. Often referred to as the *innermost secondaries*.

tibia The section of leg above the tarsus.

trinomial A three-word scientific name, the third word of which designates the organism's subspecies.

undertail coverts The covert feathers that cover the bases of the tail feathers from below. *Crissum* is a synonym.

underwing coverts The covert feathers on the underside of the wing that cover the bases of the primaries and secondaries. *Wing linings* is a synonym.

uppertail coverts The covert feathers that cover the bases of the tail feathers from above, located between the rump and the tail.

vent The region located where the belly feathers meet the undertail coverts.

wing bars One or two contrasting bars running across a bird's wing. The effect results from the pale tips on the greater and/or median secondary coverts.

Many of the glossary definitions have been excerpted from *Handbook of Bird Biology,* from the Cornell Lab of Ornithology.

Acknowledgments

Jon Dunn, the chief author of National Geographic's definitive *Field Guide to the Birds of North America,* read the entire identification section of this book, as it was being drafted and again in its final form. His world-class expertise was of immeasurable help, as were his many insightful suggestions and comments. The bird illustrations found in the identification section were originally painted for the aforementioned field guide. The artists who painted them are to be congratulated on the accuracy and artistry of those images. Credits for each of the illustrations can be found on the next page. My editor, Garrett Brown, was a pleasure to work with and skillfully kept the project on time and on point. My wife, Zora Margolis Alderfer, supplied editorial advice and made numerous suggestions that greatly improved the readability of the identification section—thank you for your gentle guidance and unflagging support.

—Jonathan Alderfer

Additional Reading

Below is an abbreviated list of books that interested readers might wish to consult; most specialized books and guides are omitted.

Alderfer, Jonathan, ed. *Complete Birds of North America*. National Geographic Society, 2005.

Alderfer, Jonathan, and Jon L. Dunn. *Birding Essentials*. National Geographic, 2007. A compact reference for improving your bird identification skills.

American Birding Association [ABA]. *ABA Checklist: Birds of the Continental United States and Canada,* 7th edition. ABA, 2008.

American Ornithologists' Union [AOU]. *Check-list of North American Birds,* 7th edition. AOU, 1998. Standard taxonomic authority for North American birds. The fifth edition (1957) is the last edition with a complete list of subspecies.

Baicich, Paul J., and Colin O. Harrison. *Nests, Eggs, and Nestlings of North American Birds,* 2nd edition. Princeton University Press, 2005. A compendium of the nests, eggs, and nestlings of all North American breeding birds; includes many illustrations.

Beadle, David, and James Rising. *Sparrows of the United States and Canada: The Photographic Guide*. Academic Press, 2002.

———. *Tanagers, Cardinals, and Finches of the United States and Canada: The Photographic Guide*. Princeton University Press, 2006.

Brinkley, Edward S. *Field Guide to the Birds of North America*. Sterling, 2007. A photographic field guide.

Burton, Robert, and Stephen W. Kress. *North American Birdfeeder Guide,* revised edition. DK Publishing, 2010.

Campbell, Bruce, and Elizabeth Lack. *A Dictionary of Birds*. Buteo Books, 1985.

Dunn, Jon L., and Jonathan Alderfer, eds. *Field Guide to the Birds of North America,* 5th edition. National Geographic Society, 2006.

Dunn, Jon L., and Kimball L. Garrett. *A Field Guide to Warblers of North America*. Houghton Mifflin, 1997.

Dunne, Pete. *Pete Dunne on Bird Watching*. Houghton Mifflin, 2003.

————. *Pete Dunne's Essential Field Guide Companion*. Houghton Mifflin, 2006.

Elbroch, Mark, and Eleanor Marks. *Bird Tracks & Sign*. Stackpole Books, 2001. A guide to identifying feathers, nests, tracks, and other bird-related signs you might find in your yard.

Floyd, Ted. *Smithsonian Field Guide to the Birds of North America*. Harper-Collins, 2008. A photographic field guide.

Howell, Steve N. G. *Hummingbirds of North America: The Photographic Guide*. Academic Press, 2002.

Kaufman, Kenn. *Lives of North American Birds*. Houghton Mifflin, 1996.

Kroodsma, Donald. *The Backyard Birdsong Guide*. Chronicle Books, 2008. Includes a built-in audio player.

————. *The Singing Life of Birds*. Houghton Mifflin, 2005.

Leahy, Christopher W. *The Birdwatcher's Companion to North American Birdlife*. Princeton University Press, 2004.

Ligouri, Jerry. *Hawks from Every Angle*. Princeton University Press, 2005.

Lynch, Wayne. *Owls of the United States and Canada*. Johns Hopkins University Press, 2007.

O'Brien, Michael, Richard Crossley, and Kevin Karlson. *The Shorebird Guide*. Houghton Mifflin, 2006.

Poole, Alan, and Frank Gill, eds. *The Birds of North America*. Academy of Natural Sciences and AOU, 1992–2002. Accounts of all birds breeding in North America, including Hawaii. Published individually by species; available online at bna.birds.cornell.edu/BNA.

Robbins, Chandler S., Bertel Bruun, and Herbert S. Zim. *Birds of North America*. Golden Press, 1966. The only North American field guide to include sonograms.

Roth, Sally. *Bird-by-Bird Gardening*. Rodale, 2006. Advice on planting a bird-friendly yard.

Sibley, David A. *The Sibley Guide to Birds*. Alfred A. Knopf, 2000.

Stokes, Donald, and Lillian Stokes. *Beginner's Guide to Bird Feeding*. Little, Brown and Company, 2002.

Art Credits

Illustration Credits

1, H. Douglas Pratt; 20, Diane Pierce; 42, H. Douglas Pratt; 43 (LE), Kent Pendleton; 43 (LO LE), Michael O'Brien; 43 (LO RT), Michael O'Brien; 43 (RT), Kent Pendleton; 43 (UP LE), Donald L. Malick; 43 (UP RT), Donald L. Malick; 44, Jonathan Alderfer; 50-51 (ALL), Cynthia J. House; 53, Kent Pendleton; 54-55 (ALL), Kent Pendleton; 56-57 (ALL), Donald L. Malick; 58 (ALL), Donald L. Malick; 60 (LO), N. John Schmitt; 60 (UP), Donald L. Malick; 61 (UP), N. John Schmitt; 61(LO), Donald L. Malick; 62-63 (ALL), N. John Schmitt; 64 (UP), N. John Schmitt; 64 (LO), Donald L. Malick; 65 (UP), N. John Schmitt; 65 (LO), Donald L. Malick; 66 (LO), Donald L. Malick; 66 (RT), N. John Schmitt; 66 (UP LE), Donald L. Malick; 68, Killian Mullarney; 69, Daniel S. Smith; 70-71 (ALL), Thomas R. Schultz; 72 (ALL), Thomas R. Schultz; 73 (ALL), H. Douglas Pratt; 74 (ALL), H. Douglas Pratt; 75 (ALL), Jonathan Alderfer; 76-77 (ALL), Jonathan Alderfer; 78 (ALL), Donald L. Malick; 79 (ALL), H. Douglas Pratt; 80, Donald L. Malick; 82-83 (ALL), Donald L. Malick; 84-85 (ALL), Chuck Ripper; 86 (ALL), H. Douglas Pratt; 88-91 (ALL), H. Douglas Pratt; 92, N. John Schmitt; 93-105 (ALL), Donald L. Malick; 106-107 (ALL), David Beadle; 108-112 (ALL), H. Douglas Pratt; 114-115 (ALL), Jonathan Alderfer; 116 (ALL), H. Douglas Pratt; 117-119 (ALL), Peter Burke; 120, H. Douglas Pratt; 121, David Beadle; 122-129 (ALL), H. Douglas Pratt; 130 (LO), Jonathan Alderfer; 130 (UP), H. Douglas Pratt; 131 (LO), H. Douglas Pratt; 131 (UP), Jonathan Alderfer; 132-138 (ALL), H. Douglas Pratt; 140-147 (ALL), Michael O'Brien; 148-149 (ALL), John P. O'Neill; 150-164 (ALL), H. Douglas Pratt; 165-167 (ALL), Thomas R. Schultz; 168-171 (ALL), H. Douglas Pratt; 172 (LO), N. John Schmitt; 172 (UP), H. Douglas Pratt; 173-174 (ALL), H. Douglas Pratt; 175, N. John Schmitt; 176-177 (ALL), H. Douglas Pratt; 178 (A), Thomas R. Schultz; 178 (B, E, F, G), H. Douglas Pratt; 178 (C), Thomas R. Schultz; 178 (D), Peter Burke; 178 (H), David Beadle; 179 (A, B, C, D, E, F, G, I, J, K), H. Douglas Pratt; 179 (H), Thomas R. Schultz; 179 (L), Peter Burke; 180-181 (ALL), H. Douglas Pratt; 182-185 (ALL), Peter Burke; 187-200 (ALL), Diane Pierce; 201 (LO LE), Diane Pierce; 201 (LO RT), Peter Burke; 201 (UP RT), N. John Schmitt; 202, Diane Pierce; 204-206 (ALL), Peter Burke; 207-209 (ALL), Diane Pierce; 210-219 (ALL), H. Douglas Pratt; 220-221 (ALL), Thomas R. Schultz; 222-225 (ALL), Peter Burke; 226-235 (ALL), Diane Pierce.

Photo Credits

2-3, Jim Zipp; 4, Brian E. Small; 15, Alan Murphy; 16 (LE), Donna Short, National Geographic My Shot; 16 (RT), Norman Dulak/ Alamy; 17 (LE), Marie Read; 17 (RT), Christopher Drake, National Geographic My Shot; 18 (A), Dwayne Boykin, National Geographic My Shot; 18 (B), Joel Sartore; 18 (C), All Canada Photos/Alamy; 18 (D), Fred Thompson, National Geographic My Shot; 19 (LE), Takahashi Photography/Shutterstock; 19 (CTR), AvianArt Images by David Hemmings; 19 (RT), Donald M. Jones/ Getty Images; 21, Eduardo Jose Bernardino/iStockphoto.com; 22 (UP LE), Richard Day/Daybreak Imagery; 22 (UP CTR), Jim Zipp; 22 (UP RT), Clark Wheeler/iStockphoto.com; 22 (LE), Steve Maslowski/Getty Images; 22 (CTR), Eduardo

Jose Bernardino/iStockphoto.com; 22 (RT), Steve Maslowski/Getty Images; 22 (LO LE), Richard Day/Daybreak Imagery; 22 (LO CTR), Judy Ledbetter/iStockphoto.com; 22 (LO RT), Gerry Sibell, National Geographic My Shot; 25 (UP LE), Brian Balster/iStockphoto.com; 25 (UP CTR), Keith Ferris/iStockphoto.com; 25 (UP RT), Jethro Loader/iStockphoto.com; 25 (LE), Dave White/iStockphoto.com; 25 (CTR), Abel Leão/iStockphoto.com; 25 (RT), syagci/iStockphoto.com; 25 (LO LE), Arco Images GmbH/Alamy; 25 (LO CTR), Morgan Lane Studios/iStockphoto.com; 25 (LO RT), Owen Price/iStockphoto.com; 27 (LE), Jeff Pinkerton, National Geographic My Shot; 27 (RT), Jim Zipp; 28 (LE), Donald Blais/iStockphoto.com; 28 (RT), Greg Hamamgian, National Geographic My Shot; 29, William Leaman/Alamy; 31 (LE), Richard Mirro/iStockphoto.com; 31 (RT), Dale Halbur/iStockphoto.com; 33, Marie Read; 34 (LE), Mark Lewer, National Geographic My Shot; 34 (RT), Jim Zipp; 36, Jerry & Marcy Monkman/DanitaDelimont.com; 37, Jon Patton/iStockphoto.com; 38, Mark Turner/Getty Images; 39, Sheldon D. Kralstein/iStockphoto.com; 41, cjmckendry/iStockphoto.com; 44, Frank Leung/iStockphoto.com; 45, Angela Sorrentino/iStockphoto.com; 47, Mathew Studebaker; 52, Rowland Willis, National Geographic My Shot; 59, Jim Zipp; 65 (LO), Bob Steele; 65 (UP), Megan Lorenz/iStockphoto.com; 67, John A. Anderson/Shutterstock; 68, Roger Dirrim, National Geographic My Shot; 69 (UP), Edward Mattis, National Geographic My Shot; 69 (LO), Edward Mattis, National Geographic My Shot; 81, Connie Fore, National Geographic My Shot; 87, Missing35mm/iStockphoto.com; 102, George Whalen, National Geographic My Shot; 103, Katherine Murphy, National Geographic My Shot; 104 (LE), Danny Brown, National Geographic My Shot; 104 (RT), Joseph Bove, National Geographic My Shot; 109 (UP), Robert Royse; 109 (LO), Brook Burling, National Geographic My Shot; 113, Steven Smith, National Geographic My Shot; 123, Brandon Broderick, National Geographic My Shot; 125 (LO), Tony Campbell/iStockphoto.com; 125 (UP), Jim Ridley, National Geographic My Shot; 128, Robert Royse; 133, Tom Vezo/Minden Pictures; 136, Bryan Olesen/Getty Images; 137, Krivosheev Vitaly/Shutterstock; 139, Rusty Dodson/iStockphoto.com; 141 (LO), AvianArt Images by David Hemmings; 141 (UP), Jeremy Dussault, National Geographic My Shot; 145, Marie Read; 150, Bob Steele; 151 (UP), Jaromir Penicka, National Geographic My Shot; 151 (LO), Brandon Holden; 152, Christopher Corman, National Geographic My Shot; 157 (LE), Bill Dalton, National Geographic My Shot; 157 (RT), Marie Read; 157 (LO), Marie Read; 163, Jeff Sanders, National Geographic My Shot; 169, Scott Leslie/Minden Pictures; 171, Kenneth C. Zirkel/iStockphoto.com; 171 (LE), Betty Shelton, National Geographic My Shot; 173, Garth McElroy; 184, Jim Zipp; 187, Jim Zipp; 189 (LE), Robert Royse; 189 (RT), Jim Zipp; 192, Garth McElroy; 193, Mathew Studebaker; 199, Robert Royse; 201, Chuck Briggs, National Geographic My Shot; 203 (LO), Pam Morris, National Geographic My Shot; 203 (UP), Paul Klenck; 211, Jim Zipp; 215, Paul Klenck; 216 (LE), Marie Read; 216 (RT), Mike Weimer, National Geographic My Shot; 217, Marie Read; 230, Renant Cheng, National Geographic My Shot; 231, David Star, National Geographic My Shot; 234, Jim Zipp; 237, Megan Lorenz/iStockphoto.com.

Index

Boldface indicates illustrations.

NATIONAL GEOGRAPHIC

Backyard
GUIDE TO THE
Birds of North America

JONATHAN ALDERFER AND PAUL HESS

PUBLISHED BY THE NATIONAL GEOGRAPHIC SOCIETY
John M. Fahey, Jr., *President and Chief Executive Officer*
Gilbert M. Grosvenor, *Chairman of the Board*
Tim T. Kelly, *President, Global Media Group*
John Q. Griffin, *Executive Vice President; President, Publishing*
Nina D. Hoffman, *Executive Vice President; President, Book Publishing Group*

PREPARED BY THE BOOK DIVISION
Barbara Brownell Grogan, *Vice President and Editor in Chief*
Marianne R. Koszorus, *Director of Design*
Susan Tyler Hitchcock, *Senior Editor*
Carl Mehler, *Director of Maps*
R. Gary Colbert, *Production Director*
Jennifer A. Thornton, *Managing Editor*
Meredith C. Wilcox, *Administrative Director, Illustrations*

STAFF FOR THIS BOOK
Garrett Brown, *Editor*
Sanaa Akkach, *Art Director*
Al Morrow, *Designer*
Matt Propert, *Illustrations Editor*
Paul E. Lehman, *Chief Map Researcher/Editor*
Sven M. Dolling and Michael McNey, *Map Production*
Judith Klein, *Production Editor*
Mike Horenstein, *Production Manager*
Robert Waymouth, *Illustrations Specialist*
Jon Dunn, *Birding Consultant*
Melissa Phillips, *Design Intern*

MANUFACTURING AND QUALITY MANAGEMENT
Christopher A. Liedel, *Chief Financial Officer*
Phillip L. Schlosser, *Senior Vice President*
Chris Brown, *Technical Director*
Nicole Elliott, *Manager*
Rachel Faulise, *Manager*
Robert L. Barr, *Manager*

The National Geographic Society is one of the world's largest nonprofit scientific and educational organizations. Founded in 1888 to "increase and diffuse geographic knowledge," the Society works to inspire people to care about the planet. National Geographic reflects the world through its magazines, television programs, films, music and radio, books, DVDs, maps, exhibitions, live events, school publishing programs, interactive media and merchandise. *National Geographic* magazine, the Society's official journal, published in English and 32 local-language editions, is read by more than 35 million people each month. The National Geographic Channel reaches 320 million households in 34 languages in 166 countries. National Geographic Digital Media receives more than 13 million visitors a month. National Geographic has funded more than 9,200 scientific research, conservation and exploration projects and supports an education program promoting geography literacy. For more information, visit nationalgeographic.com.

For more information, please call 1-800-NGS LINE (647-5463) or write to the following address:

National Geographic Society
1145 17th Street N.W.
Washington, D.C. 20036-4688 U.S.A.

For information about special discounts for bulk purchases, please contact National Geographic Books Special Sales: ngspecsales@ngs.org

For rights or permissions inquiries, please contact National Geographic Books Subsidiary Rights: ngbookrights@ngs.org

Library of Congress Cataloging-in-Publication Data

Alderfer, Jonathan K.
  National Geographic backyard guide to the birds of North America / Jonathan Alderfer, Paul Hess.
    p. cm.
  Includes index.
  ISBN 978-1-4262-0720-4 (trade paper : alk. paper)
  1. Birds--North America. 2. Birds--North America--Identification.. 3. Bird attracting--North America. I. Hess, Paul, 1940-. II. Title.
  QL681.A57 2011
  598.097--dc22
                                      2010043877

Printed in China

10/TS/1

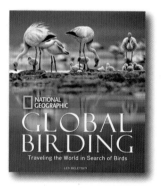

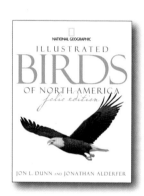
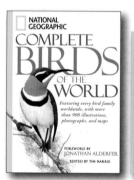

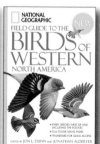
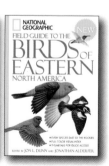